Critique of Applied Ethics

Critique of Applied Ethics

Critique of Applied Ethics

Reflections and Recommendations

ABRAHAM EDEL

ELIZABETH FLOWER

FINBARR W. O'CONNOR

TEMPLE UNIVERSITY PRESS · PHILADELPHIA

Temple University Press, Philadelphia 19122
Copyright © 1994 by Temple University
Published 1994
Printed in the United States of America

The paper used in this publication meets the minimum requirements
of American National Standard for Information Sciences—Permanence
of Paper for Printed Library Materials, ANSI Z39.48-1984 ∞

Library of Congress Cataloging-in-Publication Data

Edel, Abraham, 1908–
Critique of applied ethics : reflections and recommendations /
Abraham Edel, Elizabeth Flower, Finbarr W. O'Connor.
p.   cm.
Includes bibliographical references and index.
ISBN 1-56639-157-1 (cl).—ISBN 1-56639-158-X (pb)
1. Applied ethics.   I. Flower, Elizabeth.   II. O'Connor, Finbarr
W.   III. Title.
BJ1031.E44   1994
170—dc20   93-26981

Contents

Preface

This is a book *about* applied ethics, not a book *in* applied ethics. Its concern is not to offer solutions to particular problems but to explore our assets as we grapple with problems. Characteristically, traditional ethical theories addressed the stable over the problematic: the social environment in which Aristotle and Aquinas thought about war may not have been especially stable, but what "war" meant to them did have a remarkable stability, as it did to Hobbes and Locke. For us "war" includes a distinction between "hot" and "cold," "high-intensity" and "low-intensity," and it can be declared against drugs, poverty, and crime.

Our world is one of rapid, indeed exponential, social and technological change, and this includes a conceptual environment that is also ever-changing. While some of the problems we face are old, even perennial, others are novel and unprecedented, and perplex traditional wisdom and practice. The challenge for applied ethics today is to combine the stabilities of traditional morality and the best available knowledge of our world to create an acute sensitivity to novelty.

Critique of Applied Ethics

Introduction

It seems only fair (a natural concern of a work dealing with morality) to give the reader some preliminary idea of the kind of book on which he or she is embarking. That it deals with applied ethics is not sufficiently indicative. Publishing today is awash with books about applied ethics. Ethics used to be considered a remote corner of our everyday lives, but that is no longer (if indeed it ever was) the case. It is no longer so easy to close down debate with "Business is business" or "This is a political matter, not a moral matter." It seems as if every field has sprouted its own code of ethics, and professional schools have either introduced or re-emphasized courses in ethics. The "ethics" committees of Congress seem to be grappling with complaints constantly. And, in the strange crossing of categories of our time, discussions of ethical problems in journalism or politics or ordinary life have become attractive spectacles on television talk shows—ethics as entertainment!

This book is different from most other books on applied ethics. Most of them deal with special fields—moral problems in medicine or law, in business or the workshop, in family life and counseling, in computers and even in military matters. This book takes illustrations from the variety of fields, but it is not bent on exploring any one field comprehensively. Nor is it concerned with giving answers. Indeed, good books in applied ethics tend to avoid this on principle, the principle being that people not only should but for the most part want to make their own decisions, not to have others tell them what to do. The help they want is in exploring the problems they may be facing.

In this respect the present book is, at least in intention, like other good books in the field. The important aspect in which it differs, however, is that its primary concern is with the theory of applied ethics. It wants to convey an understanding of what is going on in applied ethics, what are the many dimensions of how it proceeds, and how they might be rendered explicit and improved.

In the 1970s and continuing through the 1980s, the notion of applied ethics became very popular. Philosophy departments began to introduce courses in applied ethics or in particular fields in applied ethics, such as bioethics or business ethics. Institutes and centers of applied ethics or of philosophy and public policy or of professional ethics were established. An occasional journal of applied ethics appeared on the scene, and even a whole encyclopedia of bioethics. In some of the established professions there were voices raised to criticize the new philosophical tendencies for making inroads on established treatments of professional matters without any special expertise; some philosophers even expressed such hesitation. In any event, the turn to applied ethics was sufficiently pervasive to count as a genuine movement.

It is somewhat puzzling that applied ethics was considered as something quite new. Most of the great moral philosophers of the past went on from their work on theoretical ethics into questions of institutions and associations as well as their legal and political forms. If the emphasis here is not on particular situations—though these are often used as illustrations—it is definitely on practical policy, on the structure and functioning of institutions and forms of association. For example, Aristotle's *Nicomachean Ethics*, the first great systematic treatise of western moral philosophy,[1] has two chapters on friendship, which is his term for human associations expressing interests, and deals with everything from the familial to the mercantile to the intellectual. And, of course, his *Politics* not only maps the diversity of political forms and the principles underlying them, but the kind of geographical conditions that make one or another form more appropriate. These ancient treatises dealt with city-states. The moral philosophy of the Middle Ages took Roman imperial form and a universal church as the context for grappling with problems of conflict of authorities and divided loyalties. Thomas Aquinas's *Summa Theologica* contains classic discussions of the morality of war, of just pricing, of responsibility to the poor, of the duties of lawyers, and many other such issues. The centralized national states that arose in

seventeenth-century Europe constituted in many respects a new phenomenon, and moral philosophers were not slow to address their
problems. Thomas Hobbes's *Leviathan* works out the political and
legal and moral requirements of such a state if it is to have a form of
sovereignty adequate to keep peace and order. John Locke's *Second
Treatise on Government*, with its defense of liberty, property, and the
right of revolution, has been characterized by Michael Oakeshott—
intriguingly, though perhaps not wholly accurately—as a handbook
for a new ruling class not born to the purple. With the expansion of
commerce and the Industrial Revolution, the need for rational change
in institutional forms inspired Jeremy Bentham toward the end of the
eighteenth century; his *Theory of Legislation* (collected by a French
disciple) sets out new laws for almost all fields of human society. But
it is his spirit that is central: legislation is the instrument for a conscious rationality, not the hangover of tradition that his contemporary, Edmund Burke, tried once more to invoke against the rationalism of the French Revolution. Immanuel Kant's *Perpetual Peace*
explored the political forms he took as necessary for maintaining just
relations between state and citizen in a liberal state based on equal
rights.

Thus, moral philosophy itself has had a long tradition of dealing
with practical moral problems. Casuistry—cases of conscience and
how to act—is an old pursuit. Even in ancient times the Stoic philosophers particularly sought out the duties, offices, and roles attendant
on particular pursuits and particular situations. For example, Cicero
recounts the argument of two eminent Stoics on whether the seller of
grain, who knows that in a day or two a large shipment from Egypt
will lower the price, ought to reveal this to still unknowing customers. Their arguments go from appeals to the brotherhood of man
to whether one is really obligated to tell all truths to all people all the
time. And it ends with the defender of reticence saying that if you
have to tell all things, then what is the point of buying and selling at
all—as if business as such hangs on the ignorance of customers. The
Stoics, too, probed the fine lines of human emotions; for example,
Seneca's *On Anger* considers whether anger is totally immoral or
whether it is a useful instrument toward others and oneself when employed with practiced control. Philosophical interest in dilemmas of
particular practical problems has never entirely disappeared, though it
may have faded into the background. Readers familiar with the legen-
dary austerity of Kant's critical philosophy are often surprised when

they encounter the contextual discussion of cases in his *Lectures on Ethics* and (although to a lesser extent) in his *Metaphysics of Morals*. In the twentieth century, Sartre's discussion of the dilemma of the French son, deciding whether to remain in France and take care of his mother or to join the Free French forces in London, falls squarely in this tradition.

In the light of this philosophical history, contemporary applied ethics is a continuation of a longstanding philosophical attempt to face practical moral problems with whatever fresh intellectual tools contemporary ethical theory may have to offer. Nonetheless, applied ethics does mark a major change—perhaps even a qualitative change—in the way we should deal with practical problems. We suggest two explanations for this, one based on what *applied* in "applied ethics" suggests, and a second based on the nature of contemporary ethical theory.

The choice of the term "applied ethics" for the movement, as opposed to, perhaps, "practical ethics," may suggest that theory is now in a readier position to help practice. It suggests that practical moral problems should be routed to the resources of ethical theory for solution. The appearance of applied ethics late in the twentieth century would then suggest that finally ethical theory has matured sufficiently to provide guidance in practical problems in a way that previously would not have been possible.

If ethical theory had matured, then, it would justify the feeling that in applied ethics we are witnessing something entirely new. It is doubtful, however, that this assumption is correct. That ethical theory is helpful in understanding particular problems is not by itself sufficient to support the claim that a particular field has been carved out, as is suggested by "applied ethics." A comparison with the established term "applied science" may be helpful. When does an area of practical work change from being helped by scientific knowledge to become applied science? Mining, bridge building, and later gunnery, were long standing *crafts*. Scientific discoveries—for example, about air pressure—helped provide pumps to get rid of water in mines and so make more extensive mining possible. That did not make mining an applied science. Perhaps the term is appropriate when a new scientific field generates fresh crafts—electrical illumination, for example, or nuclear power. But even when the whole character of production changes as a result of scientific advance, we may not think of a manufacturing process as applied science—if furniture is made by electrically powered machines, we do not think of furniture making as applied electricity. If ethical theory helps us analyze practical moral problems so that the solution takes a different path from what it might have otherwise, why should we think of it as applied ethics?

Beyond this, there is a fundamental ambiguity in the very term "applied ethics." What is it that is being applied? Is it an ethical theory, or a morality? Suppose a historian discovers that a common belief about a controversial past event is wrong (for example, that the North Vietnamese did not fire on U.S. ships in the Gulf of Tonkin, or that the Germans did not torpedo the *Lusitania*). Suppose she is writing a book about the period, and this discovery is not central to her thesis. She wonders whether she should gloss over it in the book, because the revelation will upset many important beliefs and values and may cause a reaction that will overshadow the thesis itself. Now, as she thinks about what she should do, does she apply an ethical theory (such as a utilitarian ethics of decision in terms of the greatest well-being of the greatest number) or does she apply a morality (such as the moral rule of not lying, except possibly in great emergencies)? Perhaps the notion of applied ethics can cover both, and all that is required is a contextual specification of what is being intended at what point.

The second possible explanation of the perceived novelty of *applied ethics* is that the term is meant only to signal that the concern is no longer with ethical theory alone. This has special pertinence to the twentieth century, because powerful movements in moral philosophy from the beginning of the century conceived of ethics as a purely theoretical discipline, carried on in a self-contained way, and not dependent for its results on the knowledge that the sciences provide, nor for that matter on our normative judgments. Two of the most powerful philosophical movements of the century—Logical Positivism and ordinary language analysis—though they differed in important respects, were nevertheless in agreement on this kind of isolationism for ethics. Positivism distinguished sharply between logic, science, and value. Logic dealt with concepts and their relations, science with empirical fact, and value with emotional expression in its various forms (religious, moral, or aesthetic). Ethical theory had the task of analyzing ethical concepts—the language of ethics—using logical-linguistic techniques. Practical moral utterances belonged therefore to ordinary life with its emotive reactions, with its mutually persuasive efforts: to preachers and political figures who sought to influence people. Since, moreover, fact and value were quite distinct—from something's being the case one could not derive that it ought to be the case, and from something's being worthwhile one could not conclude that it exists—science could help only on means, not on ends or ultimate obligations. In working out ethical theory, logical positivism had no special admiration for ordinary language. It looked instead to artificial systems—comparable to mathematical systems—and hoped to construct a language of imperatives or a logic of obligation (deontic logic) or of preference (axiological logic), which might have some systematic serviceability for rendering moral judgment more precise.

Ordinary language analysis (Oxford analysis) differed from logical positivism in its view of language. Its respect for ordinary language was as great as that of British lawyers for the common law—something that has grown through the ages and embodies the subtle distinctions humans had learned to make through their experience. The business of ethical theory, then, was to analyze the linguistic uses of morality, not to construct artificial systems. It paid attention to fine shades of meaning, and dissolved many broad concepts, substituting the exploration of diverse uses for attempts to set down a standard meaning. But this analysis stayed within linguistic contexts, and did not concern itself with social and historical contexts. Hence, it did not abandon the isolated character of ethical inquiry.

These movements in moral philosophy that paid little attention to practical moral problems were not so much refuted as overwhelmed by the flood of problems we note in Chapter One. The work that had such a powerful influence in bringing moral philosophy back into normative business was John Rawls's *A Theory of Justice* (1971). Soon thereafter, Robert Nozick was defending natural rights in his *Anarchy, State, and Utopia* (1974), while others were discussing the newer welfare rights vis-à-vis the older property rights, and problems of public policy and professional ethics became matters of frequent analysis.

This story of twentieth-century moral philosophy[2] readily explains why applied ethics is regarded as a new movement *within* twentieth-century philosophy. Applied ethics does represent a change of direction for twentieth-century philosophy, but, on the other hand, it does not represent an entirely new change in philosophy's traditional concerns with practical moral problems. If anything, it represents a rediscovery of past directions, with twentieth-century ethical theory itself a departure from the tradition.

As a label for signaling this change of direction, "applied ethics" is an unfortunate choice. It may indicate how difficult it was for those whose philosophical commitments were to these twentieth-century movements to distance themselves sufficiently. *Applied ethics* suggests that its core is its contrast with pure ethics and that what is being applied is a pure or systematic ethical theory. This separation of theory and practice is a holdover from early twentieth-century philosophy, which still haunts the field. If we had the power to legislate, we would prefer the label "practical ethics," or perhaps, "problematic ethics." Lacking that power, we can only indicate how we conceive of the field.

In our view applied ethics is concerned with that part of an existing morality that consists of practical moral problems, as contrasted with that part which is stable and remains unquestioned at a given time. To see the field as defined by practical moral problems suggests a distinction within the whole field between the stable parts and the problematic parts, not the contrast of theory and practice. This brings us closer to the actual contemporary concern with applied ethics. Practical moral problems have multiplied and become exceedingly complex in our rapidly changing world. Applied ethics is the attempt to solve them and consolidate ways of dealing with them, making the best use possible of the resources of ethical theory as well as accumulated human knowledge.

The kinds of problems dealt with in contemporary life appear to come from three relatively different directions. One is from the variety of professions, embodying traditional division of labor and often already associated with ethical codes. Another is from the area of public policy, where detailed questions are nowadays pressed upon us for some form of collective decision. The third, impinging most directly upon the individual, is that of personal decision. All three share the features of practical urgency and very often of immediacy. How they are related will concern us at several points in Part Two. Indeed, the three are featured in the names of the institutes that have grown up and the movement developed. A "Center for Philosophy and Public Policy" is clearly of the second kind. An "Institute for Bioethics" or an "Institute for Business Ethics" is obviously of the first. While centers for dealing with personal decisions are not to be found in standard philosophical form, the proliferation of advisory agencies, both in college and universities and in the community at large, are marked features of contemporary life, even far beyond their formal treatment in psychology and social work.

This book aims to draw on all three kinds of problems to illustrate how applied ethics goes about its work, but it is worth repeating that here we are not concerned with solving these problems but with using them as background to comments on the theory of applied ethics. Part One sets the stage and provides the background. It examines what in contemporary life has pushed applied ethics into the forefront (Chapter One), how to describe a moral order (Chapter Two), and what the concerns of ethical theory have been (Chapter Three). It sharpens our idea of applied ethics and examines the issues—chiefly about the relation of knowledge and value—that have been the stumbling blocks in ethics (Chapter Four). Part One is not so much a study of ethical theory as a philosophical pursuit of those aspects of it that impinge directly on applied ethics or provide instruments for its operations.

Part Two does the heavy work of the book. It examines major dimensions of the analysis and solution of practical moral problems. In each chapter some aspect of the processes of applied ethics or some underlying factor that plays an important role in shaping the outcome is dissected and examined: how a problem is diagnosed, how the relevant context is established, how the problem is given ethical shape, how jurisdictional regions are established and limited, what can be done about the conflict between the individual and the social, to what degree of inventiveness morality admits, and the character and types of decision. A final chapter returns to the question of the relation of theory to practice.

PART ONE

Philosophical

Backgrounds

for Applied

Ethics

CHAPTER

One

Practical Moral Problems
in an Age of Rapid Technological
and Social Change

As we look around us today, it is striking how every aspect of our lives, every institution, every public policy, every profession, almost every stage in the development of a child and in the life of an adult, generates practical moral problems. Some of these have tried and true answers. We need not devalue the stable parts of our morality just because important parts of it exhibit turbulence and indecision. It is like the observation of law in action: we focus on the courts at work, not on the public at large doing its daily round in full conformity with the law's intent. In fact, as Jeremy Bentham pointed out, social living is textured by multiple expectations we have of how others are to behave, and for the most part these expectations are recognized, or at least accepted, as legitimate. People are, for the most part, honorable, generally tell the truth, and keep their promises. Nevertheless, the proportion of urgent problems has markedly increased, which accounts for the spotlight now being refocused—even in moral philosophy—on applied ethics rather than ethical theory. The demand today is less for peremptory answers—there is that much sophistication in the modern world—than for reliable ways in which serious women and men can go about understanding moral problems in a way that may expedite solutions. Such an aim, however, itself calls for an exploration that is both theoretical and practical and that relates the two.

The features of contemporary life that generate uncertainty and indecision in practical moral problems are its increasing complexity and rapidity of change. Historians and sociologists have long been aware of what greater complexity (such as an increase in the numbers of people with whom one has commerce and increased choices due to technological advances) does to morality. This is especially clear in their studies of the contrasts between urban and rural life. The city allows an anonymity that often contrasts with the almost literal moral surveillance of the village. Mobility within a large nation relaxes the close moral ties of kinship. Now, however, within a setting of global interrelations, even those who stay in one location ensconced in a familiar environment are constantly affected by the international influences on their occupation, trade, habits, and standards. At the same time, such variety offers more complex choices in the various fields of life.

Such effects of complexity are to some extent mitigated by the growth of knowledge, and today knowledge is accumulating at an accelerating pace. This creates its own complexity, for people are decreasingly able to keep up with its growth. Even specialists now find it almost impossible to master the whole of their own field. Greater specialization in smaller areas is by no means uncommon today, and the isolation of areas of knowledge from one another is a serious practical problem, despite enormous technical advances in the storing and accessing of information.

The rapidity of technological and social change is today more obvious as a source of uncertainty and indecision than in the past. Alfred North Whitehead long ago pointed out that as long as the rate of change was generational, we had less difficulty in absorbing it; now it takes place within a single lifetime. Scarcely a generation after Whitehead, Margaret Mead, in *Culture and Commitment*, compared the situation to the experience of immigrants to America—their children rapidly absorbed the new culture, while the older generation remained with the old ways. We are now, she said, all immigrants in time, having the same experience of readjustment and failure that the older immigrant generations had. Such rapidity of change intensifies moral conflicts and moral problems, and they arise in particular situations confronting individuals and societies as a whole. The social and moral consequences of the automobile—industrial waste, suburbia, expansion of roads, drive-in movies, independence of the young, backseat sex—remain emblematic of such change. We have yet to learn how to cope with the state of affairs where rapid change is normal and how to develop moral methods of coping with moral problems.

Practical moral problems are evident all about us. For example, an older medical ethics had dealt with questions of confidentiality and whether patients ought to be told of the seriousness of their condition. It had discussed mutual obligations of several physicians dealing with the same patient, obligations in life-and-death situations, and even sometimes what attitudes are desirable toward the dying patient. (Consider Florence Nightingale's sensitive observation that it is a sin to whisper in the room of a dying patient.) The new bioethics has to grapple with definitions of death and the artificial prolongation of life, with genetic engineering and organ transplantation, and with social problems of making new but limited resources available to a larger public. The well-known Karen Quinlan case raised the issue of whether death ought be equated with the permanent end of brain functioning, even though the heart continues to work. The ability to maintain life artificially raises not only the question of whether it ought always to be employed but also whether it would be murder if, once applied, the devices were then turned off; and if they may be turned off, who is to decide—family, medical experts, courts? The Quinlan case was quickly followed by other cases raising increasingly sensitive questions. Whereas in the Quinlan case the resolution involved turning off the respirator but maintaining food and water, in the Nancy Cruzan case the request of the family was to withhold food and water. The Christine Busalacchi case involved a not fully comatose patient, and the later Helga Wanglie case reversed the previous dispositions of family and medical authorities—here the family objected to the physicians' recommendation against further life support. Organ transplantation raises questions of distributive justice: to whom should the opportunity be offered? And in what order? Who is to decide? The growth of genetic engineering raises questions of modifying (tampering with?) the basic structures of the body, of generating new modes of life, and whether (as a Supreme Court decision has allowed) a new form of life and its production can be patented as private property.

Ethical issues go beyond the domain of new techniques and reach into medical research itself. Hitherto there had been discussion of familiar problems of choosing subjects and test procedures for curative drugs—should self-sacrificing researchers first test their discoveries on themselves? Should condemned prisoners be offered life in return for undergoing tests? But now we are faced with large-scale questions of timing in licensing new drugs, pitting the risks of unforeseen dangers against the importunities of the afflicted. At the present time, the United States health authorities lean to the side of caution (justifying this stand by the historical experience with thalidomide,[1] the use of which had been forbidden in the United States). But this caution can mean that drugs are made available in countries where health authorities are less strict, and the citizens of those countries become, as it were, the test population for us. Pressure on the other side comes from the urgency of the AIDS problem, which has led to a challenge to the strict standards in the United States and eventually to a relaxation in them. Similar questions can arise over how the research is conducted. For example, research on Huntington's chorea, a degenerative disease that emerges late in middle life, required a population of research subjects from those who may be genetic carriers. To gather such a population meant assembling relatives of those known to be genetic carriers, many of whom are unaware of their state as potential carriers. So to do the research involved spreading alarm in a broad population, only some of whom were in fact at risk. In this fashion, researchers wondered whether the process of research itself sometimes might be unethical. Another problem, tied to the controversies over abortion, is the use of fetal tissue for research or therapeutically.

Other fields and professions faced similarly changing problems. Business had traditionally balanced its central aim of profit with its service aim of providing needed commodities at reachable prices. Then price and tax levels became the crux of ethical conceptions of distributive justice. Whereas dishonesty in the era of small business had meant cheating the individual customer, in the era of growing corporate monopoly and growing dependence on government contracts, it more often came to mean pillaging the public treasury. Through the 1980s deregulation became the operative slogan, but as the 1980s turned into the 1990s, scandals (cheating in the defense industry, the "revolving door" through which government officials moved into the industry they previously regulated, the savings and loan debacle, and the Bank of Credit and Commerce International (BCCI) affair, among others) called attention to the need for ethical–legal regulation on the part of either government or the industries themselves.

At every turn, business seemed beset by increasingly complex ethical demands. In the 1970s, exclusionary employment practices were challenged as discriminatory and affirmative action—understood as good-faith efforts to make openings reasonably available to all without regard to race—offered as the remedy. Then we witnessed a reversal in the 1980s as affirmative action itself came under attack as "reverse discrimination." The question quickly became polarized around sloganizing about "goals" and "quotas," and differences over the relevance of intention and effect, culminating in the 1990s with the spectacle of Democrats and Republicans fighting over a civil rights bill where, it was alleged, the differences had become so subtle that even lawyers could not tell how the positions differed. A bill that explicitly outlawed quotas was said to be a "quotas bill."

Sexual harassment, too, started as a fairly clear-cut matter, involving sexual pressure on an employee by a supervisor linked with a threat to the employee's employment. A watershed in the understanding of what constitutes sexual harassment came in 1980 with the Equal Employment Opportunity Commission's final interpretive guidelines that went beyond previous understandings to include as a form of sexual harassment practices that create an "intimidating, hostile, or offensive working environment" and placed an absolute liability on the employer for tolerating such practices.[2] In 1986 the Supreme Court entered the debate with a ruling that an employee who is not forced to participate against her will may still claim harassment.[3] And, finally, the Senate Judiciary Committee's hearings on Clarence Thomas's appointment to the Supreme Court caused the country to place the whole subject under intense scrutiny.[4] Surely, sexual harassment is not a new phenomenon, but the combination of a vast increase in the proportion of women in the workplace and of a raised feminist consciousness has resulted in a new understanding of the phenomenon.

Sometimes the ethical questions in business present themselves in a very technical formulation. It is not difficult to realize that when directors of savings and loan institutions give themselves or their friends sweetheart loans, ethical questions are raised. When a takeover artist pays an auditor to undervalue the obligations of a pension plan and then removes the "surplus," it is easy to see something is wrong. The specific rules governing insider trading, however, are not so obvious, and it takes some economic argument to establish that insider trading is bad for the market. Similarly, it is not so easy to detect the harm done by Salomon Brothers when they bid for a higher amount of government securities than the rules permitted.

From early in the century business advertising has been ethically suspect. It was one thing to meet needs, another to create needs through refined psychological devices of advertising. (The specter here was subliminal advertising.) What kind of advertising was to be allowed, what forbidden? Was it to continue a case of *caveat emptor*, for fear of lapsing into paternalism? Could doctors and lawyers advertise, or does that run contrary to the professional image of a commitment to public service? May beer and hard liquor be advertised where the primary audience is young people? Can a distinction be made between advertising products, such as cigarettes, whose *intended* use is harmful to the user and those which may be harmful as a byproduct of their use (for example, automobiles)? If such a line can be drawn, on which side do advertisements for guns fall? To what extent should advertising be judged by the harm it might bring—and to whom? Must we take into account unreasonable interpretations of the advertising? And the question of deception in advertising has almost generated a subindustry for drawing fine lines between literal truth and material or essential truth.[5]

On another front, what was to be the treatment of the impoverished? Early in the century the ethical code of ice companies had included the provision that the poor should not lack ice delivery. Today, should a gas company maintain service to those unable to pay? Is this a cost that should be borne by more affluent consumers? Is it the responsibility of the telephone company, as a public utility, to provide free telephone service to those unable to pay or to the elderly? If so, what level of service—three calls a month? Only outgoing calls?

Large-scale issues of policy in business began to take on an ethical coloration much more general than the question of regulating insider trading and limiting the use of "junk bonds" to finance takeovers. It is commonly charged that American corporations focus excessively on short-term profits—demanding three-month reports, although the value of shares rises and falls as these reports show profits rising and falling. Is this inimical to long-range research and investment in production? Will it bring its own punishment in the competition with the more far-sighted practices of other countries? Or does it require surrendering long-range industrial policy to a more general agency (perhaps the government), which threatens the moral claims of free enterprise? Here the ethics of responsibility begins to permeate the very structure and practice of business. It is perhaps clearest in particular cases of moving plants to other countries to cut labor costs although it adds to unemployment at home, in renewed attacks on labor unions, in problems of health and safety and pollution in the workplace, and so forth.

The litany of ethical issues could be continued with equal force through other professions—law, education, politics, or journalism. Issues arise even in the seemingly more technical fields where requirements seem more determinate, such as engineering, aviation, and the like. Even when risks can be calculated to fine shades of mathematical probability, the choice of what degree of risk is acceptable still remains. This was clear, for example, in the investigation of the explosion of the *Challenger*; the risk that the O-rings might fail had been calculated with precision, but the risk was undertaken nonetheless.

In this book we shall meet with many examples from all fields, not in the scattershot way we illustrated questions of medical and business ethics above, but in a fine-tuned context of specific exposition. It should not surprise us to find that every new field and every new invention generates its own realm of ethical problems. We read much these days about computer ethics and media ethics, and of how inventions upset traditional moral patterns. Thus, the video cassette and the photocopy machine (and more recently the compact disc) have played havoc with the familiar property rights in copyrights.

Although public consciousness of the new moral arena got its start in dramatic particular problems—the hard cases—of specific professions and fields, it was rapidly nourished by distinguishable large-scale issues that loomed on the practical–moral horizon in the decades after World War II. For example, as the Nuremberg trials revealed the ways prisoners were used for medical experiments, the demand for an explicit medical ethics took a place on the moral agenda, although it was some time before the medical profession responded—perhaps because it was not emphasized at the time that the experiments were conducted under the aegis of qualified and sometimes respected physicians. Interestingly enough, the immediate response to the revelations was the declaration of the Nuremberg Code, which went beyond condemning the cruelty and uselessness of Nazi experiments to locate consent at the heart of the ethics of human experimentation—whether or not the experiment is considered cruel or humane, well designed, or likely to benefit humanity, the consent of the subject is required. Slowly the lesson influenced practice and was reflected in codes and regulations. Since Nuremberg, every revelation of callousness in research or treatment fed the increasing public demand for regulation—the callous treatment of retarded children at Willowbrook caused a public uproar.[6] Among those concerned more directly than the public with regulations and research—the researchers themselves, their institutions, and those who provide the funds—the case of the Tuskegee syphilis study may have been more significant. The *New York Times* revealed in the 1970s that not only had the research, which involved leaving syphilitic patients untreated in the interests of having a "control group," been under way from the 1930s, but that it had received public funding and had been approved several times by disinterested medical practitioners.[7] The conviction grew that the research profession could not be trusted to regulate itself, and hence the 1970s witnessed a general movement toward external regulation of research.

Other fields have had their notorious cases, too. In social psychology, the Milgram experiments (ironically originating in Stanley Milgram's concern over how, in Nazi Germany, such "ordinary" people were led to acquiesce in monstrous inhumanity) caused psychologists to think about the responsibilities of a researcher to a subject, and about the role of deception in social experimentation.[8] Similarly, the case of Project Camelot caused anthropologists to reconsider their ethical obligations to those they study.[9] Agronomists have begun to debate their ethical responsibilities for the consequences of the seemingly promising "green revolution" as it has affected the Third World over the past half-century—the risk that increasing the potency of a fertilizer might cause a whole economy to become excessively reliant on one crop.

As the growth of medical ethics in the late twentieth century can be tied to Nuremberg, the Watergate scandal has had a striking impact on legal ethics. In a sense it was a scandal of lawyers, since so many of those involved were legally trained. The Watergate episode contained many moral lessons. It affirmed openness as against devious and surreptitious manipulation of public policy. It moved toward a restoration of a democratic balance of powers, as against the monopolization of power in the "imperial presidency." That the lessons were not fully assimilated may be inferred from the repeat performance of much the same debate in the subsequent Iran–Contra episode. Again the dangers inherent in secret operations were rehearsed. In a narrow sense of ethics, tagged in the media as the question of

"character," ethics in politics seems at times to have taken over political debate: disputes over sexual or financial conduct and the debate
over what standards of private behavior are appropriate to apply to a
public official; complaints that political campaigns have become triv-
ial (meaning entirely about "character"?) because politicians have become too scared to deal with the "issues"; elections being fought over
the question of which party has the least dirty advertising.[10] Some see
these issues as mere distractions from the important questions facing
the country. But ethics in politics also encompasses serious questions
of how a representative democracy is supposed to work: how campaigns are to be financed, how the line is to be drawn between hon-
oraria and influence peddling, and surely how to control the federal
deficit (this last raising questions of intergenerational fairness, which
is the elephant in the room that everyone pretends not to notice).

As we look back over the twentieth century, we can see that during
this period two massive ethical movements came to fruition. One was
the movement for *human rights*; the other, for *health and welfare*.

In the early part of the century the idea of natural rights was frequently used to protect private property and freedom of contract
against social welfare demands and legislation. Thus state legislation
to limit work hours of women or of people in special industries was
declared unconstitutional as an interference with freedom of contract.
During and after World War II, a different and more radical idea of
human rights gained strength. The idea took shape in the United Nations Declaration of Human Rights. It represented both a reaction
against the extreme cruelties of Nazism and a basis for the hoped-for
social reorganization that would justify the enormous sacrifices of the
war itself. In contrast with bills of rights of past centuries, it went
beyond civil and political rights to include substantial social and economic rights. The United Nations went on in subsequent declarations
to deal with rights of colonies, of women, of children, and of intellectuals. It could consider as broad a question as whether a people as
a whole had a right to share in the products that intellectual and
scientific progress made possible, and as narrow as whether workers
had a right to annual paid vacations. In the United States, the original
declaration did not remain merely a document. Human rights were
invoked in the liberation movements of blacks, of women, of persons
with handicaps, and of homosexuals; in the moral turmoil of students
in the 1960s with their demands for freedom and participation; in the

moral controversies over the Vietnam War; and in the issue of honesty in Watergate. Dramatic evidence of the strength of the appeal to rights is its invocation by many of the proponents of animal liberation who struggle to extend the protection of rights to nonhumans. The literature on rights and the controversy over rights in American philosophy has been both vast and deep. In its detailed exploration of specific rights it has intersected the applied ethics movement.

The public policy issue that has loomed largest as a moral concern throughout the century has been that of the opposition between the *welfare state* and *free enterprise*. While this stark opposition may have fitted those European countries where social welfare became aligned with theories of socialism and communism, it did not really fit the United States, where social security, unemployment insurance, and workers' compensation were all introduced as a response to the Great Depression of the 1930s when business itself collapsed and sought rescue by government. The government took up the slack to maintain a minimum of social well-being, in which some institutions (labor unions and federal regulatory commissions) were to act as checks and balances. Conservatives, however, did not see it this way. From the time of Herbert Hoover, they grouped communism, socialism, fascism, and new dealism together as statism and opposed to it the idea of free enterprise. During World War II, however, people at large were spurred in their sacrifices for the war by promises of greater postwar concern with their well-being. For example, in the United States, freedom from want was included in lists of rights, and a bill of economic rights specified the right to a place to live and a good education. In the 1960s the welfare conception, by one name or another, played a central part in politics, and Lyndon Johnson's "Great Society" was perhaps its high watermark. That the opposing conception was also a well-defined policy became clear in the Reagan administration's effort to dismantle many of the established controls. Most marked has been the almost wholesale movement toward privatization of traditional public tasks, efforts to transfer hospitals, schools, even prisons, into private hands for private profit, on the assumption that they will thus be run more efficiently and more economically.

It is not surprising, then, that controversies about the ethical aspects of public policy have begun to loom large: how to handle poverty and unemployment, health care and illness, access to education, safety in the workplace, and a host of other problems. To these have been added many apparently isolated policy issues of all sorts: the treatment of immigration and immigrants, matters of criminal justice, treatment of migrant workers, questions of civil disobedience (particularly those raised by opposition to the draft in the Vietnam War), and the increasingly visible plight of the homeless.

It is clear, even from this brief sampling, that the range of practical moral problems has broadened enormously. No survey of contemporary moral problems would be complete, however, if it did not observe the further feature: the stakes have gone up and moral neglect carries with it momentous consequences. The clearest case is war. In the past, war threatened at most the extinction of a people; nuclear war puts at hazard all life on the planet. In the past, pollution of the air threatened a particular region; contemporary pollution endangers the ozone layer. Once pollution of the water affected particular wells, lakes, and streams; contemporary pollution means the garbaging of the ocean. The reports of the Club of Rome marked a significant stage in the awareness of these contemporary pollution problems.[11] The reports considered not the traditional great disasters—major epidemics and plagues, failing harvests, hunger—but the extinction of humankind in global desolation. The first report, in the 1960s, was the starkest: it focused on nuclear war and nuclear accidents, on statistical predictions of the depletion of basic resources (e.g., energy), on the growth of pollution not from special causes but as a result of normal industrial activity, and on the rate of overpopulation. Although this report was widely regarded as exaggerated (the second report was more measured), its impact was enormous. Since the Club of Rome reports, problems such as that of the ozone layer and the greenhouse effect, and of the pollution of the ocean, have taken on an even greater urgency.

Morality, so often regarded as an afterthought to pressing problems, may well turn out to have a major steering role in their solution. The practical problems of the twentieth century have developed from two world wars, a cold war, the breakup of colonialism, the internationalizing of industry and commerce, the resurgence of nationalisms in a broader global world, the unbridled expansion of technology, the vast growth of knowledge, extension of education, and the spread of democratic aspirations. In this broader matrix, problems of public policy, professional action, and personal life have to take their bearings, combining knowledge and principles to meet particular situations. Applied ethics calls for analysis of moral decision and its dimensions. For a preliminary understanding of what is involved in enlightened reflection on action, a first requirement is to move toward an understanding of morality itself (Chapter Two) and to consider the resources that ethical theory offers (Chapter Three).

CHAPTER
Two

Moral Orders

A morality is part of the fabric of living, like religion, etiquette, custom, and more formal institutions like law and government. It sets limits to feelings and actions, sorts goals and aspirations for approval and disapproval, commands, advises, sanctions, furnishes models for emulation, molds character and development, monitors practices and institutions, envelops daily life in an atmosphere of civility and mutual trust, and often in individual action nods approval or offers a basis for self-criticism.

Yet, despite its familiarity, morality still remains insufficiently explored. We lack a definitive and systematic account of what makes something a moral matter, as opposed, say, to a legal, economic, political, or religious matter. The edges of a specific morality, the order of a particular culture, may be relatively clear, but it is a mistake to take the salient features of one morality—for example, that its regulation should take the form of rules, such as in a catalog of commandments, or that its sanctions should be stabs of conscience, rather than coercive law—as the defining marks of *any* morality. A great part of our own morality is explicit and conscious, stated as commands, rights and obligations, or as ideals and virtues, and it is easy to imagine that any morality must contain these elements. But we do not usually recognize how sharp is the division in our morality between right and wrong, leading us to the expectation that a debate is satisfactorily resolved only when we know definitively who is right and who is wrong. In other cultures, a decision for one side might be seen as a moral put-down of one participant; for example, in some north African Mediterranean societies the moral solution would be to work out a compromise such that both parties could honorably accept it. Is our insistence on sharp judgments a shrinking from ambiguity? Is it inimical to moral dignity?

Morality is not alone in eluding mapping. Comparable difficulties arise over describing and differentiating religion, and delineating the exact nature of a legal or political system. Narrower categories, such as marriage or the family, raise similar questions. Even some who regard as legitimate only marriages of one man and one woman, are willing to allow as a "marriage" a polygamous or polyandrous union, while refusing to consider the union of two persons of the same sex a "marriage" at all.

Religion is most instructive for the task of defining the makeup of a moral order. In the attempt to define religion, some philosophies of religion focus on beliefs (systematically elaborated, whether formal theologies or myths about the gods), others on distinctive feelings and emotions, others on standard rituals, others on the quality of attitudes to life. How this is decided has practical consequences. For example, if we are to assess the charge of "atheism" against Socrates in ancient Athens, and avoid anachronism, we need to know whether to the Athenians religion is a matter of belief (in which case, we should inquire into what Socrates believed) or a matter of conduct or ritual (in which case we need to ask how Socrates behaved). In our century, seemingly abstract questions of definition have played a vital practical role during times of war, whenever courts had to assess claims to be excused from military service as a "conscientious objec-tor"—should we regard a man who had given ample evidence in his attitudes and actions of a sincere and fundamental objection to killing and violence, but who did not believe in god as a supernatural being, as having a religious objection to violence? The affirmative answer given by the courts resulted in broadening the legal concept of reli-gion. Indeed, there is some similarity in the later claim of those who wanted "creationism" to be taught as an alternative to evolution in the schools that "secular humanism" is a religion and so both the biblical account and the scientific account are religious! A particularly diffi-cult case is that of parents who, on religious grounds, refuse surgery for their children in the face of unanimous medical advice that with-out it the child's death is likely. Are we to regard that element in their position as no longer a religious one, but a trespass into the medical? Or is it wholly a matter of religion and any interference with it an infringement of religious freedom? The precise definition of "religion" and comparably that of "morality" thus may be an important practical matter in applied ethics.

First a linguistic interlude. The domain of the moral is sometimes designated by *moral* and sometimes by *ethics*, and much confusion arises from the fact that in contemporary usage they sometimes seem to have the same meaning and sometimes not. *Moral* has a Latin root and so is etymologically a later arrival than *ethics*, which has a Greek root. The Romans used *mores* to translate the Greek *ethike*, and so in some original sense they have the same meaning. Since then, however, they have sometimes gone their own way. In Western philosophy, the convention arose of using *morality* to refer to patterns of conduct and belief—a morality is possessed by persons or a people and is investigated by observing what they do or believe—and using *ethics* to refer to theorizing about morality. We shall follow this convention.[1]

Even when we have distinguished the ethical and the moral, another ambiguity lurks in *moral*. Sometimes *moral* is used to express approval, to suggest that the conduct judged is right and good, as opposed to *immoral* or "morally wrong." At other times, *moral* is used as a classificatory term and is opposed to *nonmoral*. It is this second sense that is invoked when we say such things as, "Preventing AIDS by distributing free condoms is a medical and not a moral matter." The potential for confusing these two senses of *moral* arises not just from the fact that there are two senses here, but because *moral* in one sense is a subcategory of *moral* in the other sense. It violates the standard principle of classification that the same term should not appear at different levels. In this chapter the sense of *moral* we have in mind is the classificatory one that opposes *nonmoral*. To identify something as part of a moral order is not to approve it but to consider it a matter for moral judgment, whether that judgment be positive or negative.

For a time in the twentieth century moral philosophers sought to give precise necessary and sufficient conditions of *moral*. The search was for a single defining mark of the moral. Candidates for this single element included: a distinctive emotion (e.g., that moral disapproval is carried by a distinctive kind of resentment or indignation, or by the sense of guilt that accompanies moral infractions, or basic human sympathy), or the form of moral rules (that moral rules are distinctively universal, applicable to all rational beings everywhere), or ultimacy (e.g., that moral rules override other types of rules—legal, medical, business), or a distinctive use of a designated vocabulary.[2] On the whole, these unitary proposals did not prevail. Quite apart from the inadequacies of the specific candidates put forth, the search itself was cast into question by the ordinary language school of philosophy with its Wittgenstein-inspired skepticism over the possibility of finding necessary-and-sufficient-condition definitions for any ordinary social terms.

The search for a single mark has fallen into abeyance especially because of developments in the general theory of social institutions. In the early part of the century it was tacitly assumed that social, political, legal, and educational institutions had a stable existence in the form in which they were then found and that a study of them would elicit their defining marks and the laws of their operation. Their study was characterized by a kind of intellectual separatism. In the nineteenth century, unsuccessful attempts had been made to discover the separate evolution of these institutions, but despite their failures, the institutional separatism was carried over into the twentieth century. In some cases the separatism was supported by ideological interests. For example, if economic institutions were separate from political, then it was easier to argue that government should not interfere in business (a favorite argument in the 1920s, dashed by the Great Depression of the 1930s). But genuinely intellectual interests were pursued with a continuing assumption of institutional separatism. For example, social scientists might inquire how social institutions pressed upon one another, struggled for control of aspects of human life, provided occasions for enrichment and aggrandizement. These investigations required fairly sharp definitions that would keep the borders of institutions clear.

Morality never quite fit into this scheme; it could not easily be isolated as a separate institution among many. It could apply to business (cheating), politics (bribery), marriage (infidelity), the family (incest), and indeed to any nonformal interpersonal—and even intrapersonal—relations. Morality can apply anywhere. Accordingly, there was a strong tendency to regard it as a general spirit or atmosphere rather than a particular institution. On the other hand, no one denied that law is an institution, and yet it too could be found anywhere. So morality could still be regarded as general in its scope and still maintain the character of an institution.

In the second half of the twentieth century, many of these issues of institutional definition and jurisdiction more or less evaporated. Social theory focused instead on the needs and functions that institutions serve. It then became clear that several institutions could serve the same function and that a single institution could add and subtract functions. Production could be organized through the government as well as through private economic institutions. Conflict resolution could be undertaken by arbitration or mediation as well as by law. Education could be provided by corporations as well as schools. Educational institutions could serve some health needs. Some of the functions hitherto handled by the family were met by other agencies. Boundaries that had been sharp became vague, and even the general need to sharpen them diminished. Today the very idea of institutions has become relaxed. We speak of practices and institutions to cover patterned repeated actions and social organizations in a highly general way.

At any rate, moral considerations may be raised today in any area of human conduct, and hence no institution can be walled off from morality. We can no longer say, for example, that something is purely a matter of business, as if business occupied six days of the week while morality entered only on the Sabbath.[3] Whether one views this theoretically as showing the especially general character of moral institutions or as the intrusion of a moral dimension in nonmoral conduct matters little for practical purposes. The important point is that it is not adequate to simply deny morality its jurisdiction ("This is a medical, not a moral matter; morality has no say here"). We have to show that *morality* allows the problem to be decided on specific (economic, political, familial) nonmoral grounds. It is partly a moral decision to allow a business matter to be decided on purely business grounds.

Thus, neither the philosopher's search for necessary and sufficient conditions of the moral nor the social theorist's search for the defining features of a distinctive institution of morality has resulted in a definitive characterization of what makes up a moral order. Yet this is not a counsel of despair; we do not come to the question empty-handed.

Although a definitive and systematic account of morality is not yet available, we do know a good deal about it, especially our own. For our purposes, it is not necessary to have a precise definition of morality. A working model will suffice to indicate how the moral domain differs from the economic, religious, or legal. To avoid the mistake of confusing the specific characteristics of our own morality with those of morality in general, it is best to take a comparative view from which we may be enabled to see features of our own we might otherwise overlook. From a comparative view we can see that a moral order contains at least these elements: means or steps and goals and ends, called *goods* and *evils*; types of acts usually classified as *right*, *wrong*, or *obligatory*, to be done or not to be done; and character traits usually called *virtues* and *vices*. The italicized words indicate the *concepts* usually employed in English in talking about *moral orders*.

A more detailed account of what goes into a moral order can be achieved by attending to the differences among the moralities of different societies. Perhaps most obviously, moralities differ in their particular evaluation of conduct. But they also differ in which distinctive *mechanisms* they use to enforce regulation, in *scope* (the extent of the moral community or who counts), in the vocabulary used, in the types of justification offered, and in how each morality is configured.

Early anthropologists attended to particular differences: different notions of modesty and of which parts of the body may be exposed, differences in marriage pattern (monogamy, polygamy, polyandry), different models of the praiseworthy human being (boastful arrogant type, the accumulator of wealth, the great warrior, or the wise elder serving as judge and peacemaker), different patterns of distributive justice (for example, rules for distributing products of the hunt—some Plains Indians did not consider food as private property, although horses were held privately). There seemed no end to the variety of moral selection among types of behavior and character traits. Later anthropologists turned to more systematic themes, focusing on underlying tasks and functions. While all moralities are concerned with maintaining the necessary conditions for the existence of community, the sources of turbulence may be seen differently and the modes of addressing them varied. One society may worry mostly about aggression, another about sexual relations, another about property and acquisitiveness, and still another chiefly about warding off illness or ensuring rain for the crops. Both the language and the structure of morality will also show differences. For example, in our society, the term *thief* refers to stealing and private property, but among some African societies one term covers both stealing and inhospitable behavior. (Compare the binding together of poor and lazy in our *shiftless*.) Each culture has its own chemistry for linguistic moral combinations. It is not always easy to analyze the components. For example, does *charity* cover giving money to help out a fellow worker, or only the well-off helping the poor? As to the structure of moral discourse, our contemporary morality gives central place to universality of moral rules, while an earlier period, with marked distinction between the aristocracy and common people, had class-differentiated moral rules.

If we look at morality in this comparative way we note features that might otherwise escape us—for example, its use of distinctive *mechanisms* and its appeal to different *sanctions*, and beyond these, perhaps the way in which a morality sees its world and takes on *configurational properties*. The common source of mechanisms is human feelings and emotions. One morality produces guilt feelings for trespass, which haunt a trespasser even if no one else is aware of the lapse. Another stresses the social feeling of shame, a shrinking before others, with the miscreant sometimes being met with ostracism.[4] Regret may mushroom into remorse, out of which—as conscience—philosophers have sometimes tried to construct a whole view of the moral structure of the world.[5] In any case, different moralities draw on a whole range of social sanctions, rewards as well as punishments. If we are told that "virtue is its own reward," it means that morality is also tied to inner feelings of self-esteem and the way a self is molded in its development.

Moralities as a whole have markedly different configurational properties. For example, one kind of morality is repressive. Its rules are sharp commands, allowing of no deviation. The feelings it elicits are guilt, with little mode of expiation. The modes of decision are authoritative in tone, demanding strict obedience. Its justifying theory may picture a vengeful deity or ancestral spirits. Its vocabulary is one of duties and obligations, not ideals. In contrast, a second kind of morality may emphasize love and sympathy. Instead of rules, it may have models of the saintly person. It offers forgiveness and expiation. To one in distress it offers a community of helping hands, not the pointing finger of condemnation. Its vocabulary is one of virtue rather than of duty. A third kind of morality may feature the individual aspiring to success, with ideals of achievement and the growing well-being of the community. Its vocabulary is one of goods—individual and common—and its virtues initiative, industry, and self-improvement.

Morality has sometimes been compared to language. There are hundreds of languages, differing in sounds used, in vocabulary, in rules of construction and rules of utterance. Similarly, as we have seen, there are hundreds of moralities worldwide, also differing in vocabulary and rules. But the analogy with language is especially illuminating if we attend to two features displayed by natural languages. One is that any given language is characterized by constant and inevitable *change*, and this change encompasses not just the more obvious changes in vocabulary as words are added and subtracted, but also more deep-seated change in rules of construction that may become clear only to the historian of language development. One language might even be compared to another on their ability to change. One of the glories of the English language is its adaptability and readiness to change (although the Académie Française might consider changeability a weakness rather than a strength).[6] On the other hand, languages also show an impressive *stability*. The common tasks of language—communication of ideas, of feelings, of efforts—are strong forces for conserving the conventional.

In the same way as languages, moralities change. Perhaps the best overall example is the growth of the moral community, the idea of who counts and who participates in the common life. While the dream of the brotherhood of man (or perhaps now correcting for gender, the "siblinghood of the person") was found among the Hebrew prophets, in early Christianity, and in Stoic philosophy, the practical growth of the moral community depended on the degree of communication and interaction between different parts of the world. The place of hospitality in most earlier moralities (when obligations largely extended to the kin group only) was an accommodation of the necessity of social intercourse for trade and marriage when arrangements for strangers such as hotels are lacking. In due course, we find the broader communities of village and city, of nation, of class, of race, all of which come to be seen as unduly narrow, and even (when they become virulent, as racism did in our century) morally devious. The transition has been to the moral idea of respect for every person or for humankind. (Even this is labeled "speciesism" today by those who would extend moral consideration to nonhuman life as well.) We can readily tie the contemporary broadening of the moral sphere to the growth of one world, and its increasing unification through trade, communication, transportation, and the movement of peoples. Humankind has also tended to increase the number of those actively participating in the moral and political process, particularly with the growth of democratic ideas, increasing individual freedom and autonomy, as well as expanded educational opportunities. Thus "to participate" has shifted from merely being counted to playing a part in decisions and in determining what is right and wrong, good and evil. The marked individualism of modern life and thought has put on the defensive all patterns of authoritarianism, in morals as well as politics.

The recognition that variety and change characterize morality as well as all else in human life has often led to tirades against moral "relativism" (see Chapter Four) and the charge that it makes all morality arbitrary. These responses reflect the anxiety of persons whose footing is insecure. The focus on change, however, tends to obscure the *stabilities* that underlie morality. It is natural to fasten attention on points of difficulty and challenge, rather than on stable attitudes. The same tendency can be observed in the way people think of the law as a matter primarily of courts and courtroom battles and the conflicts of hard cases. The result is to underestimate the degree to which the law depends on unquestioning acquiescence by most people of most rules of law. Perhaps it is because present challenge is more stirring than past solutions, or because greater joy is found from the momentary thrill of creative solution, that we focus on the problematic rather than the stable. Whatever the explanation, it is a mistake to dismiss either element.

There is no lack of stabilities in the history of the moral life. They can be of longer or shorter duration, but they are *givens* for their time. Indeed, the stabilities fashion the human being at any given time. They dictate how far he or she is in a community or stands apart from it, what the typical goals or attitudes ingrained in the culture are (for example, basic mutual trust or suspicion, cooperative or go-it-alone attitudes), fundamental regulation of types of action (moral rules of honesty and fairness), approved character traits (faithful follower or independent judge). Bentham emphasized the degree to which human expectations rely upon stabilities to the point that he thought a bad law in general use preferable to a new uncertain one. Thus it may be underlying stabilities that give a people its distinctive character or a community its atmosphere. There are also deeper stabilities (kinship loyalties and responsibilities), characteristic of all human history, that tap fundamental features of community as such. The key question about stabilities is where to look for them. Too often historically they have been sought on the overt level of action and character, as if there could be just one model for the good person. Often, too, moral judgments are too closely tied to the institutions of the time and place, as they are conveyed through education and socialization. Here the stabilities assigned to the institutions come to be regarded as permanent in human life. With the recognition of the shifting, markedly instrumental roles of institutions, moral constancies can be sought in the needs, requirements, and tasks found in all societies.

Although the most agonizing problems arise when the stabilities are strained, and while applied ethics is not about the stable parts of morality, it looks among the stable parts for ways of dealing with moral issues as they arise in practical problems. To do so with greater understanding, it is useful to go to the resources that moral philosophy, that is, ethical theory, provides.

If the moral life were entirely smooth going, the demand for ethical theory would be less urgent. This demand arises when people are led to think about their morality. Ethical theory is thus a second-order inquiry. This need to rise to a second-order level is not distinctive of morality: it can happen in any field. For example, children do not always catch on when we first try to teach them something. We might attribute this to some failure of theirs, but then we ask whether our teaching is effective, or whether the level is appropriate, or whether the language is clear. And so, over and above the teaching itself, we inquire into teaching and its methods. Thus educational theory is inaugurated. Had our method been effective in the first instance, we might never have gotten to theory.

What are the points in a morality and its functioning that prompt reflections generating ethical inquiry? There are many, quite different points, indeed, a plethora. There is no telling where or how an inquiry can be initiated. One can, however, judge that ethical theory has three sources: the need for consistency and clarification, the facts of disagreement, and uncertainty.

The pressure for consistency is a prominent source. You feel it wrong to tell a lie, but you are still ready to lie to save a life, and doubtless you have no qualms about the order of importance of the two moral precepts on this occasion. You tell a lie to spare a person's feelings, but when she or he gets into trouble afterward by repeating what you said, you may begin to wonder what the justifiable exceptions to truth-telling are in situations of conflict and you begin to consider whether you can develop a consistent set of principles governing truth-telling. Soon you are offering clearer rules, definite exceptions, ordered priorities among the rules. In short, you are well on the way to making morality more systematic, and this is to enter on ethical theory.

Again, there is disagreement. It may occur within the group whose morality it is, or it may arise from the encounter with outsiders whose morality is different. It is a rare culture, self-confident and tolerant, that can simply say: "That's their morality, but we have ours. Let them follow theirs and we'll follow ours." But even with insiders there is conflict, which requires the effort at justification. Most moralities do have some built-in beliefs about how to justify moral judgments. Some appeal to tradition, others to the gods, and still others to the success that has resulted from adhering to the existing pattern. Embryonic ethical theories are thus already to be found within the moralities themselves.

Then there is uncertainty: uncertainty as to what the consequences of an action are, which rule to apply, and which authorities to trust. Uncertainty focuses attention on the process of decision itself. Is it a logical procedure of deduction from rules or is it a digging procedure with principles as instruments? Is it guided habit or fresh learning and inventiveness? This emphasis in theory was a late development, and its problems have opened fresh paths in contemporary ethics.

Purely intellectual investigations have provided another source for ethical theory. Socrates wanted to know what justice is, and he posed the problem as a problem of definition—how does one define justice? In modern times linguistic interests have called attention to the entire range of moral concepts, or (in more linguistic fashion) the whole vocabulary of morality. (Where Socrates worried about the meaning of *justice*, we worry about the meaning of "justice.") Actually, the linguistic concern could have been reached more directly under practical necessity. To ask, "Is it right to tell a lie on such-and-such occasion?" may be met with "But what do you mean by 'right'? What are the criteria of rightness?" Or again, we find such questions as, "It'll surely have the best results for all concerned, but is it right?" To those employed in the analysis of meaning, this is framed as the problem of how the meaning of *good* is related to the meaning of *right*.

Philosophers have, on the whole, found linguistic or conceptual analysis more attractive than the practices of experimental science.[7]

We see later in the book how philosophers themselves parted company on issues of meaning and how these differences have affected ways of dealing with practical problems. Moreover, particularly in the twentieth century, ideas about language were invoked to turn ethical theory in one or another direction.

A further stimulus to ethical theory is important in contemporary thought. As knowledge—anthropological, sociological, and historical—grew about the various institutions of society, similar questions were raised about morality as a whole. Is it a natural expression of the human self, operating through feeling or will and guided by reason? Or is it simply a mode of control by which a population uses whatever it can to maintain its survival and enhance its social life? The range of possibilities developed in ethical theory is, of course, much wider than these two examples. But the problem is always the same—to assess morality as a whole among varying human ways.

Whatever its various stimuli or sources, over the centuries ethics has maintained a large reservoir of theories, many overlapping, but many at odds with one another on beliefs that may be metaphysical, religious, epistemological, logical or scientific, or valuational grounds. Because applied ethics is often taken to be the application of ethical theory to solving moral problems, and in any case different ethical theories are invoked in the process of solution, we have to establish some familiarity with ethical theory. We proceed accordingly to character sketches, not so much of specific theories as of the families of theories that have been prominent on the ethical stage—some taking center stage (though changing their costumes in different ages), with others only waiting in the wings.

Three

Ethical Theories: Intellectual Tools for Applied Ethics

Those great systems of thought we know as Western ethical theory consolidate responses to those pressures—those deriving from inconsistency, incompleteness, conflict, and lack of clarity—that cause conventional stabilities of the moral order to break down. Here we find the familiar figures—Socrates, Plato and Aristotle, Stoics and Epicureans, Augustine and Aquinas, and such seventeenth- and eighteenth-century figures as Hobbes, Locke, Spinoza, Hume, Smith, Bentham, and Kant. And if we are to enrich our understanding of current moral problems, not just as an aid in our seeking of solutions but as an aid to the very framing of the problems, the reservoir of funded wisdom represented by this portrait gallery of the past is of inestimable value.

In this chapter, though perforce in a schematic way, we look at some aspects of what is contained in this reservoir of theories, first with some general remarks about characteristics of ethical theory— illustrated mostly from classical (pre-Enlightenment) theories—then, more narratively, the story of ethical theory from the Enlightenment.[1]

The history of ethical theory is both broad and deep. As is true generally of philosophy, the classical theorists remain vital participants in current debates. It is hard to imagine a debate on the nature of a community that will not be enriched by Aristotle's treatment of the *polis*, or one on human relationships that will not benefit from his reflections on types of friendship. One would not go to Aristotle for illumination—except perhaps in a negative way—on public roles for women, but Plato's advocacy of the right of women to serve as guardians in his *Republic* does still speak to modern issues. An important lesson is that, in turning to classical writers on moral problems, we need to be sensitive to the context in which they wrote. The different directions taken by two theories may reflect not just different choices of basic concepts, but also the mark of their different associations. Thus, Aquinas's and Augustine's ethics exhibit a strong institutional association with religion or theology; they tend toward the legalistic and an emphasis on other-worldly virtue; the ethics of Locke and Hobbes reflect their thinking on government and sovereignty and their concern over how to give a secular basis to government; the Stoics and Bentham have law in their background association.

Theories also respond to the larger intellectual climate and the scientific and philosophic resources of the time in which they were developed. Thus Plato and Aristotle start with a commitment to a metaphysical and objective reality, though they may differ over the nature of that reality—ideas for Plato, and natural purposes in the operation of the world for Aristotle. The Stoics assume the reality of a natural law reflecting Reason in humans and nature. By contrast, the ethical theories of the seventeenth and eighteenth centuries reflect the turn in philosophy generally from metaphysical questions to epistemological questions and the intellectual tensions caused by the growth of science. As philosophy turned toward epistemology, the ethical theories focus on the question of how morals are apprehended. As the power of mathematics, especially in the deductive method of Euclidean geometry, was appreciated, it was extended as a model for all knowledge; this was especially influential on the European continent, as developed in the Rationalism of Descartes, Spinoza, and Leibniz. It shaped the French legal system and of course touched our own Declaration of Independence with its self-evident truths. The British followed another course in epistemology, and consequently in ethics: they appealed rather to sensory experience, regarding scientific law as built out of sensory blocks with our knowledge thus resting on sensory reports or observations. Hence, they allied moral learning with cognitive learning generally (although among the empiricists there were some, like Hume, who held that "moral matters were more properly felt than judged of" and stressed the role of feelings such as sympathy, resentment, and fittedness). In attempting a synthesis of these Rationalist and Empiricist epistemologies, Kant argued for an active role for the mind in constructing our picture of the world out of content provided by experience.

Finally, the great systems also bear the mark of the particular emergencies and pressing problems of the day. Plato and Aristotle both write to the problems of the political community, Plato blaming the democratic form of Athens for the destructive war against Sparta and challenging the competence of the people (*demos*) to rule in favor of the claims of the "meritorious," while Aristotle, facing the Macedonian-Greek city-state conflict, calls for moderation and placing authority in the hands of a stable middle class. The Stoic ideas of law reflect a preoccupation with the seeming loss of a role for the individual and family in a universal empire ruled from Rome. Augustine writes to a world in social chaos as the Roman empire collapses—Rome itself literally going up in flames. Hobbes and Locke write, and participate, in the conflicts over authority between parliament and king during the British civil war. Hume and Smith, writing in a country finally stabilized after a century of discord, turn to the challenge of mercantile economics, while Bentham is motivated by what he sees as the corruption of "sinister interests" in legislation. Ethical theories are not created in a vacuum: they are responsive to civil discord (e.g., the revolutions, French and British and American); conflicts of church and state (or empire); the force of the popular; enfranchisement of new classes, such as the commercial class; and—perennially—war.

ETHICS AT THE ENLIGHTENMENT: DEONTOLOGY VERSUS TELEOLOGY

By the time the enthusiasms of the Enlightenment had faded, or at least by the early decades of the nineteenth century, much of the vocabulary and many of the key concepts found in modern moral discussion had been laid down. The revolutions, social as well as political, ensured a central place to the notions of contract, popular sovereignty, social utility, and some version of natural law or natural rights, as well as the constellation of ideas that grow around the idea of freedom—liberty and equality. Even fault lines—very broad lines of division among ethical theorists that make for opposition and allegiance—that mark out present options and make for theoretical rivals and antagonisms are already in place. Two fault lines through ethical theory are of particular importance. One, using the standard somewhat ponderous labels, is the division into *deontological* and *teleological* theories, the fundamental self-conscious division of the nineteenth century. The other, dividing ethical theory in the twentieth century, is the division between *naturalists* and *non-naturalists*, that is, the division between those who use explanations for moral phenomena that are continuous with ideas of experience used in the natural sciences and those holding that moral ideas require explanation in non-natural (for example, religious or idealistic) terms.

As we look back from the vantage point of the twentieth century, it is clear that the Enlightenment represents a watershed in the history of ethical theory when theorists self-consciously divided themselves into the two opposing camps of teleologists and deontologists. We can easily identify the great modern representatives of the positions—for deontology it is Immanuel Kant, and for teleology it is Jeremy Bentham.

The deontological[2] position—especially in its legalistic or juridical forms—takes morality to lie primarily in rules or laws or rights. For Kant, the central moral concept is the concept of duty—indeed, he was willing to concede only one motive that was entirely creditable from a moral point of view, namely, acting for the sake of duty. Duty, he felt, had the nature of a command and was experienced as such in the voice of conscience, and it permitted of no excuse or even mitigating circumstances. The paradigmatic moral experience is that of an individual, fully aware of what the right thing to do is, but tempted to do otherwise. For the most part, Kant felt, people already know perfectly well how to identify right and wrong; hence, ethical theory has the role not of discovering what is right, but of "grounding" it—justifying it and explaining it and analyzing what lies behind it. Above all, for Kant, ethics is a nonempirical matter. Duty does not vary with circumstances or consequences. Rather, the sophisticated moral actor determines what is right by applying the "Categorical Imperative," which, in a way akin to the Golden Rule, asks one to consider whether one could consistently will to concede to everyone the right to perform the action one is contemplating. This is not an appeal to the consequences of actions; rather it is a demand that one be logically consistent in one's moral behavior. Thus, in Kant's famous example, to tell a lie is never justified, no matter what the consequences, even when the intention is to save a life. The reasoning is that if you lie—and are justified in so doing—then you must, in logical consistency, permit others to lie also. But, says Kant, if everyone is permitted to lie, then lying itself becomes impossible; lying presupposes a background expectation of truth-telling. Note that the reasoning is not an appeal to the detrimental consequences if everyone *did* lie. Kant would presumably agree that the consequences would be socially chaotic, but, then, one might reasonably argue that not everyone will lie. But it is not the putative consequences that make the lie wrong; it is what happens *conceptually* to the ability to lie when the expectation of truth-telling is removed.

Another way to regard Kant is to see him as explicating a conception of the moral equality among human beings, an equality that he signals by writing of the "dignity" of the human person, by insisting, in one version of the Categorical Imperative, that we may not treat other human persons merely as means to our own ends, which today is labeled as the requirement that we "respect persons." To claim the right to lie when one refuses the same right to others is, to Kant, to claim a special status for oneself that violates this principle of equality. It may not be a historical accident that, just as Kant is developing an ethics based on a commitment to human equality, revolutions are under way based upon ideas of equality and basic rights—the American Revolution, but especially the French Revolution. Now Kant's ethics has as central concepts duty or law (and has in its historical antecedents both the Stoics' idea that there is a moral law binding on all people and also the medieval Christianization of natural law in Aquinas), not the concept of a right; yet a theory based on rights is in the same family of theories. As with duty, rights speak peremptorily and imperatively; they demand, require, insist, "no matter the consequences." To assert a right is to claim what one is due, not to request a favor. To receive by virtue of a right is not to receive a gift or largesse for which gratitude is appropriate—just as, for Kant, doing one's duty does not call for gratitude on the part of others. It is, simply, the "right thing to do." Natural rights theory, originating in the later Middle Ages with William of Ockham, and then developed by Hobbes, Locke, and Jefferson, became the conceptual framework for the revolutions of the eighteenth century, perhaps because the needs of the time called for extraordinarily forceful language. In

Locke and Jefferson these natural rights are intuitively self-evident and have an integrity and authority of their own. They are also associated with social contract theory, as in Hobbes, to give rights the binding character of a promise or contract. These rights are deontological in the sense given above, whether their foundation be considered God-given, engrained in human nature, or even constitutive of the idea of a person.

The other great family of ethical theories is the *teleological*,[3] and here the teleologist *par excellence* is Jeremy Bentham and the paradigmatic teleological theory is Utilitarianism, of which Bentham is considered the modern founder. Unlike Kant, Bentham had a vital role in the political reform movements of his time. His followers, a group called the "Philosophic Radicals," dedicated themselves to influencing legislators in a progressive direction, including the reform of the legislative system, extending the franchise (though not all philosophical radicals agreed with Bentham himself on the need to include women in the vote), abolition of slavery, and so on. Although the Philosophical Radicals did not constitute a political party, their program was carried on in Parliament by the Whig Party (and later by the Liberal Party), and they provided the intellectual direction for much of the reform of the nineteenth century in Britain—in particular, the extension of the suffrage to the commercial middle class in the Reform Bill of 1832, the consolidation of courts of equity, and reforming the Poor Laws.

Bentham himself saw his role as that of introducing reason to an area that is notoriously permeated by privilege (in his phrase, "sinister interests") based on no ground other than custom and tradition. To be successful, he conceived, he would have to get his contemporaries to *think* differently about legislation. In the Britain of his time, law was considered something that was *declared* by the legislature, rather than being created by the legislature. The legislature discovers what had always been the case, and announces it. Clearly a large conceptual shift was necessary if he was to move from the view that legislators discover law to the view that legislators invent law.

Bentham searched for a criterion by which he could assess social practices, and he came upon it in the form of the principle of utility. The essence of the principle is that law, and social practices generally, should be assessed by their probable consequences on everyone affected. It establishes, therefore, both a future-oriented outlook on legislation and an egalitarian outlook—"everyone to count as one, and no one to count as more than one," he wrote. It is also a thoroughgoing individualistic outlook: the interest of the community, for Bentham, is simply the sum of the interests of the individuals that make it up.

The utilitarian approach to legislation appears commonplace today. What could be controversial about insisting that laws be evaluated by their effect on people? And to the extent that it so appears, Bentham was entirely successful. But, of course, "the devil is in the details," and in this case the details are extraordinarily difficult. How are the consequences on the people affected to be calculated? What counts as an effect? Are individuals to be counted as privileged observers in counting the effect on themselves, or can they make mistakes? How do we compare effects on one person with effects on another? These questions, and others, are answered in different ways by different utilitarians. Bentham's own answer is hedonistic (pleasures and pains are the only ultimate values), and he attempted to solve the calculation problem by the notorious "felicific calculus" (which proposed an entirely quantitative calculation of pleasures and pains in terms of degrees of intensity, duration, propinquity, certainty, purity, and extent). He devoted much attention to systematic classification—much as a chemist might—of types of motives and types of pleasures and pains. For Bentham, all these efforts are in the practical interest of guiding legislation and reforming institutions.

This outlook is very different from the deontological one.[4] Recall that for Kant what is right is independent of consequences; for utilitarians it all depends on the consequences. For Kant, human beings by and large know what is right and the paradigmatic moral situation is temptation; for utilitarians, what is right is known only as the result of an intricate calculation of consequences. Still, it should be noted that the impact of a teleological approach and a deontological approach can be the same in a particular situation. Bentham was wholeheartedly in favor of the revolutionary movements of his day. Indeed, his sympathy with the aims of the French Revolution[5] led to his being declared an honorary citizen of France. Similarly, he favored independence for the American colonies. But he was entirely at odds with the reasoning, or as he thought, the lack of reasoning, offered in justification of these revolutions. The appeal to natural rights, as a self-evident property of human beings or as givens, he considered merely the abandonment of reason, "nonsense upon stilts." How can we assess whether a right exists? To say it is "self-evident," he thought, is only to assert it again. No reasons can be given one way or another.

NINETEENTH-CENTURY ETHICS

Deontology and Utilitarianism were the basic fault lines established at the end of the eighteenth century, and for the most part they define the positions taken through the nineteenth century. This is not to say that no new paths were opened or new options explored, but the general lines of allegiance were settled. Established theories were refurbished and updated, and old concepts took on new meanings under the impact of the vast changes that altered the nineteenth-century's view of human beings and their world, among them, the shift of population from agricultural to urban life, from commercial to industrial economies, with changes in the notion of work and the commodification of labor, globalization of communication, and developments in science and technology, including the professionalization of knowledge itself.

Kant's theory of obligation continued to find adherents in the nineteenth century, including its introduction into literature by Coleridge, Emerson, and the Transcendentalists. Often those in philosophy who were sympathetic to Kant's ethics dispensed with the heavy epistemological and metaphysical baggage. Among these were the Intuitionists, often not profound thinkers and usually members of the dissenting clergy, particularly Unitarians. Men of enormous integrity and undoubted influence, they steadily opposed those who determined morality by some form of calculation, especially in terms that involved self-interest. They succeeded in capturing what many of us feel in daily life situations: we just *know* (intuit) in daily encounters what the right thing to do is, what kinds of actions are good, and which of our motives are admirable.

But if there is any idea that is distinctive of the nineteenth century it is the idea of change and the search for the laws that govern it. We see it in geology in mid-century and in biology toward the end of the century. In philosophy it is associated with the work of G.W.F. Hegel. On the face of it, Kant's theory of duty and obligation—reason is a law giver, legislating what could become a universal law, good for all times and situations—is not especially congenial to change, and Hegel criticized just this part of Kant's theory for ignoring historical processes. Interestingly enough, Kant's own historical writings, *Perpetual Peace* and *Idea of History*, prefigure the search for laws of historical change. Kant held that international peace may become effective in history as a governing ideal—that is, may lead to the development of institutions like a federation of states that may give us a reasonable hope of securing peace, dependent on our own decisions, actions, and resolve. The ideal of peace then may be feasible while not in any way inevitable. It is this feature of inevitability that Hegel imports into his notion of history. Kant's individualistic theory, with overtones of Protestant conscience and stern obligation, is but a prior stage that will be superseded by a stage in which individual interests will be welded, under the driving power of Spirit or *Geist*, with the social in the state. At mid-century Karl Marx was to elaborate these ideas into a social-economic theory. Whereas for Hegel the moving force of history is idealistic, Marx looked to how socioeconomic natural laws shape a succession of institutional forms under the motor power of economic processes and the resulting class divisions.

The British Hegelians (for example, T. H. Green), loosely following Hegel, looked to the self rather than to history. They abandoned Hegel's grandiose all-embracing World-Spirit moving dialectically through history and determining it; they proposed instead a more modest view of individual ends and objectives. There is a spiritual principle of development in humans, that is, self-realization. But the *self* here refers not to a narrow individual but a social self extending over the whole of spiritual reality and manifesting itself in each of us, as well as taking social form in our institutions. Thus the problem of egoism versus altruism is less a conflict of opposing forces than two forms—a wrong and a right form—of willing the good.

In the family of deontological theories, it is the younger relative—rights—that has had the more flourishing career over the past two centuries and has enjoyed spectacular prosperity in the late twentieth century. The United Nations Declaration of Human Rights established—or perhaps merely acknowledged—it as the preeminent conceptual framework for social progress. It is hard to imagine carrying on a current discussion of abortion (consider choosing "choice" or "abortion rights" as the label for one position), pornography, political correctness, feminism, experimentation on animals, or torture, without the concept of rights. Earlier in the twentieth century rights-theory played a critical role in the movements for equality for all racial groups and for women.

The idea of natural rights also has associations with the ideas of liberty and justice, and as it veers more to the one or the other it can change the direction it takes. At the end of the nineteenth century the idea of rights veered toward liberty and the right to property—the liberty to acquire it without government interference and to dispose of it as one wishes—became for many people the preeminent right, and with this association, especially when couched in the individualism of the nineteenth century, the idea of rights tended toward conservative uses. In the twentieth century the idea of rights, particularly the idea of human rights, became more intimately linked to justice, with the result that its direction shifted from the protection of property to the advancement of other human benefits. The career of the rights concept through the last two centuries shows how ideas can get stretched over the course of time. In the American Revolution, although the basic idea of natural rights had been laid out, the appeal to rights tended to careen uncertainly from the more traditional notion of "rights of Englishmen"—traditional rights of citizenship—to the idea of rights possessed merely by virtue of being human. The language of the French Declaration was of human rights; in practice the rights extended to men only (as was pointed out by Olympe de Gouges's, in pained protest, publishing an alternative, "more inclusive" [as we would now put it] Declaration, and by Mary Wollstonecraft's *A Vindication of the Rights of Woman*). Gradually over the centuries the idea of rights moved from that of civil or political rights, with a limited domain of membership, to the wider concept of human rights. First, rights were held only by a restricted class of men (say, owners of a specified amount of property or some racial group), then they were extended to a larger class of men, then to include women, then to include children, then to include animals, and now, to some in the ecology movement, natural objects. Similarly, the content of the rights has been stretched from civil rights to a concern with the dignity of the human person, and that dignity construed to include a concern with the wherewithal to live a decent life—sufficient food, medical treatment, and education. At each step along the way, rights struggled against one another. The rights of parents to control the destiny of their children struggled with the rights of children; the right of sovereignty becomes breached by the need to reach across national boundaries for redress of inhuman treatment.

The utilitarian outlook also underwent modification and deepening in the nineteenth century, primarily at the hands of Bentham's godson, John Stuart Mill, who developed it into a full moral and social philosophy. His *Logic* helped shift simple empiricism toward Experimentalism, a shift that was important for the developing social sciences as well as ethics. His *Political Economy* and *Representative Government* were used both as texts and policy manuals, and ensured that Utilitarianism was a matter of discussion not only in Britain but also in Europe and America. These discussions engaged a wide range of people, for the question of whether Utilitarianism was the right approach was not seen as merely academic.

Mill's work involved important emendations to Bentham's. Most important was Mill's modification of Bentham's fairly crude account of pleasure/pain. Mill insisted that qualitative pleasures/pains be included also in the underlying psychology; for example, aesthetic pleasures, sympathy, and reputation. It should also include, he thought, "fellow feeling," which was to help to resolve the egoism–altruism dispute. This enlargement enabled him to convey the insight that the individual's good is best served by advancing the social good. Of course this is so only if the institutional arrangements, political and social, support the realization that the individual's good is best served by advancing the social good. This social good, he argued, required extending the franchise to labor (and not just to guild workers but to those laboring in factories) and, at the time more controversially, to women. (As a Member of Parliament for a short period, Mill was proudest of his intervention in the debate over Benjamin Disraeli's Reform Bill of 1867 to propose that all occurrences of the word *man* in the bill be replaced by *person*. His amendment failed, but he succeeded in placing women's suffrage on the agenda for serious discussion.)

Utilitarianism in the nineteenth century was understood in two ways, depending on the attitude toward the idea of laissez-faire, the idea that government should take a "hands-off" approach to the economy. All utilitarians accepted the principle of nonintervention, and fully concurred with Adam Smith's arguments against mercantile economics. The differences among utilitarians had to do with their willingness to tolerate exceptions to the principle. The early Philosophic Radicals of Bentham's generation were not reluctant to assign a role to government in the face of pressing social needs. This more progressive interpretation was the one taken by Mill. Although his *Political Economy* vigorously defended laissez-faire principles, he softened the impact by distinguishing between the question of economic production, the laws governing which, he insisted, were natural and beyond our control, and the question of distribution, which is open to human decision. Since laissez-faire assumes consumer sovereignty, in cases where the consumer is not in a position to judge the value of goods, the government may be obliged to intervene, if the value of the goods involved is of great social interest. A primary example is, for Mill, education: here, he said, consumers cannot judge, and so the government must play a role.[6]

A second wing of Utilitarianism took a harder line on exceptions to laissez-faire: the government has a role to play, it claims, only in matters of criminal justice and in national defense. It was this wing of Utilitarianism that came under attack by European economists even before Marx. The critics argued that Utilitarianism appealed only to broad and abstract laws without taking into consideration a more complex and systematic understanding of particular situations. What was needed was a more profound understanding of such things as depressions and the general impact of changing modes of production with the displacement and impoverishment of large populations. Worst of all, the critics charged, the utilitarian equating of happiness with wealth-getting and wealth-use is much too simplistic.

Herbert Spencer was an adherent of this second, harder Utilitarianism. He was the prime mover in Social Darwinism, a movement that brought biological theories of evolution to the support of laissez-faire. In the competition for survival the fittest will survive, and the mark of superiority is precisely that the fittest occupy the seats of power and wealth. Intervention by government to ease the impact of economic change is interference with the operation of natural laws and, in any case, bound to fail.

The Darwinists' view of social history did not always lead to such dire consequences of policy. Even T. H. Huxley, who agreed that competition in nature was indeed a matter of "red in tooth and claw," held that in human societies a moral order requires us to combat gladiatorial ways of life. Later Peter Kropotkin, taking the lead from Darwin's own writings, argued that mutual aid and a sense of solidarity were as natural a part of evolution as competition. This sense is more than a feeling, more even than sympathy, for it arises as a property of natural participation in group living. It is state-imposed power that conflicts with genuinely free association and naturally occurring concern for and cooperation with others.

Developments in the natural sciences during the century were to alter significantly the view of the world, of ourselves, and of our place in it. Thus the Wöhler synthesis of urea from inorganic materials in 1828 effectively destroyed the distinction between the organic and the inorganic. Other discoveries weakened the popular Vitalism by showing that no distinctive kind of energy was necessary to account for animal heat—it could be explained adequately as a case of combustion. Still others pointed out the similarity of plant and animal cells and even of vertebrate and invertebrate embryos.

More popular in its impact were the developments in geology, beginning with the work of James Hutton and later that of Charles Lyell, friend and adviser to Darwin. Our earth, they showed, is not the recent and unchanging reference point it was generally taken to be, but had a long history of gradual, progressively monumental changes—and was even now slowly changing, under our very feet as it were. Lyell found sea fossils in mountain sides and primitive utensils in company with bones of extinct animals.

The social sciences were to develop their own techniques and subject matters. For example, sociology beginning with Émile Durkheim came to a more subtle understanding of personality as an interaction of the individual and the social. Wants, beyond the barest necessities, are not just given, but are colored by the community in which we live. We internalize the social pattern as a central feature of our own personality. Moral authority is partly internalized on the individual side, as a distinctive kind of obligation, but there is an objective side rooted in the actual cultural pattern.[7]

Unquestionably the most important scientific contribution of this period was Darwinian evolution. *The Descent of Man* traced the continuities in the animal world in general—even the external expression of emotions (of anger, subservience, friendliness, and social cohesion) exhibit functional continuity and utility, especially for communicating, with animal postures. The natural social condition for animals and humankind is in groups, and the extent of cooperation or conflict depends on the environment, both social and physical, that they find or make for themselves. Human nature and social institutions are thus both products of human capacities and provide opportunities as well as constraints. Each is subject to change and development. Morality itself is a social product to be understood in terms of natural laws. But neither Darwin nor Huxley was a social Darwinist. Indeed, T. H. Huxley, "Darwin's bull dog," and even Alfred Russel Wallace, the co-discoverer of natural selection, were not sure that the moral sense, the imperious ought, could be captured entirely in terms of natural selection. They believed there were important differences between biological evolution, on the one side, and social and cultural evolution on the other.

Throughout the century, science remained the model for knowledge, but science itself came to have an increasingly sophisticated view of what was involved in method, learned from the practice of scientists themselves. In its popular impact, no scientific work exceeds that of Darwin's. But below the threshold of popular attention, methodological changes were just as significant in their effect, above all, the discovery of non-Euclidean geometry. In the eighteenth century, there had been only two models for knowledge, one rationalist and deductive, which took mathematics, especially geometry, as its measure and emphasized the purely cognitive and intellectual; and the other inductive and empirical, based on observation. In the nineteenth century, the rationalist model was seriously upset. It had taken as its model Euclidean geometry, which begins with self-evident axioms that, together with what could be consistently derived from them, provided a uniquely true description of space and the properties of figures in it. But nineteenth-century mathematicians began to try out different axioms, only to find that equally consistent, alternate geometries with curious properties resulted. (Shortly after, alternate logics were also explored.) In consequence, the axioms of geometry came to be regarded as conventional decisions for given purposes, subject only to the criterion of consistency, rather than uniquely applicable to reality.

Although they may seem somewhat remote from moral theory, these developments in geometry shook the belief in intuitive axioms, or universal rational principles. Euclid's deductive model had found favor with the French and American revolutionaries, who had asserted the self-evident rights of equality, property, and liberty. When the universal validity of Euclidean axioms was challenged, how could geometry provide any support for the claim that the existence of natural rights is intuitively given as well?

The nineteenth century also began with many embracing a relatively naive empiricism: that the mind is a blank tablet upon which sensible experiences write. All knowledge rests upon observation processed by rather limited laws of association—of combining, abstracting, comparing, etc.—to arrive at the generalizations that constitute scientific knowledge. Now it became clear that both the practice of scientists and the reasoning of lay people belied this simplicity. The new appreciation of the complexity of inquiry came to be called Experimentalism. More is involved in inquiry than simple observation: inquiry is selective, guided by hypothesis and interest. When practice, testing, and action are added, then we need to take into account motivation and the control that focus on a particular problem may exert, including inventiveness and discovery. It is clear that a more creative role must be assigned to the organization of experience than that provided by associational psychology, and that psychology must look further to understand such abilities as we have, even to the talents that go into framing theories themselves.

As interest in science became more general, it began to become more professional. Royal societies were organized, academic posts were established in the social sciences—in anthropology, sociology, and economics—as well as in the natural sciences. This breaking off of disciplines from philosophy was to have its impact on moral philosophy. Gone were the days when a Hume or a Kant could contribute materially to knowledge in general. One impact was that moral theorists were now forced to define their domain, methods, and relations (if any) to the rapidly accumulating sciences and sometimes to show what qualifies as expertise. In short, ethics was to become professional and academic (in both senses). Further, evolutionary theory was to divide twentieth-century moral philosophers into the two camps noted earlier: naturalists, who regarded morality as a natural social product open to study by methods continuous with those of science, and non-naturalists, who would reserve a part, and sometimes the whole, of human experience, history, and morality as immune from explanation by such methods.

TWENTIETH-CENTURY ETHICS

At the beginning of the twentieth century, the character of the discussion in ethics changed to give a central role to concerns about the distinctiveness of moral phenomena. This discussion—largely between naturalists and non-naturalists—was precipitated by G. E. Moore's vigorous attack on all moral philosophies that identified value with any natural or metaphysical or religious property whatsoever, instead of recognizing the uniqueness of the idea of *value*.

The naturalists, on the other hand, believing that the human resources and capacities that are employed for solving problems generally are available and sufficient for moral problems, too, moved away from purely biological questions toward questions of the evolution of cultures and societies, the interplay of character and social milieu, and the kinds of social cohesion, as well as questions of individual responsibility and the role of guilt, shame, respect, and sympathy in human beings.

Of course many philosophers of different schools agreed that moral phenomena were distinct, that moral knowledge differed from that furnished by science or even ordinary experience of the world around us. Arguments centered to a great extent on the relation of fact and value, of the normative and descriptive, of the *is* and the *ought*. While one might hesitate to regard this as a single tradition, these thinkers disagreed with the naturalists about the continuity of moral experience with experience generally, and they all believed morals to be a separate domain.

Idealists and naturalists (especially the utilitarians) were challenged by Moore's arguments. Moore took seriously Henry Sidgwick's view that the task of moral philosophy was to analyze and clarify concepts, and like Sidgwick he spoke of moral properties, especially of *good* and *value*, which he took to be central to ethics. But Moore denied that these properties are the sort that science and ordinary empirical experience deals with: hence he called them "non-natural." As in the case of color perception—yellow was his favorite example—we can be sure of what we perceive or intuit. Non-natural properties are as experiential as color perception is: judgments about their presence or absence cannot be established by the evidence or ordinary or scientific experience. To attempt to explain or define these moral properties—for example, in ordinary terms like usefulness, pleasure, or even self-realization—is to commit what Moore called the "naturalistic fallacy." It is to cross categories, a line as inviolable as Hume had taken that between *is* and *ought* to be. *Rightness* and *obligation*, in Moore's view, are not quite in the same category, for they may be considered instrumental to the good—what would in the long run yield the greatest good as consequences, but since consequences are endless and not really calculable, the better policy is to trust common morality as presumably a lesson of experience.

The realism of Moore and his view of non-natural properties were too precarious to survive for long. For a while his moral view influenced the group around him, which included John Maynard Keynes, whose *Memoir* of Moore recounts his impact: the group found it refreshing that one could simply intuit the goodness of friendship, love, and even the good itself. What did survive for a long time, however, was the charge of committing the naturalistic fallacy: criticism in its name could unnerve any attempt to understand moral terms in non-moral terms, that is, in the language of ordinary human experience. Of course, one would first have to show that the division into natural and non-natural was a useful, not a chance or random, one, and for what purposes it could be used.

Moore's realism bowed before the whirlwind entry of Logical Positivism. This sterner movement, with its members known as the "Vienna Circle" and largely European (primarily Germans and Austrians, though with Polish contributions, especially in mathematical logic), protested the fuzziness that they found in German metaphysics. They pointed to Johann Fichte's view of a World Self differentiating itself into an empirical self and a nonempirical Other, or to Hegel's notion of a Real as an all-embracing unity that transmutes into a higher synthesis the partial, fragmentary, and "self-contradictory" purposes, thoughts, and values of finite existence. While many Idealists were more sensible than such grandiose conceptions might suggest, there were enough excesses to prompt the logical positivists to search for more exact and refined criteria of meaningful discourse and sensible questions. While this exposition was undertaken by a number of European philosophers who were refugees from Nazi persecution in America—including Rudolf Carnap, Hans Reichenbach, Herbert Feigl, and others—the most popular attack on metaphysics in the 1930s appeared in A. J. Ayer's *Language, Truth, and Logic* (1936), published in Great Britain but even more widely received in American university circles (though often as an object of attack).[8]

The criterion that the positivists offered for meaningfulness was that a statement uttered must be translatable into immediate sense experiences. This was moderated later to allow general or highly abstract theories to be meaningful by stipulating that the logical consequences of such theories would have to be testable in experience. Philipp Frank allowed a broader criterion—utterances would be verifiable in *common*, not just *sensory*, experiences. For moral statements, the difference was crucial. Ayer argued that no sensory experience established the validity of a moral utterance (for example, that lying is wrong), and therefore that such utterances were not statements, just emotional reactions. (This exposition gave the name "emotivism" to the positivists' view of morality.) Frank's formulation in terms of *common experience*, on the other hand, might seem to allow a Millian utilitarian principle in that it would allow "Lying is wrong" to be analyzed as "Lying causes a greater unhappiness to people in general than telling the truth."

Ayer's own view moderated with time. His association with Bertrand Russell in political action led him to see, as Russell had seen, that when people advocated a social policy they did not mean only that they liked it. Ayer was knighted (by a Labour government in Britain), appointed to an Oxford chair, and welcomed once again in America.

The further explorations of the functions of moral language were carried out by a group of largely Oxford philosophers in the late 1930s and 1940s, among whom the best known are Gilbert Ryle and John L. Austin. At Cambridge, for a time, the center of interest was the work and lecturing of Ludwig Wittgenstein.

On the face of it, it seems unlikely that moral discourse, with its general sensibleness and its utility in guiding our lives, should be only, or even largely, emotive. Even in its own terms, the emotive theory was too narrow to explain all the uses and complexities of moral discourse. The inquiry had been formulated as one into the uses of language, and as it was carried further, an increasing number of different uses were brought into focus. Language could be used not only to express feelings, but also to give commands, affirm agreements, make promises, turn agreements into contracts, deceive others, instruct, learn, express wishes, and a host of other uses. The same words, in different contexts, may have different import: for example, "not guilty" is an acquittal. Compare with this, "He's out," said by the pitcher, and by the umpire. "I declare thee husband and wife" in a wedding ceremony marks the first moment of the legal marriage. Even the use of the same word in different contexts or in association with words has various meanings: for example, pronominal differences may change the meaning of "ought"—"I ought" is deliberative, "you ought" may be a command, "he ought" offers advice. Linguistic expressions may thus assign responsibilities, make claims, and in some forms (e.g., "I ought to have . . .") express regret, sometimes with feelings of guilt and remorse. Complex formulations may be geared to all sorts of different contexts: for example, "I have a right . . ." probably both makes a claim and registers a complaint, and it may be accompanied with justifying reasons.

This largely academic tradition, whatever else were its gains and internal differences, had the general effect of estranging moral theory from practice as well as isolating it from cooperation with the social sciences and psychology. In contrast, there were many philosophers who believed that moral theory was concerned with the purposive strivings of human beings and the qualities of their experience in their lives and associations, not with something other-worldly or non-natural. Hence they are regarded as "naturalists." They differed in the particular phenomena of human experience they emphasized. Ralph Barton Perry spoke of human *interests*; Edward Chace Tolman of human *purposes*; Charles Sanders Peirce, William James, and John Dewey of *values* and *human experience* and human *practice* and *action* (hence they were called "pragmatists"). These differences did not affect their shared opposition to views such as Moore's or the logical positivists', views which narrowed down morality to a non-natural quality or a special noncognitive, emotional, or linguistic utterance.

Of these naturalistic movements, perhaps the easiest to identify is Pragmatism, but it is better regarded as a general outlook rather than a school. It began in informal club or group meetings in Cambridge (Massachusetts) in the 1870s. The original members brought different interests and expertise: science and logic (Charles Sanders Peirce), psychology and philosophy (William James), and law (Oliver Wendell Holmes, Jr.). Their shared commitments are general: that knowledge has a functional role in diagnosing and solving moral and social problems, that learning is dependent on action and practice and their interplay, and that neither theory nor practice is ever complete, for new problems always lie ahead. The spirit of Pragmatism is well represented in the beginning of Holmes's *The Common Law*:

> The spirit of the law has not been logic: it has been experience. The felt necessities of the time, the prevalent moral and political theories, intuitions of public policy, avowed or unconscious, even the prejudices judges share with their fellow-men, have a good deal more to do than the syllogism in determining the rules by which men should be governed. The law embodies the story of a nation's development through many centuries, and it cannot be dealt with as if it contained only the axioms and corollaries of a book of mathematics.[9]

Peirce, who had already distinguished himself as a chemist, was primarily interested in scientific method and philosophy as a subclass of the sciences of discovery. Inquiry does not just happen: it is generally initiated by some doubt or hesitation when established intellectual habits, consolidated as beliefs and expectations, are blocked. A problem and its diagnosis serve to limit and to determine what is relevant. Insofar as this is a public undertaking, public criteria are needed for the critical terms and concepts. This need leads to his notion of operational definition: the meaning of a concept is exhausted by the set of operations or tests together with the observable consequences that result. Peirce usually illustrates his arguments with observational terms like *weight* and *length*, but the point can be made with *tallness*—clearly relevant to tallness are the instruments used to measure that property, no less than the context and the interest that led to the measuring in the first place. It makes a difference whether what is at issue is the height of basketball players in an attempt to predict success in the NBA or of Somalian children in a study of the effects of malnutrition. And, as we learned only too late to avoid acrimonious debate, the measure of intelligence is not independent of the tests used and the purposes to be served, whether to predict success in college or in the military.

James took advantage of Peirce's failure, at least at first, to specify the kinds of properties or predicates he was dealing with (e.g., moral terms and even *truth*) as well as what kind of experience was to count as confirming. James was to enlarge both. He clearly included moral terms and *truth*; and he allowed as verifying experiences the sense of failure, of satisfaction and achievement, of reasonableness and relevance, of hope that things are marching well, and even those peripheral feelings of self and continuity that accompany all our experiences. In effect, Peirce's criterion as liberalized by James, holds not only for the meaningfulness of a concept but for intelligibility itself. Reference to experience, immediate or remote, actual or possible, is involved in all meaningful discourse.

This begins James's successful challenge to the then-reigning faculty and associational psychology. Against faculty psychology, he argued that it is only late in our experience that we compartmentalize reason, will, and emotion. Against the associationists, he argued that we are more than simple inductive generalizers: learning has an active character. We are more talented than the associationists allow, above all in our capacity for deliberate action that is presupposed in all serious undertakings (including psychologizing). Experience, asserted James, initially comes undifferentiated in a stream of feelings, wishes, and desires. Only afterward do we carve out concepts, repeatable tastes, colors, and even faculties like reason and emotion. From the outset we are selective. If we see a billiard ball next to an egg, we may notice shape, but next to a tennis ball, we are likely to notice texture. For the most part, the likenesses and differences we perceive are related to interest: an architect, a social worker, a police officer, or a politician looking for votes would each likely describe an urban block differently; and while their descriptions may not be contradictory, they may not mesh very well, for virtually any scene, occasion, or event will outrun any description of them.

But we are constructive as well as selective. In the interest of the search for a stable world of predictable objects and events, we transform sensibly given materials into thoroughly different orders or worlds. The most useful, of course, is the world of common sense—of solid objects and relations by which we negotiate our way in everyday living. The penny *is* round, the table *is* square, although they are seldom experienced as such. But we also construct worlds of literature, science, business and exchange, even of art. Each of these generates different expectations, relations, and habits; each subserves different interests and is consolidated by historical experience, vocabulary, custom, and expectation. These worlds are not independent, but we navigate among them casually. Thus we may easily suspend ordinary causal laws when reading fairy tales or science fiction, while even a particle physicist plays hockey with a solid puck.

Under consideration here are the legal and moral orders of good and values, of conflicting ideals and desires, or responsibilities and relations. Although we claim for them a kind of objectivity, we do not expect them to answer to the standard modes of verification and prediction, since these worlds serve regulatively in refashioning the world as we want it to be. The moral world in particular is unfinished and in the making; no previously fashioned ethical rule will suffice for meeting the ever-new dilemmas that betoken a unique situation and that may call for novelty and increased knowledge in moral decision.

From a somewhat younger generation, C. I. Lewis and John Dewey write directly to ethical issues. In both cases their positions were developed before the impact of Logical Positivism; while they were sympathetic to its main scientific objectives, each in different

ways sought to show the continuity of values and facts, of the normative and the descriptive, within experience. Of the two, Lewis writes
more technically—appropriately enough, since his earliest work was
in mathematical logic.

At any given moment, according to Lewis, we are equipped with
presystematic commitments to what is true and real, good and satisfying, or just and fair. The job of philosophy is not to create such
commitments but, starting from them, to seek to formulate what is
already implicit in those judgments and decisions that we respect.
Utilizing Peirce's notion of operational definition, Lewis traces the
long route from particular reports, say of what looks red, to a judgment of what is objectively red, as well as the even longer route from
observation and experiment in empirical science to theory. Valuations, judgments of objective goodness and of what is truly satisfying
or grievous, are established in the same way; that is to say, valuations
are a kind of empirical knowledge not different from empirical judgments generally in their modes of verification and justification.
Clearly valuations are more complex, since the kinds of experiences
of what is satisfying, enjoyable, or painful, are more diverse than
judgments of color, weight, or solubility. Further complexities are
introduced by the variety of modes of evaluation, as predictions of
what may be found immediately good, as instrumentally valuable, or
even as contributing to a larger span of experience such as a good
marriage, a satisfactory sequence of experiments, enjoyable under-
graduate years, or even a life good on the whole. But this is not
sufficient to disqualify valuations as empirical knowledge. In any
case, valuations and empirical judgments are seldom packaged separately; even the scientist has interests and values while no valuation
is justified independently of reliable empirical knowledge.

Had Lewis stopped here he might be thought to have contributed
to a utilitarian analysis of good consequences. There is a further dimension to knowledge, namely, rules that help consolidate experiences and serve as guides for decision. Such rules are pervasive:
not only *Robert's Rules of Order* and the like, but rules of logic, of
chess, of baking, and of etiquette, and indeed of musical scores, which
provide directives for playing, say, a trio. Rules seldom prescribe
a single course of action, leaving no leeway for interpretation and
innovation. Further, when the enterprise is important, we may review and assess the rules in an effort to make them more comprehen-

sive and consistent, that is, to offer a critique. Where we have confidence that they are the best we can provide, such rules carry authority or obligation.

Such critiques are binding only if and when we choose to run meetings or play chess or trios—that is to say, their force is hypothetical. But where there are activities in which, as humans, we have no choice but to participate, the rules and the necessity of criticizing them become categorical. Since we cannot exempt ourselves from correct inferring and concluding, the rules of logic, incomplete though they be, are categorical. Though harder to formulate, we are also bound to do what we find effective in the execution of our plans and projects. This is formulated, although still incompletely, as a critique of cogency, best reflected in scientific method.

Lewis's point here is that we are also imperatively social. We cannot live unheeding of the claims that others make on our actions, nor of our need of them. Here we may be embarrassed by an excess of rules: "Honesty is the best policy," the Golden Rule, the charge of Jesus and Hillel to "love your neighbor," and even Kant's Categorical Imperative. All these except the first encourage impartiality, but they are too often unhelpful when we need a concrete decision: they need to be supported by knowledge of human nature, of reliable valuations (predictions of good consequences), and even of what is possible. Yet whatever we take to be the *right* decision carries with it authority, that is, the imperative to conform our actions to its directives.

Yet moral critique is broader than justice as impartiality; it involves as well the quality of associated living. Science and technology depend on capitalizing on the successes and failures of the past. Thus the quality of living depends on social memory and on the agencies that preserve and transmit them, including the supportive social structures such as education, freedom of inquiry and communication, and even the encouragement of individual talent.

Moral critique, in the broadest sense, must not merely look for imperatives that come from the status quo, but also look to the human aspirations for participation and for richer community, to the forging of shared goals and ideals, and to fresh norms of what we could be. These aspirations, goals, and norms are constitutive of morality and involve the institutionalizing of criticism itself.

Lewis comes to the social late in his work, but for Dewey it is there from the start. Dewey holds that reflection starts when there is a *problem-situation.* If all is going well, he says, following Charles Sanders Peirce, there is no hesitation in action and no problem-situation. When there is a problem-situation already, we have a sense that something has to be done but we cannot see immediately what action to take. Moral reflection arises when there is a problem-situation. Dewey holds that morality is social: I may think when I struggle with a moral problem that it is a purely personal matter, but there must be a background of social approval or disapproval to make it a problem in the first place. That social origin of a problem makes it a moral one. Society also specifies (overtly or tacitly) how moral problems should be dealt with.

The morality of a given society is a complex matter. It includes not only what to do and not to do, but also grounds or reasons for the injunctions. These involve conceptual elements—ideas of good and bad, right, wrong, obligation, and virtue and vice, as well as applications and specific forms of these ideas: for example, the obligations listed in the Decalogue, such as not to lie, and the corresponding virtue of honesty. The morality also provides procedures for occasions when there is doubt or hesitation about what to do. These may vary culturally, such as to consult an authority figure (parent, priest, or rabbi), follow customary ways, or think for oneself. And the morality may also tell us how to recognize a moral situation, in which we are expected to follow moral rules, as against a merely practical situation of resolving particular difficulties with no special moral import. Reflection on all such questions is usually called "ethical theory."

Dewey uses another vocabulary when there is a comparison, not merely of ethical theories but of various institutions in a society—religious, political, economic, artistic, social, and so forth. He writes of the *values* in each field and *valuation* as the process of determining value. He employed these ideas for many decades. He began developing them in 1913, when a committee of the American Philosophical Association posed as the topic for a meeting the question of value. Dewey argued largely against the utility of the idea of value: it seemed to him to be of use only in stating the results of a calculation or evaluation of the benefits and losses in a given situation. He proposed instead to speak of *prizings* and *appraisals*, to be regarded as active attitudes on the part of an individual or society. In fact, he doubted whether prizing meant more than *desiring* and thought the latter a preferable term because desire usually involves action toward achievement, whereas prizing might be merely a feeling. The notion of desire through its reference to action would bring us back to the basic notion of a problem-situation. This whole line of thought was presented by Dewey in his *Theory of Valuation* (1939).

Although problem-situations occurred in personal life, Dewey thought that this occurrence required the presence of problem-situations in social life. For example, a society that values getting rich highly may present problems to the individual that do not arise in a society that is equalitarian; similarly, for an aristocratic society as against a democratic one. A society that expects a conflict between individual and social values will differ markedly from one that expects them to harmonize: the former may higly value being different. Thus the character of people reflects in large part the kind of society in which they live.

Dewey's idea of *community* is not simply that of a society in a given territory; it is a mode of association. Association may rest on different features: a crowd, a mob, or people walking on the street are quite different forms of association. A group does not become a community until it has some problems in common that require associated action for their solution. Of course the kind of problems also determines in part the kind of association: for example, what makes people friends may differ from what makes them business associates.

Dewey's concept of democracy, developed in the first half of the century, resembles more closely the idea of participatory democracy that emerged after mid-century. In the earlier period, the general idea of democracy was *representative* democracy: the citizens elected their representatives, who then governed. Participatory democracy called for constant awareness of what the legislators were doing and putting constant pressure upon them to advance citizen aims. It involved expression of conflicts in the community as well, and similarly in the legislature. For Dewey, the aim of consciousness of values was central—not merely the values of the national community but of the international community as well. He recognized the dominating influence of business in America, so he did not expect his values to be realized in his lifetime, but he expressed a Jeffersonian faith in common people.

Throughout his work, Dewey points to a major defect in American thought: thinking in dichotomous terms rather than recognizing the complexity of our problems. He thought that the opposition of fact and value, the religious and the secular, even the individual and the social, hindered desirable social action. Thus, for example, he wrote a work on religion in which he tried to show that the human emotions and aspirations found in religion are also found in pursuing non-religious social aims. And in the economic realm, he pointed to social goals sought in individualistic societies and individualistic goals promoted in socialist societies—for example, he noted that socialist Russia encouraged high individual achievement in production, while private enterprise in America was moving toward cooperation (in the case of business, toward monopolistic cooperation; in the case of unions, toward national federation). Judgment of what was desirable on a particular issue was therefore not to be deduced from a general social position; it required careful examination of the particular situation and of the specific goods and harms of intended action. General slogans did more harm than good, in his view.

ETHICAL THEORIES: PROBLEMATIC APPROACH

Given the diversity, abundance, and conflict among the theories we have just reviewed—and the number of available theories is greater than we have considered here—the question of how to regard them is itself a serious moral issue. Moral discussion in our time is replete with appeals to rights, sanctity of life, social consequences, and to serious obligations such as telling the truth and keeping promises. Whole moral outlooks are in conflict, and we have to decide between them.

Notoriously, in spite of centuries of efforts to devise one, there appears to be no decisive way of choosing between ethical theories— *if* we think of ethical theories as putative claimants to provide the whole and only truth in the domain of morality, and *if* we conceive the task as that of choosing one theory among mutually exclusive rivals (much as people commonly think of choosing among competing scientific theories). But to conceive the task in this way presupposes that ethical theories are related to one another in the way, say, that the oxygen theory and the phlogiston theory are related in chemistry—they cannot both be correct. They are rivals in the very distinctive sense that they seek the same object (explanation, prediction) in relation to the same phenomenon.[10] The phlogiston theory and the big bang theory are not rivals in this sense. More apposite for our purposes is the relation between Newtonian mechanics and relativity theory: although the latter is said to have "replaced" the former and in some sense is a "better" theory, Newtonian mechanics continues to be used in preference to relativity when dealing with restricted domains of physical reality. For some purposes, we are told, Newtonian mechanics is the better choice, even though for other purposes it is not so good as relativity.

Now, one reason it is so difficult to choose among ethical theories may be that they are not rivals in the way phlogiston theory is related to oxygen theory. Instead, they are often dealing with different parts of the moral field. Thus, Kant may be concerned with the inner self-judgment of a human being and the feelings accompanying it, while Bentham may have his eye on legislation for the general welfare. If so, then the conflict between different schools of thought may not be so deep nor disagreements so grave as they appear at first. The theories may be going past one another rather than meeting in open conflict. The tasks performed by one theory may be different from those of another and the theories may also differ in the field they cover; in effect there is a division of labor among the theories. Hobbes and Locke, for example, are writing to institution building, while utilitarians are generally concerned with reforming existing institutions. Kant and Sartre, in their different ways, may look to matters of personal decision, modern contractarians and Mill to the limits of social invasion, and communitarians to counter excessive individualism. And the emotivists do well to remind us, especially when analysis falls on guilt, sympathy, or feelings of respect, of the critical role of interpersonal relations.

We need to reconsider how we use theories in applied ethics. Our job may be less making choice of one theory over another than exploring where a given theory provides help in solving or addressing a particular problem: we select *from* theories rather than *among* theories, we draw from theories. In the spirit of the pragmatic approach given above, it means we regard theories less as providing rival truths and more as instruments or tools to be drawn on to solve problems. And it is the problem itself that is governing, that dictates the best tool.

We mean to take this metaphor of tools quite seriously. When we are dealing with ordinary household problems, we have a general sense of problem types—electrical problems, plumbing problems, carpentry problems, and the rest—and correspondingly there are tools associated with each type. When setting out to solve an electrical problem, we may begin by reviewing the tools we have that are appropriate to the task. But we also invent—we may find that a plumbing tool is adequate to an electrical task; we may even find that a tool from one type is better than any tool we have available from the relevant type. It is the specific nature of the problem that determines whether the tool we choose is adequate.

In just this way, we suggest, the materials found in ethical theories can be used to solve problems or, at least, to move us toward a solution. These materials—concepts such as rights, duties, obligations, laws, character, consequences, pleasure, pain, common good, community, interest, needs, desire, justice, virtue, self-control, liberty, happiness, self-realization, equality, and so on, and their relationships—are our tools. As a result, a pluralism of theories is most appropriate for the domain of morality, not only because morality itself is so complex, works so differently in different contexts, is so intertwined with the workings of other institutions, but also because human nature is so rich in its potential, and the interplay of character and culture so little understood. Different theories fit different problems.

Taking this approach—centering ethical reflection on the problem and drawing on the theories, rather than choosing a theory and applying it—has some distinct advantages for our present undertaking. It introduces the theory–practice relation at the very outset and it opens the door to issues that are too infrequently attended to, especially the sociohistorical dimensions of moral problems. It may be that there is a reluctance to open this door because people are afraid of being accused of committing the "genetic fallacy"—that is, substituting an account of the origins or socioeconomic basis of a theory for an account or evaluation of the theory itself. Yet such issues, when raised, give us a very different perspective on the conflict of schools and the points at issue in the conflict. They point beyond the question of the truth of theories to questions of the adequacy of the theory in solving particular problems, practical as well as theoretical.

Four

Knowledge in Moral Decision

A final preliminary task is to consider more directly the question of how knowledge and experience enter moral decision, consideration of which is implicit in much of the theoretical discussion of the preceding chapter. In part this question involves our identifying intellectual pitfalls that may impede the study of applied ethics and—more constructively—offering some suggestions on how knowledge *does* enter moral decision. This chapter—aiming to clear the decks—begins with the pitfalls. These come from the intellectual culture of our time. They are different in kind: some are entrenched assumptions operating silently to frame the questions, some are dichotomies that send us in one direction only and hinder the fruitful interrelations of inquiry, and some are traditional or hardened formulations that assume universal relevance when they possess only a restricted pertinence. Among the ones particularly likely to lead us astray are assumptions about *ultimate authority*, and strict dichotomies of objectivity–subjectivity, relative–absolute, reason–emotion, and fact–value.[1]

ULTIMATE AUTHORITY

"I'm in command here," said Secretary of State Alexander Haig to the press soon after the attempted assassination of President Reagan. No one had asked him and the assertion was immediately contested. Where does ultimate authority lie when the President is disabled? In the sphere of ethics the candidates for such an office are legion—religious beliefs, moral axioms, societal demands, individual assertion—and the struggle among the contenders has been an ongoing story in ethics. It is important, however, to raise the prior question of whether the very framing of the debate is misconceived. The sad fact is that answers are at the mercy of the question asked, and advocates for these various candidates for ultimate authority sometimes become so consumed by their advocacy that they fail to consider whether the office they seek to fill is legitimate in the first place. Why seek for an ultimate authority if there is no sufficient warrant for such a search, and if all the candidates proposed have feet of clay? The heavens do not fall because the earth is no longer seen as the fixed center. Political life has been improved by the replacement of monarchical or imperial authority with complex democratic processes, in which even the "will of the people" is subject to learning and revision of methods and beliefs. Philosophically, the lesson has been that there can be a relatively stable system in which no part is assigned ultimacy, any component is subject to change, and the system as a whole is self-corrective.

No domain of human thought, endeavor, or devotion—from religion and political life to science and logic—has escaped this sad lesson. Religion, perhaps the most far-reaching in its claims, has suffered the hardest blows. The history of ethics in the Western world is in part the story of efforts to emancipate morality from religion, and even to claim a priority for morality. In the ancient world, Plato's *Euthyphro* has this as a central issue, Socrates arguing that the standard of the virtue "piety" must be independent of the will of the gods: the relation of an act's being pious and the gods' approval of it is not that divine approval makes it pious, rather it is its being pious that explains the gods' approval. In Bentham's work, religion is one of the sanctions for morality, effective for those who believe in it—nothing more. In Kant, religious as his thought is, there is a great reversal of religion and morality: instead of divine law laying down morality, it is morality that determines how we are to conceive of the divine. (For this reversal, Kant was placed on the Roman Catholic Index of forbidden books.) Note the basic agreement of Bentham and Kant that morality does not come from an external authority; for Bentham it is humans' reckoning their own well-being, and for Kant it is the self-legislation of the will. In short, the Enlightenment of the eighteenth century brought morality into the arena of human self-legislation.

To the religiously oriented layperson, the saddest fact of recent years has been the strife of religious dogmatisms—Iran's Ayatollah Khomeini announcing a reward for Salman Rushdie's assassination because his *Satanic Verses* is deemed pernicious in its treatment of Mohammed; extreme Jewish Orthodox groups in Israel reading Reformed Jews out of the faith and seeking to limit their secular privileges; the Moral Majority in the United States attempting to straitjacket the teaching of biology in the schools. Opponents of "relativism" could find no better example of arbitrary relativism than religious sects today. If religious philosophers still seek an ultimate religious authority for morality today, they may perhaps turn to the existentialist, for whom we decide in "fear and trembling," for we can never be certain. As Vercors put it, "God is always silent."[2]

The history of mathematics has furnished its own dreams for morality. Prominent among them has been the search for moral axioms, certified by their intellectual clarity and self-evidence. Among the examples scattered throughout the history of morals, the more important usually have been more than self-evident: for example, it may be affirmed that all persons are born equal and entitled to freedom of speech, but this status and such rights are also defended in many other ways—for example, Mill's argument for liberty as productive of invention and progress. Many self-evident truths are conveniently ambiguous. That "merit deserves reward" garners such universal agreement that it might seem self-evident, but it is riddled with ambiguity. The notion of merit itself is notoriously a matter of contention. Aristotle noticed this in pointing out that in his time disagreements over what constitutes merit lead alternatively to democracy or aristocracy or oligarchy. Medieval and modern theologians have explored many senses in which "merit in the eyes of God" might be taken. In the nineteenth century Mill observed that as a principle of justice "remuneration according to merit" might mean by effort, or ability, or work done. And one need only attend to the conflicting views in our own time over merit pay for teachers to realize that merit is far from a simple notion. There is also the question of merit in what—surely not in tiddlywinks? And even "reward" is nonspecific—does it mean money or praise or satisfaction? In the long run, the authority of self-evidence reflects rather the entrenchment of habitual acceptance. (Who would now find it self-evident that a man of honor when insulted should challenge his insulter to a duel?) The axiomatic character is invoked largely where there is either a challenge to or an interest in logical formulation.

Logic, too, has its dominating values—consistency and system (insofar as possible). The logician's dream for morality is that with consistency there will be no conflict, with clarity there will be no ambiguity or vagueness, with deductive consequences there will be no indeterminacy. Only in the late twentieth century have moral philosophers imbued with that dream come to realize that ambiguity, indeterminacy, and conflict are to be found within morality, not just beyond its borders.

Science also is a source of dreams. Biologists dream of secure foundations in a definitive account of human nature, as in the search to locate altruism in biological needs. A knowledge of human nature will reveal human aspiration as unavoidable tendencies in feeling and action, in short, the raw material out of which culture fashions a portrait. As long as the religious idea of humans having been made in the image of God prevailed, human nature and its tendencies were thought of as basically good, except where matter as evil was sharply divided from soul as good. With growing secularization implications of the natural as the foundation of the moral came to the fore and the association of the natural with the good came into question. Interestingly enough, the negative connotation of "unnatural" seems to have retained greater moral force than has the positive associations of the "natural." For example, "unnatural sex" invites approbrium while "natural sex" passes without comment. This may be changing as the "natural" (as opposed to "artificial") takes on the laudatory sense in the area of food. In any case, the evolutionary view of human development and ingrained tendencies that serve as survival mechanisms under specific environmental conditions left the moral critique of natural tendencies open. The ultimate moral authority of human nature, although it lingers in popular thought, has come philosophically to an end.

Moral philosophers, too, have had professional dreams, as is evident in the history of ethics. Most prominent has been that principles or moral laws could determine the outcome of moral decision, just as scientific laws determine results of experimentation. This dream rested on the assumption that in moral reasoning the minor premises (concerning the "facts of the case"), like the "state descriptions" of a scientific argument, were fairly simple and could be dealt with as a matter of course. But the failure of the minor premises has been serious. Just as in science, there is a long march from theory to prediction, with all sorts of intervening assumptions and measurements, so it is in moral decision. The road—we shall see presently—leading through diagnosis and context and regionalization makes the journey from problem to decision long and arduous. Principles have an important part, but no longer a monarchical one.

So much for the dreams of ultimate authority. It is time to wake up. Perhaps political history may point a way with an example: from the sixteenth-century theories of the divine right of kings to the twentieth-century theory of participatory democracy. In its early modern form, political democracy was taken to consist of the substitution of elected representatives for autocratic hereditary rulers. Significance is attached to the size of the electorate, which is successively enlarged until, early in the twentieth century, it comes to include women, lowers the voting age, and in some countries bypasses even the requirement of literacy by the use of symbols to stand for parties—in short, the march is toward a larger and larger electorate. At this point, the idea of the ultimate authority—in political theory captured in the notion of sovereignty—lingers as the collective will of the people, while the actual authority at any given time is the governing leader or group. The idea and the actual, then, are brought closer together as a result of several developments. One change is a shift from the electorate's infrequent participation at infrequent intervals to its continuing pressure on its representatives, thus causing a more constant participation. A second shift occurs when the idea of the will of the people is converted into statistical majorities and measured continuously by polls (which reinforce the first change of providing a continuous voice to the electorate). A third is a focus on the individual but with no assumption of constancy in an individual's position; rather, the individual is free to alter his or her interests in a changing world and to learn what best promotes those interests. We are not concerned here with evaluating these changes, nor with working out moral criteria for voter responsibility and voter participation. The point is simply that the idea of ultimate authority—even that of the individual as a constant ultimate authority—has gradually dimmed to the point of virtual extinction. In its place new categories of political processes have arisen, which are much more complex than the above description has been able to suggest. Contemporary democracy is a going system, often regarded as the best political system so far achieved by humankind, one in which checks and balances, division of powers, change and improvement, and learning and reorganization are all possible without locating an ultimate authority.

Keeping in mind this account of ultimate authority in the political realm, we might ask how far the pattern might hold in morality. As in politics, it appears that morality can thrive even in the absence of a fixed ultimate authority. Indeed, that is what seems to be happening at the present time. Doubtless many will regard this as an abandonment of morality (as monarchists might regard the complex and inefficient mechanisms of modern democracies as the abandonment of authority itself),[3] but one might regard it instead as an intensification of morality. For one thing, it leads to increased assumption of moral responsibility on the part of the individual. Just as the individual vote counts (as we eventually learn), so the individual decision counts. Advice may be sought from others, and their moral judgments weighed and even accepted; but that acceptance and the choice of one advisor over another are themselves moral decisions with an accompanying responsibility. Again, in a complex and changing world, a decision may prove to be wrong, and yet have been the best option available. Certainty does not necessarily attach to the moral decision. We examine such features of decision in Chapter Eleven, but here we observe that to abandon the dream of ultimate authority is to abandon the hope of absolute correctness in moral decision. This brings to prominence the virtue of humility in moral decision, quite different from the arrogance[4] that often accompanies a stern moralism—"Let him who is without sin cast the first stone."

OBJECTIVITY AND SUBJECTIVITY

The sharp separation of the objective and the subjective is an offspring of Descartes's philosophical dualism, which takes matter and mind to be, in effect, separate substances. The "outer" world's physical phenomena are ascertained indirectly by their effects on the mind, while "inner" phenomena (sensations, ideas, feelings) are grasped directly by introspection, looking into ourselves. Different categories are associated with each realm; for example, values or purposes exist only in our consciousness, not in the material world. So too, physical nature has no "meanings" or "intentions"; these are acts of the subject. Of course philosophy since Descartes has refined and multiplied theses embodying such contrasts; but the fixed lines of separation have held firm. Science, either physical science or other sciences modeled in its image, is thus value-free. Values belong to the domain of consciousness. They are subjective and have all the variability and uniqueness—and often inscrutability—that mind shows in its exercise of its freedom.

It is worth contrasting this outlook with the one-world approach found among ancient philosophies, most markedly in Aristotle's account of nature. Psychological phenomena of sense and feeling occur as events in the natural world: the modest maiden's blush is as natural an event as the color of a rainbow in the sky. Changes are classified as qualitative, quantitative, substantial (coming-into-being and passing-away), and spatial movement, but while the last unvaryingly occurs when any of the others take place, it does not have superior objective reality, with qualities like color and sound rendered subjective. Indeed, color and sound occur under determinate conditions of movement as all qualities do, and in some qualities the human organism is involved.

Philosophical dualism, which still directly or indirectly permeates contemporary thought, was spurred on by its seeming ability to serve two quite opposing objectives: on the one hand, to preserve a religious view of the soul against the inroads of a secular physical science; on the other, by reading purposes out of nature to protect physical science from teleological interpretation.[5] But it also kindled aggressive ambitions in various enterprises: the reductive materialism that hoped to reduce all biological and psychological phenomena to patterns of molecular movement; the idealist philosophies that translated matter into a collection of sensations; and the vitalist outlooks that reduced science to practical means rather than authentic knowledge. But most critical for ethics was the separation of values from the rest of human phenomena, so that "intrinsic value" was considered as either a special kind of quality (a "non-natural" quality, in the terminology of G. E. Moore) grasped in an isolated intuitive act unrelated to occurrence and historical relations or else a realm of ideals reached in some special affective act.

Fortunately, it is not our task here to explore the implications of dualism for ethical theory generally. It is important, however, that applied ethics somehow bypass the conclusion that values are isolated by virtue of their alleged subjectivity. If they are to be isolated from the general run of human phenomena, either in specific contexts or in some general way, the need for it will have to be shown by careful analysis of the needs of applied ethics, not by initial postulation as a philosophical dogma. For example, whether the method of knowing our own values differs from the way we know other people's values or the properties of the world around us[6] cannot be settled by insisting it *must* be different because values are subjective and subjectivity involves direct knowledge. The general picture of knowledge and how it enters applied ethics is the major task of the present chapter.

Perhaps the best way to avoid the pitfalls of the objective–subjective dichotomy is to substitute a different distinction that will keep questions open and allow them to be settled in the examination of particular contexts, not even postulating a general solution. For this purpose, we propose the categorial distinction, *public* and *private*. If something is public, it is more open to general knowledge processes; if private, these become difficult, but there is no general assumption in the distinction that items in physics are always public and items in the psychology of consciousness always private. In particular, actions, which are so important for applied ethics, may be one or the other, and in both areas. You can wear my shoes but you cannot do my wearing of them; you can, however, know a great deal about my wearing of them, sometimes even predicting better than I can how comfortable I shall find them. You can also, usually, see the green color I see—sufficiently to avoid auto accidents; and with careful testing and knowledge of optics (physiological, physical, and psychological) get close to reproducing the color as I see it. Of course, there are large domains of ignorance; but that holds liberally for all fields. Should it be charged particularly against the sensory-affective phenomena? Experiences may vary, and each will require investigation to see how public or private it is. Sometimes, indeed, public investigation helps improve private discernment. For example, the distinction between feeling sympathy as fellow feeling and feeling pity, a feeling from above, became much clearer after Tamara Dembo's inquiries into the reactions of disabled war veterans to people visiting them in the hospital.[7] Indeed, a sensitive person cognizant of her findings would find his or her own reactions sharpened and made more subtle. Investigations by social psychologists on racial attitudes and discriminatory behavior had the same effect on a larger scale.

Use of the private–public distinction instead of the objective–subjective will help shed the dogmatic presuppositions that have hindered inquiry into the role of knowledge in all its forms in moral judgment.

RELATIVE AND ABSOLUTE

Probably no term is used more widely, variably, emotionally, and confusedly in discussing morality than *relativity*. Yet the root idea—that of relation—is simple and familiar: terms that cannot be described or understood or described by themselves without reference to something else have their relations as part of their meaning. For example, a person is an *uncle* only if he has a nephew or niece: that makes *uncle* a relative term. *Distance* of a specified place from here is also relative, although in a more complex way. We need the context of inquiry to suggest whether we are simply measuring the earth or determining a mode of transportation—too far to walk, near by car. Plato was very puzzled by the great and small, and wondered how the same thing could be both great and small, and what made a thing great-in-itself. Aristotle more soberly listed relation among his categories.

Relativity may seem to have strange and variable usage. For example, we do not consider language relative just because different languages are found in different human groups, but precisely under those conditions we speak of morality as being relative. At least we can say that variation—among groups or among individuals—is one of the requirements of being relative, though that is not a sufficient condition. Perhaps we use the term when unexpected variation surprises us, because we had a previous belief in constancy or universality. When, in the not too distant past, morality was generally tied to religion, those who held theirs to be the only true religion also held their moral beliefs to be the only correct ones. As this moral parochialism diminished, people were left without a basis for proclaiming the superior validity of their ways, and the stage was set for a broader conviction of relativity.[8]

The use of *relativity* is not without considerable confusion. Fundamentalist religions consider themselves absolutist and often fulminate against relativism; but to the onlooker the variety of religions and sects—even within a single religious movement—clearly betokens relativism. The obvious perception that different peoples have different customs—which even Herodotus in early Greek times stressed—

made the acceptance of relativism not uncommon; it was usually formulated as the denial of the natural in human behavior or the exaltation of the notion of custom, or simply as skepticism about going beyond appearances or surface phenomena. What characterizes recent relativism is that it is individualistic or personal rather than collective or group. Indeed, at times this extreme of relativism—that moral autonomy means every person deciding for oneself with no rational appeal beyond his or her decision—yields an individualistic absolutism.

The popularity of the actual term *relativity* in the twentieth century is doubtless due to its use in the physical theory of relativity. But as physicists point out in their philosophical spare time, this relativity in physics has a precise meaning—the fact that a "frame of reference" is required in what had appeared hitherto as universal and absolute features of the world. Thus we cannot make judgments of place and time for actual objects in our world without giving some specific physical interpretation to the terms used in pure mathematics—for example, taking the path of a ray of light as the interpretation of the abstract idea of "straight line," or assuming defined movement of objects over time as standards for measuring time. Different physical standards may thus give not merely different results but even different meanings to our ideas.

The view that morality is relative leads us to expect—which of course is the case—that there have been and are still different moralities on the face of the earth (perhaps hundreds of them, just as there are hundreds of languages). Once scientists and scholars got over the shock and began to examine these moralities, they found important similarities among them—for example, in such crucial areas as mother–child care. Different institutions might be seen as different historical devices accomplishing the same function. For example, every society has to have some way of distributing the necessities of life, whether it be through trade, gift giving, chief ownership and compulsory modes of distribution, or communal production and ownership. Every society has to have some arrangement for care of children and for maintaining sufficient peace to allow production to go on. Despite relativistic formulations, it is possible in the comparison of institutions to see which are more effective, though the judgment has to be made with an eye to consequences throughout the society, not just in an isolated function.

It is also worth noting that the cultural facts stated in the language of moral relativism may also be seen in a different way in terms of the existing ideals of the society. Thus a relativism that accepts the moral differences of different cultures may be seen as having the positive ideal of tolerance; and one that accepts the moral authority of individual decision has the positive ideal of individual liberty.

Contemporary tirades against moral "relativism" and the charge that it makes all morality arbitrary—which arises from the recognition that variety and change characterize morality as well as all else in human life—can be regarded as the expression of panic in one whose footing is insecure and is fearful of falling. But to say that something is relative is incomplete: it invites the query of what it is *relative to*. A morality cannot simply be relative, it has to be relative to something, and a serious inquiry has to look for the factors on which dependence is implied. In this sense, judgments of relativity in morals are at best a halfway station in inquiry. Whether the outcome is instability or not depends not on the fact that the morality is relative but on the character of what it is relative to. Even the sternest religious morality has to present the deity's plan to which morality is relative; otherwise, nothing saves the human soul from hanging from a gossamer thread over a bottomless pit or anguishing in fear and trembling. If morality expresses human nature, then we need a dependable picture of what that nature is. If it is social custom, we have to look to the source and function of the custom. If it is individual decision, we have to turn to the nature and complexities of such decision itself. If it is related instead to the human situation, then what are the tasks imposed on humans by the world in which they find themselves? Hence, behind the insecurity of morality in the modern world lies the demand for greater knowledge of that world and the ways in which it impinges on or helps shape morality itself.

REASON AND EMOTION

The rational and the affective are only two "faculties" that have competed for prominence in the history of philosophy. *Reason* usually comes out on top, *emotion* on the bottom. *Will* has at times made a spectacular onslaught, while *sensation* has on the whole been content with its foundational character. Psychologists sometimes line them all up as the *cognitive*, the *affective*, the *conative*, and the *sensory*. When so presented, they may more readily be seen as different aspects of a comprehensive notion of *experience*. When in dramatic versions of what it is to be a human being they are presented in their more glamorous titles, their performance becomes tragic more often than comic. Reason, in Plato's *Republic*, is the essential part of the soul, is capable of absolute knowledge, and those in whom it is strong are given complete rule over the society, keeping the mass of the people in their place as workers and farmers. Reason in Hume is utterly different: the absolute knowledge it possesses consists of empty mathematics and tells you nothing about the world; its function is instrumental, to be the "slave of the passions." The reason logicians talk about tolerates no inconsistency, but its domain is narrow, for the moment we turn to actions and purposes and make note, for example, of "inconsistent aims," we mean not that they cannot exist together but that they cannot be achieved together. Indeed, increasingly reason as a faculty and rationality as a property of the human being gave way to "reasonableness," which, so far from constituting a special source of knowledge, became primarily the habit of mind of a person who is guided by the accumulation and lessons of experience.

In the long tradition of the separation of the faculties, *emotion* was cast as the opposite of reason; it has the blindness of passion and in its pure form is just feeling.[9] In the history of ethics, British theory in the eighteenth century made much of morals being affective rather than rational. But its idea of the affections included some intellectual components. Adam Smith's view of *sympathy* was that it is more than a feeling; it involves some cognizance of the circumstances of the person with whom one sympathizes. Yet surprisingly, in the early twentieth century, when the emotivist theory of ethics emerged from reflections about the uses of language, moral language was given a purely emotive function—to express the feelings and impart them to others in a persuasive effort. It was contrasted—particularly in logical positivist theory—with logical statements (purely rational) and empirical statements (ultimately resting on the sensory). Hence, moral judgments were neither true nor false, they were simply emotive.

The difficulty was that the emotive theory had no theory of the emotions to offer. It simply took for granted the sharp division between reason and emotion, giving the former no affective content and the latter no cognitive content. Compare the opposing argument offered by Sartre in writing of the emotions. A young girl coming to be psychoanalyzed bursts into tears, and so the analysis cannot go on. Shall we say she is so overcome by the situation that she cannot help crying? Sartre suggests instead that the emotion she has is purposive: she is overcome affectively *so as* not to have to talk! Now, purposes have a cognitive content, and his point is directed against the notion of pure affectivity. A reasonable case can be made for the cognitive content of feelings: sorrow, sympathy, and anger all involve some recognition of the character of the situation as saddening, harmful, dangerous, or fearful. The idea of pure emotion without cognitive content is rather what has to be explained.

This brief account suggests that when the separation of components in human experience becomes an absolute division, it is likely to restrict the scope of theory in ethics and to route an inquiry in only one direction when it ought to have access to the full range of human experience. What is required is a more integrative and comprehensive view of human experience, in which the various functions separated so rigidly will be seen rather as phases temporarily explored by themselves. Such a broad conception of experience was developed in William James's *Principles of Psychology*. There are not only cognitive elements in the sensory as it occurs, but purposive components in the selection that goes on in the experience itself. The consciousness itself is set in a context of action in response to hesitations and problems in the flux of experience. It is by a reflective abstraction that we separate the purposive–valuational, identify sensory items that point to specific action in the context, and winnow out comparative principles that we can then explore on their own.

The notion of *experience* should not, then, be reduced to one or another of the analytic components we can extract from the flow of consciousness. To appeal to experience—as all knowledge eventually does—is thus a complex matter. It cannot be parceled into the separate contributions of reason, sensation, emotion, and the sense of action.

FACT AND VALUE

One of the most entrenched dichotomies in twentieth-century moral philosophy has been that of fact and value. It may be more recognizable by its alternative description as the distinction between science and ethics. Science is said to give us the facts about the world, without any moral evaluation. Ethics is concerned not with *what is*, but with *what is valuable* or *what ought to be* whether it exists or not. In 1889, Rudyard Kipling wrote, "Oh, East is East, and West is West, and never the twain shall meet," expressing the now-discredited imperialism by which the West held the East in bondage. Now it is out of date: perhaps the same is true for the separate empires of Fact and Value in moral philosophy.

The need to question the distinction is made especially urgent because the method of deciding moral matters is often cast in its terms. First, it is said, line up on one side whatever is likely to happen, attaching a probability to each envisaged state of affairs. Then, on the other side, line up your value preferences in order of weight. The decision requires coupling the two, but according to some strategy— for example, to achieve the greatest total value or the least total harm or disvalue. Decision is thus seen as a kind of gambling among states of affairs with attached values and disvalues, in line with a preferred risk pattern.

The crux of the matter is how independent facts and values are, and for this we have first to ask what are they. One view sharply separates them: they are seen as utterly different. The world consists of events and qualities or else things and relations and qualities. When we make statements reporting on the world, we purport to describe some features of the world and what is going on; the content of our report consists of *facts* if our statements are true or our reports are correct. On this view science is our best way so far to ascertain the facts. In principle a statement of fact is verifiable and agreement could be reached about it by competent inquirers; actually, there are many statements we cannot decide that in principle are decidable. Facts are therefore objective, impersonal, and public. Values are different. They are private, subjective, and in the case of disagreement, incapable of being resolved by any procedure that deals with truth or falsity. People can share them or differ over them; that is all. They represent personal attitudes or expressions of will, of preference, of feeling, or purpose. They guide or at least influence action; they are not essentially telling us what the world is like.

This utter disparity between fact and value is indicated in common language by our inability to go from one domain to the other: you cannot derive values from facts or the converse; or, in a slightly different context, you cannot decide what ought to be from what is, nor what is from what ought to be. Hence ideally we can separate our value assertions from our fact assertions, although many terms in our language may have them combined or scrambled; careful analysis is required to carry through the separation. For example, role-words are particularly prone to confuse us: we talk as if we could derive the value assertion, "X ought to support child Y" from the biological fact that X is the father of Y. We fail to carry through the separation and see that we have to put into the social role of "father" the value judgment that fathers ought to support their children. Other societies might have it that the mother's brother ought to do the supporting, or that society should provide automatic family allowances where there are children. Clarity seems to demand separation of values or purposes from facts.

There are indeed many contexts in which such a distinction proves highly useful, when a careful customs inspection might disclose a value or a purpose being smuggled in surreptitiously, as in the example given. Some central notions in psychology and the social sciences that play a prominent part in moral decision have often been suspected of being covert value-vehicles: for example, *human nature*, *needs*, *deviance*, *mental health*. Let us take the case of *needs* as paradigmatic. Appeal to *needs* (and similarly to *wants*) has a stable position in morality—needs call legitimately for satisfaction; to satisfy human needs has sometimes been regarded as a basic moral demand. Such notions, however, are highly complex: something is a need if its not being satisfied will result in death, illness, or frustration—or perhaps even just discomfort. There is enough ambiguity in the idea of *wants* that if something is a (genuine) human want it has some warrant for satisfaction; but if a person just says truthfully "I want it," practically no moral mandate is involved. In short, *needs* in its strictest sense, and *wants*, only in a comparable sense, may make a moral claim, but in their attenuated sense they have no initial moral capital and require concrete evaluation. Even a moral claim for satisfying needs calls for further evaluation in terms of the kind of need and the consequences of satisfying it. Hence, in sum, *need* does contain value or purposive components.

Yet when all this is revealed, and any smuggling thwarted, does what is accomplished amount to the separation of fact from value? Not necessarily. Just as readily it can be seen as the rejection of what in the context is an *intrusive* value (e.g., avoidance of discomfort), while an essential purpose (e.g., life against death) is retained, though now clear as a purpose. It is not certain that our purpose in the customs inspection is really to separate value as a general category from fact as a distinct category, rather than to draw attention to some overlooked particular value in a given problem. Thus, in all these cases comparable to our analysis of *needs*—cases of *natural* and *unnatural, conformist* and *deviant, normal* and *abnormal*—we want to uncover the smuggled value because we want to face directly and evaluate the kind of actions involved, not because we want to be left with pure fact. What we are really doing is criticizing the entrenchment of the particular value in a complex of knowledge in which there may be many resident appropriate values. What is *abnormal* thus comes to be seen as what is *unusual* rather than what is *wrong*; and *deviant* is no more lacking in value than *conformist*. Indeed, sometimes conformity is more immoral than deviance. Deviance includes, for example, the case of a person who is deviantly mild-tempered, that is, who is disposed to remain calm in circumstances in which most people would get angry. Whether to be mild-tempered is a good thing or a bad thing for a human being is a distinct matter for evaluation: it may be a good thing in a complex society, bad in a frontier shoot-it-out society. It might even turn out to be an innovative good thing in extreme conditions, as for example, when it leads to peaceful picketing in spite of provocation or to Gandhian pacifism as a means to achieving independence for a nation.[10] Hence the removal of the value aspect from the idea of deviance does not show that the idea of normality is value neutral. The normal is still positive when desirable, as in the value of reliability. Thus Darwin pointed out that sympathy—as a natural reaction entrenched in the evolutionary development of the human species—is a value asset: even when overridden by a stronger passion (for example, anger), it later exerts an effect when the anger is dissipated. The entrenchment of a passion like anger in human nature requires a more complex evaluation.

Many views stand opposed to the fact–value dichotomy. A simple one is that while there are both distinct values and distinct facts, they are so intermixed in human life that separating them is a hopeless task; only in an occasional case can it be carried through. To try to build a method of moral decision on the separation is folly; we need to develop more contextual methods by which to carry out the customs inspection where it is appropriate. A second view offers a more sweeping rejection of the dichotomy, arguing that facts and values are not different "materials" of investigation; the materials are the same, but they are dealt with in different ways or in different enterprises. For example, "I am pleased" is a fact datum for psychology as an introspective report. But in my own life stream, it is a value item in my ongoing moral economy (viewed in Benthamite fashion). A third, and still more far-reaching, critique of the dichotomy finds that it rests on a mistaken analysis of the character of *experience*. The dichotomy taking it for granted that the cognitive, the sensory, and the affective (feelings and emotions) are three distinct realms aligns facts with the cognitive and sensory realms, leaving values aligned with the affective. On this critique, the sharp dichotomy is regarded as based on an unwarranted psychology that misunderstands the comprehensive integral character of human experience. The positive position here indicated is examined later.

In view of these observations about the theory of fact and value, it is obviously unwise policy to adopt any initial commitment in applied ethics to a method that rests wholly on a sharp dichotomy of fact and value.

LEARNING

We now turn to the question of how knowledge enters into the moral decision—whether it enters in one way only or in a variety of ways, how far it extends into self-knowledge as well as knowledge of the surrounding world, and whether there is anything to be relied on beyond its cumulative effect. That such questions are not remote from the processes of practical decision can be seen readily. Consider, for example, decisions about punishment and responsibility, an area of morality that stands out sharply on the historical scene. It is a long intellectual–moral march from the ancient British judicial practice of throwing an accused witch into the water, where guilt or innocence is established by floating or sinking, to the recent and even contemporary use of the criterion (in the mode of the M'Naghten decision) of whether the accused knew the difference between right and wrong while committing a crime. We might also look at whether we have learned enough from the history of leprosy and the cruelties of its treatment of sufferers to be morally humane in the treatment of AIDS victims.

Doubtless it is agreed that what we deliberate in applied ethics are the lessons of human experience. Even the vast edifice of the sciences ultimately rests on the same ground, albeit more analytically and systematically. Yet different aspects of experience are tapped in different accounts of it. Ancient philosophers thought of experience more in the sense in which we speak of the "person of experience," focusing on the learning outcome. Philosophers of the seventeenth and eighteenth centuries thought in terms of the immediate act of sensation and feeling. Different problems thus became important to different approaches. For the ancients, the unreliability of the senses meant that the scene we looked at might change when we turned away; it (the scene) could not be relied on, not that our senses could not be relied on when we are looking at it. (Hence they sought knowledge in mathematics that was outside time and change and dealt with the eternal.) The moderns worried whether what we saw while we were looking adequately reflected an *outside* reality. There is no reason we should not learn from both worries. From the ancients' concern, we conclude that the world may be undergoing changes we do not know about; our present knowledge has a tentative character and may be corrigible in terms of future experience. From the moderns' concern, we can learn that we may not have focused on all the elements that are relevant to the problem at hand, that we may be approaching it with the wrong conceptual tools, so that reassessment of our present experience is always in order.

Another fundamental change in the philosophical outlook may be relevant to our present questions. The ancients tended to ally knowledge with the eternal and the unchanging, so that mathematics stood out as the prototype of successful knowledge. The rest was dismissed as belief or opinion—a second-rate kind of awareness that might be right or wrong. Correspondingly, what exists in the world was separated sharply into the eternal and the changing; and the changing itself was divided into the regular, which somehow participated in or reflected the eternal, and the accidental. The regular could be studied in science; but, said Aristotle, there is no science of accident. The advance of the sciences and of the theory of knowledge over the centuries has softened these sharp distinctions. Pure mathematics has come to be seen more as empty constructions than as ultimate truth about the eternal. A separate domain of heavenly objects above the moon, with absolute regularity of motion, was absorbed into a uniformity of nature by Isaac Newton. Regularities in natural processes and changes eventually lost the glamour of being fixed and eternal "laws" and emerged as probabilities in a world of continual change. The notion of probability in its rise to respectability brought the accidental within the scope of science as well. Today even the turbulent and the chaotic attract the mathematician. This esoteric and fascinating story has important implications for applied ethics: that applied ethics is always dealing with special circumstances and possibly unique conditions and acting on policies that may have to be changed in the light of growing experience. It no longer need oppose invoking experience. To the extent to which such experience has been systematized, we are invoking knowledge to help resolve moral problems.

When we ask how knowledge enters into moral deliberation, we are prone to forget that it already is a constituent of the world we are operating in and the ways we have formulated our problems, the ways we understand our fellows, and the ways we understand our selves and our values. Knowledge thus permeates; it does not enter, make a contribution, and bow out. The scope of its permeation is worth canvassing.

Compare—to take an extreme example—the unseen world of the medieval human being, peopled with angelic and demonic beings, witches and their curses and spells, with the late twentieth-century unseen world of radiation and radon, with our view of sunshine shifting from the column of the wholly beneficent to the column of the dangerous. The difference between these two worlds is a difference caused by the growth of the physical and biological sciences. Think too of the world of vegetation, from the slash-and-burn methods of much primitive agriculture to the tended fields of later centuries to the contemporary world in which the city is so far from resting on farming, while farming rests on the industrial preparation of seed and fertilizer; and in which threats to the rain forest have recently become a global threat. Or, again, the "unbounded sea" of old with the threat of a garbaged ocean. Or the many successful herbs of the early medicine man—which still yield an occasional surprise for us—with the methodical surveying of chemical compounds with the object of hitting on a specific drug for a specific malady. It is not merely that today we depend to a very high degree on the products that have resulted from scientific inquiry, but that the very world around us is already—so to speak—scientifically woven fabric. It is the same world that we have for deliberation in applied ethics, but as background in action, not just as object of contemplation.

The difference between the context of contemplation and that of action may be seen simply in linguistic usage. Suppose we describe the blade of a knife in terms of the precise angle of its sides and the hardness of its material. We relate it to a systematic body of knowledge about materials and properties of metals. If, however, we think of the knife as *sharp* or *dull*, we are relating it to a specific function in action, namely cutting and efficacy in cutting. This is the kind of knowledge we have in mind in problems of applied ethics. In sum, the knowledge that enters applied ethics, stemming from the sciences, is a view of the world as geared for action. It is a mistake to think of the contributions of science to applied ethics simply in terms of whether scientific laws will enter as premises in arguments that conclude with moral imperatives or statements of moral advice.

The world in which we act is also one of living beings, of animals and humans, and the biological and psychological sciences help us to prepare for the kinds of encounters we anticipate. Sometimes applications have been beneficent, sometimes partially beneficent but at a great cost—as the history of many pesticides showed. Sometimes harm comes from selective concentration on the new, or the too hasty application of insufficiently established knowledge. Concentrating on the automobile undermined railroads and urban rail systems. Development of nuclear energy sidetracked investigation of solar energy. (In all such cases, economic entrenchment in one direction actually engendered hostility to possible competition.) The prestige of science has sometimes led to hasty application of its generalizations as well. For example, psychological behaviorism appeared to indicate that the child should be conditioned early to good regular habits; infant care and nursery school procedures for a time were subjected to strict and undeviating regularization. The onset of Freudian theory, with its exhibition of the distortions that repression might produce, modified the behavioristic strictness but in turn often led to abandonment of all discipline: for example, fighting children might not be stopped because it was deemed good to let their "aggression" run its expressive course.

The social sciences come closer to the immediate problems of applied ethics, partly because they reveal the themes and structures of what is going on and partly because they can provide case studies of what has proved useful under what kinds of conditions. Take, for example, the report that in India today the development of amniocentesis has produced a situation in which this test for the sex of the fetus has led to increased abortion of the females. Would a general prohibition of abortion remedy this evil or would it be a failure? An attempt to differentiate intentions and motives in abortion would be futile—in general, law is better concerned with actions. An understanding of the culture and its problems makes it clear that the desire to have boys rather than girls is in some measure related to the fact that girls marry into other families and drain the family resources with dowries, while boys remain with the family, continue it, and provide for the old age of the parents. Would a system of old age pensions—which India with its vast population cannot afford—alter the present cultural preference? At least understanding the problem prevents our treating it as an arbitrary sexual preference. But perhaps other deep strata have to be exposed. For example, the theory of transmigration of souls in India teaches that souls are incarnated as women first and later reappear as men in the succession of lives leading to the ultimate release from the round of mortality. A useful direction of effort—drawing on the experience of other countries— might be encouraging a more militant feminist movement. These considerations merely suggest how proposed actions have to be based on an understanding of the cultural situation. In short, actions must be *knowledge-saturated*.

An important dialectic is to be found among various bodies of knowledge themselves. For example, sociocultural knowledge sharpens and corrects biological theses about humans that are relevant to moral understanding. The use of ideas of human nature as a moral sanction shows this clearly. In the early twentieth century, the view that human nature could be summed up in a list of instincts was used to justify corresponding institutions: a sexual instinct for marriage, an aggressive instinct for war, and so on. Growing knowledge of cultural variation on the same biological base led to a view of human nature as providing raw materials for cultural fashioning, removing the moral stamp from the presumed natural expression. But an even deeper analysis was available for moral understanding from a historical–evolutionary perspective. T. H. Huxley long ago pointed out that aggression entrenched in human nature gains no moral sanction from its presence: it was a useful response for survival in earlier evolutionary periods, hanging on in a comparatively organized world. It may remain as a fact or problem to be dealt with, but it has no special moral status from its persistence. The moral respect for human nature as such, whatever it might contain, came largely from the religious assumption that the nature of man was a divine product. This explains also why the question of whether there were contradictions in the human makeup itself, such as hate in the midst of love, was so late in coming.

How assumptions about natural reactions work themselves out in practice can be seen from the kinds of regulations found governing special social situations. For example, Texas had a law that a man killing his wife's lover would not be considered to have committed murder if the killing took place within forty-eight hours of the discovery. Contrast this with the growing tendency to deny a person who has been robbed the right the shoot the fleeing robber when there is no threat to the victim's person—obviously based on the disparate value of life and property.

Our consideration of the way in which knowledge in the various sciences enters into practical judgments has moved seamlessly into how the same modes of knowledge acquaint us more fully with our own values. This can be seen in values that range from the widespread social to the personal—indeed, first-person—ones.

Take, for example, the intense—one might almost say epidemic of—nationalism that is sweeping the world. Nationalism is obviously widely valued among vast populations. But how is it to be understood? Is there an intrinsic value in closeness and similarities, in a "home" group? Perhaps it is the intimate part that having a common language plays in human groups. Or a reaction against growing globalism and the fear of loss of bearings. Or a traditional reaction against change. Or, as with Belgium or Canada, the response of a population that had been discriminated against or disadvantaged. Or the reaction, with the additional influence of traditional religion, against Westernization, as in Iran. Or as in many areas of Africa, the reaction against boundaries of different tribal societies drawn by previous imperialist powers without attention to native differences in customs. Or the breakup of long dominant empires. Perhaps nationalism is not a single phenomenon but a host of overlapping but widely differing phenomena. Extensive research utilizing the best methods of social science will be required to determine whether nationalism is a temporary phenomenon of the twentieth century or a permanent feature of human life. It cannot be settled by strength of feeling or by the pattern of life of selected groups. Meanwhile, nationalism influences fundamental life decisions within such selected groups. They act (or decide) on the basis of the understanding they have of the phenomenon at the time.

In countries like the United States, with the growth of democratic participation in political life, it has become important for those engaged in politics to know what the electorate wants, how it feels about critical questions, and how it will vote. The techniques of polling as the science of discovering the values of the present are highly esteemed and widely invoked. Polling has become a highly refined, scientifically guided method, with considerable predictive success. (It overcame early howlers, such as selecting its informants from telephone directories and thereby missing the opinions of voters who could not afford a telephone.) Yet there are clearly both special values in its construction and practical effects in its mode of operation. For example, a pollster asks how the person questioned would choose or vote on a given matter; he or she does not usually ask for reasons and so does not get a picture of the long-range goals and desires, which are the basis of the person's opinion. Instead, the pollster may rely on repeated polling to determine changes in popular attitudes. In this respect, its product resembles the daily report of the stock market, tempting prediction of trends from the data rather than from fundamental analyses. As for practical impact, it has been found that exit polls on election days tend to affect behavior in time regions where the polls are still open; for example, people do not vote because they believe the election is already settled. (Accordingly, there are calls to ban such polls.)

The lesson of such examples is that when the social sciences get close to matters of practice, differential value-attitudes and value-orientations loom large. In looking to the knowledge that they bring to a situation, there is need for a critical estimate of how far special values may have become entrenched in the scientific operations. If they are explicit, they may define for us the limits of interest of the science as applied or its techniques. If they are hidden, they may be carriers of a surreptitious ideology. Interest in the momentary or short range is fairly explicit in America. It is found both in the press and on television, in the stock market with its daily and even hourly rise and fall, in the imperative that corporations show a quarterly profit, and in political campaigns that hurl forty-five-second slogans rather than debate fundamental issues. It has almost reached the point where special deliberative institutions may have to be set up to counter the momentary and the forgettable.

Consider a theoretical modern analogue to the Committees of Correspondence that flourished during the American Revolution, by means of which questions of policy were discussed in detail. Suppose every Monday evening were declared public policy evening (not politics evening) and radio and television programs wholly, and newspapers partly, were devoted to deliberative debate about important public policies—with mention of political party prohibited, so that issues would be the center of attention. Can we conceive of family circles gathered around the television set, patrons of bars eagerly listening to pros and cons, continuing the debate after the program was over? (We omit the mechanics of arrangement, assuming them to be workable by common agreement.) Would such an institution raise the level of public political concern?

Part of the attempt to know our social values and our national character, insofar as there are common traits or a pluralistic diversity, has been found in the work of social psychologists and sociologists and in the comparative studies of anthropologists. Tocqueville's *Democracy in America* was a foundational work on our national character, and visitors and travelers have often made sage remarks. Bertrand Russell once facetiously compared American rats in behaviorist experiments (scurrying here and there in a maze until they found what they were looking for) with German apes (in the studies of the Gestalt psychologist, Wolfgang Köhler) where one animal sat and thought till it got a bright idea (the "aha" phenomenon) and put two sticks together to reach a distant banana. Martha Wolfenstein and Nathan Leites, in their book on the movies, contrasted the United States cinematic method of resolving a "love triangle" by having one of the parties killed in a traffic accident with the French method of having a heart-to-heart discussion, and one of them finally walking off into the sunset.[11] Anthropological contrasts of Americans' and other peoples' general value-attitudes have been particularly insightful: for example, a view of nature as a resource to be exploited rather than (as among many Native American tribes) a gift to be cherished and tended; an orientation toward the future rather than the present (which may be changing in the present generation) or the past; an outlook on problems as composed of mechanical elements to be freshly reconstructed, as contrasted with a British agricultural metaphor in which problems mature over time and solutions grow. To view ourselves as others see us may often be an enlightening technique. For example, corporal punishment of children (particularly spanking) came to be understood as an aggression rather than as an expression of "spare the rod and spoil the child," and with such learning, this form of punishment has been reduced.

We turn finally from the attempt to know our social values to the first person attempt on the part of each of us to know him- or herself—the Socratic "Know thyself." How far is such knowledge continuous with the kinds of knowledge we have been examining, or how far is it a privileged personal insight? In one respect, it seems more like a quest to have the limitations that we found in the social arena—it is too often reduced to a formulation of our momentary preferences. These preferences are given a finality that varies from self-legitimating decree to fundamental insight into the self's values. Doubtless preferential acts are the testing points, the observations we make of ourselves in action, that help establish our more general views of our values, just as observational tests are the end points of scientific experiments or judgments. But just as the latter are meaningful because they are enmeshed in a network of theory, so preferences point to values as they are analyzed in terms of a way of understanding our selves. For example, is this preferential choice here and now a compromise or a wholehearted movement of the self? Does it reflect a momentary passion or whim or an abiding long-range interest? Does it correspond to a deep-felt need or a hardened habit? These are the concerns that help me—not just somebody else—determine the value-meaning of my preferences. And each of these questions in turn may lead to more extensive theoretical probing.

The recognition that first person inquiry into one's values is extremely complex—and we have mentioned only the transparent surface of philosophical probing, without raising familiar and traditional issues about the nature of a self—and carries with it a web of already established knowledge (including much that is theoretical in character) has important practical implications. It means that in spite of any certainty we may have in immediate preference, it remains hypothetical until it fits into the background framework or we make a specific change within that framework. It follows that we cannot use the central role of preferences in ethical analysis to go from their observed variety in different persons or groups to a general moral relativism, if the latter connotes any arbitrariness in morality. For such an ethical theory takes it that we cannot go beyond differences, that "each is right from his or her point of view." Whatever the historical merits of this philosophical theory in promoting tolerance, or its historical demerits in promoting individual or group egoism and arbitrariness, it has no relation to the present analysis. (Indeed, it seems more like individualistic or group absolutism than relativism, for it gives every unit, individual or group, the right to confer moral status on its wishes.)

As contrasted with a relativism that stops with the fact of preferential difference, the attempt to "know thyself" leads to the two paths already noted: either to integrate present experience within the background of ordered knowledge (including knowledge of values) or to propose an alteration within that background system. Interestingly, these are the same alternatives that the scientist faces in dealing with the results of an experiment, particularly a crucial one that may prove the birthplace of a fresh theoretical direction. (Of course, this scientific context is not the source of the same ethical process. Indeed, both reflect the common feature of experience as a source of learning.) The history of ethical theories in modern times shows the interplay of integrative and innovative elements. Thus in the late eighteenth century (when in Britain the Industrial Revolution was under way, and on the Continent the Enlightenment was heading toward revolution), Bentham gears his systematization of morality into a method for evaluating and altering social institutions and practices, while Kant focuses on bringing human choices within a systematic moral–rational framework. In the twentieth century, when rapid technological and social change, as we have seen, releases a stream of new moral problems, the act of choice changes from a self-contained, self-revealing act of preference (to be much plotted but little analyzed) and becomes the bursting point for major philosophical outlooks. Now it is the innovative rather than the integrative aspect that occupies center stage. In Europe, closer to extreme social struggle and world wars, it took the dramatic form of Sartrean Existentialism. In America, it was found in the more reflective mood of Deweyan Pragmatism. A glance at their central focus underscores the activism found in both.

Sartre's Existentialism in many ways elaborates Kierkegaard's replacement of Socrates's "Know thyself" with "Choose thyself." The self is always in the making, and moral choice is not a coherence with an established self, but a now-making of the self; nor is it ever finally a made self. To follow a moral rule in this situation without reaffirming it is to enslave myself and to deny my freedom. Human beings are absolutely free in each decision: absolute choice with absolute responsibility. In effect, Sartre draws the line in time with everything of the past, its fixities and its system, reduced to raw materials for present choice. Dewey is more attentive to the use of the past, not to govern the present in an automatic fashion but as lessons of experience for reflective analysis of the present. But the analysis is a present task, for it involves new relations and new situations, and the paths to be taken may themselves be innovative. The emphasis falls not so much on improving the background system in the light of new experience—that is taken for granted—but in the readiness for innovation (see Chapter Ten), almost as fresh experiment.

The outcome of such contemporary probing of choice and preference in relation to the integrative and the innovative is far from traditional views, which held that the self has immediate certainty in its introspection, that self-knowledge is a realm of direct knowledge, not one of indirect and patient accumulation that strengthens self-understanding. Certainly I am closer to self-knowledge than I am to knowledge of things farther out, but the depth of this self-knowledge is continuous with what I have learned of the wider world and its ways, with myself among its constituents.

The one possibly unsettling aspect of such understanding is that it brings to self-knowledge the same property of tentativeness—the realization that we are dealing with probabilities in every corner of our awareness, not certainties. Even with that realization, we go from day to day and plan for the future with a practical notion of "practical certainties," among them being judgments where we have greater and less such practical certainty. Curiously, in the history of philosophy, though such probabilism in Hume's eighteenth-century skepticism was felt as devastating in European thought, in the America of that time, concerned with the practical task of making a home in a new country, the reliance on such practical certainties was not felt to be paradoxical but simply recognition that humans are not omniscient. And this holds for self-understanding as well as the understanding of the rest of nature.

Such philosophical lessons do not of course automatically solve the practical problem of dogmatic disagreements in applied ethics, but they can help the effort to dissolve the dogmatic attitude that finds expression there. Intellectual clarity here is of practical importance: one must not equate an attitude of scientific enlightenment with entrenched dogmatism. The call by the Ayatollah in Iran for the assassination of novelist Salman Rushdie was a startling reminder that older notions of heresy as betokening inner corruption and deserving death are not wholly of the past. But it would be belying human learning to equate the Ayatollah's attitude and contemporary freedom of inquiry as just two valid preferences in social relations and social regulation. The theoretical step of understanding our knowledge of values—personally as well as socially—is of vital practical importance.

The answer to the question posed in this last section—how knowledge permeates moral decision and enters applied ethics—is thus that every decision in applied ethics, whether a determination of public policy, a professional judgment for action, or a personal embarking on a path of conduct, is continuous with a resident body of knowledge of world and self that grows and is tested in continuing experience.

PART TWO

From Diagnosis

to Moral Decision

Five

Diagnosis

Since applied ethics is concerned with resolving practical moral problems (dilemmas, quandaries, impasses, complex difficulties) in decision, we now have to examine the basic characteristics of a practical problem, what makes it a moral problem, and how its diagnosis gets under way.

When a practical problem arises in the course of a life's activity—for such problems do not simply exist on their own, but arise out of the ongoing course of activity and the obstacles it encounters—we may already distinguish three aspects: a *purposive background*, a *problem formulation*, explicit or implicit, and an *existing situation*. Since in the history of moral philosophy moral problems have been analyzed in many different ways, guided by different interests and outlooks, we must provide some preliminary indications of the character of the present distinctions.

We speak of a *purposive background* because problems arise only for persons for whom some things matter and where some active effort is going on in some direction. If a person did not care what happened, there would be no problem for him or her—life, death, pain, pleasure would all be one. We call it a "purposive background," not just "having values," because a practical problem occurs in the midst of effort and purpose; it is not a matter merely of pro- and con-attitudes. Purposes are dynamic, embody some awareness of what the world around one is like, and are constantly reacting to the course of events in which their activity is enmeshed. Moreover, the purposive background should not be reduced to one simple philosophical category. It is not sufficient to label it "teleological," or "purely causal," or just "historically descriptive." Where it plays a part in resolving a practical problem, it may do so in different ways: sometimes by pointing a direction, sometimes by enabling us to turn knowledge of past causality into instrumental action for the future, sometimes by explaining, sometimes by offering evidence; and in many more ways that we have not yet explored.

When we become aware of a practical problem, it has already taken some shape, that is, we have already in some sense formulated it. A traditional formulation of many practical moral problems is to see them as temptation to violate the moral law under the strong pressure of desire. A more formidable type is the conflict of two goods, as illustrated in the familiar example of a patriotic young man conscripted for a war that he firmly believes his country is wrong to wage. There is always the possibility of different formulations of a problem. For example, opponents aiming for the same object may construe the problem as conquering, or alternatively as working out a compromise, or even as cooperating to multiply production of the object in question. A major theoretical question to be explored is whether there is a correct formulation or at least some way of judging alternative ones as better or worse.

An *existing situation* is, of course, the matrix in which the problem arises. It is what applied ethics is being applied to. If we had to choose between telling the truth and lying *in general*, the choice would be morally easy, and there would be no problem. The practical moral problem exists because of special features of the situation.

In the first place, the situation is quite literally a chunk of the present. But it has relations to the wider present, to the traces and effects of the past, and it will have consequences in the future. How much of our knowledge of these broader relations must we bring in to understand what is happening, to choose among formulations, to decide upon action? Granted that the situation must be bounded if we are to reach a decision, how much of the past, present, and future shall we sweep in within the boundaries? This is the aspect of *context*. If the situation is the matrix of the problem, context is the matrix of the situation. In many respects, the judgment of admissible context in resolving practical problems is like the judgment of admissible evidence in a legal trial—the judge has to decide on its relevance to let it in or rule it out.

PURPOSIVE BACKGROUND

All problems begin with a recognition that there is a problem and with some provisional identification or description—it is *under a description* that it is felt as a problem. This initial identification may be exceedingly thin—felt only as a vague unease or sense of difficulty—or quite rich (as when a mathematician immediately identifies the problem as a differential equation problem). At that stage, we have two options on procedure. One option involves focusing on how we have identified the problem, questioning whether the formulation is inexact or misleading, and whether alternate formulations might be more helpful. A second option involves accepting the preliminary identification as given and exploring its ramifications. We shall call the first *diagnosing* the problem, and it is the subject matter of this chapter. In the second option, we explore the *context* of the problem, particularly the sociocultural and historical circumstances, and this is the subject matter of Chapter Six. It should be emphasized that these routes are not entirely independent of one another, nor do they nor should they proceed in a fixed sequence. What we learn from exploring the context may lead us to reconsider the preliminary description, as efforts to reformulate may point us toward looking for additional contextual information. Whatever results are reached by either route are always considered preliminary until the whole process is completed.

In speaking of problems in this and the next chapter, we have in mind problems of any sort, not exclusively moral problems. We move to consider the peculiar features of moral problems in Chapter Seven.

Before proceeding to these tasks, however, we should consider the relations of the three aspects to one another. Our differences with the more common approaches of twentieth-century philosophy lie partly in the vocabulary of problematics we adopt, but more fundamentally in how we think of the three dimensions. Where we designate the subject matter of applied logic in terms of purposive background, problem formulation, and existing situation, it is more common for philosophers to speak in terms of values, facts, and meaning. What we call the *purposive background* has been treated as if it were an inventory of relevant *values*: in a practical problem those involved might be listed separately in advance and ordered in terms of weight or importance. The question of problem formulation has been treated as a matter of *meaning*, and this in turn as a topic for *language and logic*. The existing situation and any kindred segment of evidence from relevant context have been identified as the *facts*, and the task of resolving a practical problem has been explicated as finding a method of bringing together value and language and fact.

This confluence is particularly important because philosophers in the twentieth century have often made isolated fields out of each. No such isolation is envisaged here. On the contrary, it would appear that the three aspects we have distinguished are separate from one another only relatively. The formulation not only expresses purposive components but may also change as the context of the situation is broadened or narrowed; and the context may widen or narrow in response to a reformulation. What we have is an interactive whole, whose interaction is an integral part of resolving the practical problem, and whose formulation expresses the diagnosis of the problem.

These abstract considerations deserve some illustration. We choose a case that at first sight seems trifling, but turns out to have surprising depths. Some women want to wear their hair short and some men want to wear it long; some men want to wear beards and others do not. Why should these preferences be construed as practical problems? Today, they are considered for the most part as matters of individual preference and accepted as such by most people in the United States (though not in all parts of the country). In this country, then, they should not be practical problems at all. But let us survey the century.

Women in the United States began to wear their hair short after World War I. Now take an individual woman contemplating a change of hair style. What was the nature of the problem she faced? It might be entirely a matter of aesthetic preference, as it might be today—did she like short hair? Enlarge the context, however, and the problem becomes reformulated. Long hair had been the mark of femininity, and to reject it was to risk the disapproval of husband or family. Then the problem cannot be confined to a matter of aesthetics. There is more. Short hair on women appeared when they emerged from the home to join a work force reduced by the conscription of men to fight the war. At work, long hair was a nuisance, sometimes even dangerous. With this as context, she might see the problem as a requirement of the job, perhaps even as a sacrifice to be made for the sake of employment, and conceivably, if engaged in war work, an act of patriotism. But a further enlargement of the context is possible. There is another reason short ("bobbed") hair caught on. The context is not just a-country-at-war-in-need-of-workers. It was also a period of agitation for expansion of equality for women. It was at this time that women in the United States achieved the right to vote. Thus, to wear short hair had an emancipatory quality; long hair had been a mark of femininity, and to depart from it signaled a move toward equality. (Another mark of the same emancipation was the shorter skirt. It was still too early for women to wear pants in public.) Thus, a woman posing the problem of whether to cut her hair at that time, in that situation, was not facing simply a question of aesthetic preference, or even the wider question of what her husband's or family's reaction would be, but the often-daring movement into emancipation.

A man wanting to wear long hair faced a different problem. Early in the century, the problem was whether to risk being thought as having feminine inclinations. In the 1960s long hair became part of a deliberate revolt against the traditional attitudes and values of an older generation. To choose long hair was to rebel, but this was not an act of undifferentiated rebellion; instead, it involved a specific revolt against specific standards of a previous generation that sanctioned the inequality of men and women. Thus, long hair on men served as a cultural symbol of a specific historical moment. With greater or less awareness of what was going on, a young man facing the problem of hair length was making a decision of what standard to raise.

Now what about beards? The first half of the century was rigidly set in its attitude against bearded men, especially if they were young. A common game among children in the street was to look for a beard: the first child, on spotting a beard, to call "Beaver!" scored a point. The wearing of a beard had commonly accepted excuses: medical, in the case of hemophilia; or religious, in the case of an Orthodox Jew. But otherwise to grow a beard was to be suspect—it is hard to say just of what, but at least of not being right, of being deviant. The disapproval of beards was supported by ready rationalizations—for example, that cleanliness required shaving. In some areas, for example, the military, regulation was explicit. In any case, before the 1960s a young man contemplating wearing a beard was dealing with a social problem, not just an aesthetic problem.

There were practical problems in the other direction as well. Take the situation of an Orthodox Jew considering whether to shave or not.

If he is not living in an ethnic enclave of a large city but moves freely around in the general community, the wearing of a beard has consequences he finds uncomfortable. He might formulate his problem as how to reconcile religious edict with the demands of modernity and his wish to enter the wider community. The alternatives admitted at the time clearly followed the lines of how the problem was formulated. Some religious Jews regarded the prohibition of the use of the knife on facial hair as one of a large class of traditional prohibitions whose social purpose was to maintain community cohesion in centuries of oppression; they felt these prohibitions were not at the core of Judaism, were no longer needed in a free country, and so could be dispensed with. Those who saw the problem in these terms shifted to Reform Judaism. Those who wished to stand by Orthodoxy but shave had to find another way. Some achieved this by a strict interpretation of the prohibition. What was forbidden, they said, was the use of the knife, the application of a blade, including a razor. But Orthodox tradition sanctioned the use of scissors, and the (misnamed) electric razor really operates like scissors; therefore, the use of the electric razor is not forbidden. In this case the fact that alternative conceptual formulations are possible, which often tends to complicate the problem, helps solve the problem.

These examples might seem merely relics of a pre-enlightenment era. In some respects perhaps they are. This does not mean that similar issues are not pressing at the present time: the recent history of Iran and the growth of dogmatic orthodoxies in all religions and their campaigns to dominate social life are by no means negligible. The response of the Islamic world to Salmon Rushdie's *Satanic Verses*— violent demonstrations, attacks on embassies, assassination of an Islamic leader in Holland, Ayatollah Khomeini's proclamation of a death sentence for blasphemy, and a reward proclaimed for assassination, not to speak of the effects on publishers and booksellers in the United States—is a vivid reminder. But it is best to look at ourselves, so that we see that this is not an alien matter.

Early in 1989 the Supreme Court's decision that burning the American flag was to be deemed symbolic political speech—and therefore fell under the protection of the First Amendment—unleashed a storm of criticism. What was going on here? What practical problem is posed by flag-burning? The dominant reaction in the country, and certainly among politicians, was to look for some legal way to forbid flag-burning. The argument in Congress immediately turned to whether legislation or constitutional amendment was the preferable route. It seemed to be taken for granted that the act is universally abhorrent—even those very few politicians who opposed congressional action voiced their opposition with introductions such as, "No one is second to me in honoring the American flag, for which many young men gave their lives, . . ."—and that this abhorrence is sufficient ground for legal repression. But if flag-burning is speech, as the Court ruled, then universal abhorrence is insufficient to forbid it. Is the flag different by virtue of being a symbol of patriotism? Perhaps so. But what we are not asking is what the frame of belief and values of the individual who chooses to burn the flag is. Is he deriding patriotism or saying that there are higher values than patriotism? Is it an act of defiance or of despair? Is it comparable to the cases where Buddhist monks in Vietnam poured gasoline on themselves and set themselves afire in specific protest against the corruption of the South Vietnamese government? Would our reaction have been different if the flag-burner had wrapped her- or himself in the flag before burning it? Would we still have considered it an act of desecration?

Once we begin to ask what is going on here, once we go beyond the simple formulation "flag-burning," the practical problem of what to do about flag-burning becomes more complex than it had seemed. In the purposive background is our desire to maintain respect for the flag and what it stands for. But respect is a highly personal matter, like conscience, and legal enforcement may not be the best way to promote it.[1] Moreover, legal enforcement risks a broadening tyranny over the person, since it tends to cast too broad a net: how much respect for the flag is shown by its use as part of a garment,[2] as background to advertisements for beer or automobiles? If the object is to maintain respect, perhaps we should look to an educational rather than a legal approach, which directs us toward finding out why the person resorted to the act in the first place. If it is an outburst of aggressive violence, it calls for psychiatric consideration. If it is to call attention to evils in the state of the country, then dialogue about the country and its problems is called for. We can easily understand now, and even sympathize with, a slave's burning the flag in the early 1800s. Even if we thought the flag-burner was blind to patriotic values and was obdurately unappreciative of the beneficent aspects of the nation, does it call for punishment? We do not punish alcoholics. Even those who most oppose abortion and seek to criminalize it ask that punishment be directed to those who perform the abortion, not those who have it. So why the flag-burner? Is it relevant—that is, should we expand the context to include—that the issue is being debated just after an election widely regarded as unparalleled for its triviality and its substitution of symbol for substantive debate? Is the Vietnam War relevant to the context, "the first war America lost"? Is it relevant that the Cold War has thawed, removing the comfort of stable hostilities, while an unmanageable terrorism universally threatens America?

It is unnecessary to pursue at great length alternative diagnoses of the practical problem of flag-burning to see that the surface is barely scratched by the immediate uniform reaction to it. Increasingly, as we probe, we are led to ask what *we* are seeking in the situation as well as what the situation is in its actual context. We may be helped by our own past. Just as the United States entered World War II, a comparable furor developed over saluting the flag in school, inspired by the refusal to do so by children of the faith of Jehovah's Witnesses. The Supreme Court permitted these children to be expelled on the ground, as Felix Frankfurter wrote, of the need for unity in a country embarked on a struggle for survival against Nazism. But in reversing itself a few years later the Court in effect acknowledged the hysteria of its previous response. It had become apparent that common sense could find some other way for children forbidden by their religion from saluting the flag to express their patriotism.

Other paroxysms in our history in the twentieth century—the Palmer raids against radicals during and after World War I, Senator Joseph M. McCarthy's investigations of subversion in the 1950s—as well as our recovery from such episodes, suggest that, no less than the dogmatic theocracies of the Near East though less drastically, our social life is subject to the strains of readjusting traditional modes of thought and ways of life. The stresses of inevitable change and fear of change lie deep in many of our practical problems. To diagnose practical problems, critically considering their formulation and context, is to seek out these issues and identify their place in the problem focused upon, whether at the center or at the periphery.

In the remainder of this chapter we turn to the analysis of formulation, alternative formulations, and the bases for selection among them.

FORMULATION OF THE PROBLEM

From the preliminary examination of diagnosis it is clear that the results of diagnosis at any given stage are expressed in the formulation of the problem. However the formulation is analyzed, one central topic will be the *meaning of its terms*. For example, we speak of the problem of *war*, and we recognize a body of literature dealing with the ethical problems of war, running from Plato and Aristotle through Augustine and Aquinas, Hobbes and Locke, and later writers. But is the problem the *same problem*, with perhaps a shift in degree, if the consequences risked are total annihilation and not the limited consequences of hand-to-hand combat? Does war remain the same problem as we move from spear to cannon to nuclear missile? Traditional ethics of war takes the distinction between combatant and noncombatant as the pivot for many a moral judgment. As war becomes total—a conflict between populations rather than between small mercenary armies in the employ of competing ruling families— does the distinction become irrelevant? Traditional ethics makes much of a rule of proportionality, and distinguishes wars of aggression from wars of self-defense. Do these distinctions remain relevant to the problem of war in the twentieth century? How do we classify the Israeli doctrine of "aggressive self-defense"? In the conflict in Nicaragua, who was the aggressor—the Sandinistas, the Contras, or the United States? Indeed, should the relation between the United States and Nicaragua have been perceived as a matter of war? Instead of an ethics of war, should we now think in terms of an ethics for nuclear war, an ethics for conventional war, for guerrilla war, for antiterrorist war, and so on? If what we face is the same problem, then we have resources to tap from the past: to see the problem as one of war is to invoke a label that triggers rules and principles and distinctions that have a substantial history. Otherwise, there is a call to query whether old labels are adequate to classifying or conceiving these conflicts and to invent or find new ones.

Such examples can be multiplied. Is poverty the *same problem* when the understanding of its causes changes, moving from merit and moral stigma to dislocations in the economy at large? Or when production itself shifts from craft to assembly line? Or when responsibility for alleviating poverty shifts from being a personal duty, as in charity, to become a task assigned to public institutions? Or when we have developed new distinctions, such as the feminization of poverty? Is the separation of church and state a response to the same problem if it is seen as protecting the secular from religious inroads or the religious from coercion by a single sect? Does famine cease to be a natural disaster and become a moral problem when there are unused resources sufficient to provide for many more if not for all? When may we treat as the same problem-situations proposed at one time as matters of right and at other times as matters of good or evil? When may we say we have uncovered a hitherto unnoticed problem or say we have discovered a new problem (for example, sexual harassment or child abuse)?

A way of beginning to unravel these issues and their complexities is to raise the question of how concepts function to guide inquiry, which locks into longstanding interests of philosophy in definition, categorization, description and identification, interpretation and significance. These questions have been a concern to philosophy since Socrates first had a try at defining justice—what it means, and how to identify a case as just or unjust. It is an issue for everyday experience, but it is critical for moral questions since so much depends on how we *perceive* a situation and under what ideas or *concepts* we construe it. We need, therefore, to attend to how we identify, classify, and recognize a problem, and *how we come to see that it is a problem*, as a necessary preliminary to the search for solution, resolution, or answer.

THE EXISTING SITUATION

That the manner in which a problem is conceived—the way it is labeled and described, how it is understood and its nature explored— is critical to how it is treated is a very old story. Indeed, a situation is transformed into a problem only relative to some conceptualization or interpretation. Ordinarily, the experiencing of pain marks a problem, and its conceptualization as a toothache or a stomachache routes a solution. But the pain of a pinprick felt under the conditions of a test for paralysis is cause for relief, not alarm. Whether we think of a missing book as lost in the office clutter, lent to a forgotten student, or stolen suggests three quite different patterns of response. The story is told of farmers in California, troubled by the number of tomatoes lost in the harvesting by the machine tomato-pickers bursting the skin, asking a California university for help in designing a more sensitive tomato-picker. They had conceptualized the problem as an inefficient tomato-picker. After efforts to redesign the machine failed, someone thought of reconceptualizing the problem—not that the machines were badly designed but that the tomato skins were too weak. The objective was redefined as one of redesigning the tomato so that it would fit the machines. That was successfully achieved—at least, successfully for the tomato growers, although not necessarily for consumers.

The choice of description can have tragic consequences. In the summer of 1985 officials of the city of Philadelphia attempted to deal with provocations by members of a radical group called MOVE. It resulted in the burning of several blocks of a neighborhood and the deaths of eleven people, children among them. Later what the officials did was described as "dropping a bomb" on a neighborhood. At the inquiry, the mayor said that when he was informed of what the police intended to do, he had not been told they were going to drop a bomb. He had been told it was an "incendiary device." When pressed on the question of whether the police were aware that children were in the house, the police commissioner said the situation had been classified as a "barricade situation," not as a "hostage situation" (apparently classifications from official police policy manuals). The fact that the children were with their parents led him not to think of them as "hostages." By the later testimony of these officials, had the situation been described then, or thought of, as "dropping a bomb" or as a "hostage situation" they would have acted differently.

The most powerful single influence on how we conceptualize is language. Through it we become accustomed to slicing up the world in standard ways that are shared with others in our language community. Philosophers have been attentive to the dangers resulting from words carrying an affective penumbra: some words are positively charged, and others negatively charged. This feature, what Francis Bacon called the color of words, is well-known and skillfully used by propaganda analysts, public relations experts, and of course legions of advertisers. In the earlier part of the century, a popular *semantics* movement made people conscious of the way words are used to secure some special effect, convey some special purpose, or get others to treat things or situations in a given way. A rose by any name would smell as sweet; but would people smell it if it were described as stinkweed? If something is a weed, it goes to the waste pile; if it is a vegetable, it goes to the kitchen or market. Sometimes, under the same name, there may be a change in use: horseradish, once a gardener's pest for the way it spread, became an acceptable food, if not quite a delicacy. Weakfish is as good to eat as flounder; is it now "seatrout"? Catfish ascended the scale of delicacy with remarkable gusto, and is now "farmed" for export; its taste, once known, more than compensates for its name. In political life, to be a liberal at one time was to be in the respected center of public life. Now the same liberal becomes a "moderate" or "progressive conservative" and carefully distinguishes her- or himself from "right liberal" and "left liberal."

Attention to the instrumental characterization of language is not new to philosophy. Jeremy Bentham's *Table of the Springs of Action*[3] is a systematic classification of types of pleasures and pains with corresponding motives, and the names for those motives listed as neutral, eulogistic, or dyslogistic. For example, in the domain of the pleasure of taste, hunger is neutral, love of good cheer is eulogistic, gluttony is dyslogistic. In the domain of the sexual appetite, sexual desire is neutral, and lechery is dyslogistic, but Bentham observes that no eulogistic terminology exists. Bentham's awareness of the power of language is clearest in his notes on homosexuality, published only in the twentieth century. It was in his time difficult even to mention the topic: for William Blackstone, homosexuality was "that horrible sin, not to be named among Christians."[4] When described, it was with dyslogistic language only: "unnatural" and "impure." From the use of such words, says Bentham, "has flowed a mass of misery altogether beyond the reach of calculation."[5]

> The truth is that by the epithet *unnatural*, when applied to any human act or thought, the only matter which it affords any indication that can be depended upon is the existence of a sentiment of disapprobation, accompanied with passion in the breast of the person by whom it is employed.[6]

It is significant that Bentham goes beyond the propagandistic effect of language—which considers the effect on others—to suggest that those who think by such language are themselves victims of it. "It is by the power of names—of signs originally arbitrary and insignificant—that imagination has in good measure been guided."[7] As a remedy he seeks a more neutral vocabulary, distinguishing types of sexual intercourse as *regular* and *irregular*, rather than *natural* and *unnatural*, and *improlific* appetite rather than *unnatural* appetite.

That language communicates attitudes and that those attitudes and the choice of words have social consequences is no longer in dispute, especially in an era of increased sensitivity to sexism in language and to ethnic slurs. Nonetheless, efforts by Bentham and later philosophers to construct a neutral language is troubling in the assumption that if we could only get rid of the distortions of language motivated by special purposes, we could reach a proper understanding of what was going on. If all purposes are removed, would we have a language left? The predicament is like the use of "special interests" in political language today. We are constantly warned not to yield to "special interests" and to keep the good of the country as a whole in mind. Yet the identification of special interests becomes voracious. By the time it has covered minorities and labor and consumers and business and moved on to women, there is little left that is not "special" for the "general good" to work on. While simple analysis reveals the difference between "gay" and "queer," or between "girl" and "woman," a great deal more is involved in S. I. Hayakawa's discussion of the difference between a sum of money given as "relief" to the unemployed as a "handout" in the Depression and an "insurance payment" earned by years of labor in the community. Even more subtle was the "spin" placed by the White House early in the Reagan years on a potentially damaging story. David Stockman in an interview in the *Atlantic Monthly* had revealed that as director of the Office of Management and Budget he knew that the figures in the budget did not add up. A meeting between Stockman and the President was described as Stockman's "trip to the woodshed," so that the story was not about an economic scandal but about a disloyal son. It is not that one story was true and the other false; it is that it was in the interest of the White House to have people conceptualize it one way rather than the other.

Language users would do well to learn the lesson that William James's psychology propounded for all experience and all thought: that purpose and interest are not added to a purpose-free and interest-free or neutral experience but constitute an intrinsic part of the selection that is characteristic of all experience, and indeed of all conceptualization. Our seeing and our thinking are already perspectival in their very concurrence. From such an understanding it follows that conceptualization has always structured material in some way and that there are other ways in which it might have been structured in the light of other interests.

It has taken philosophy a long time to learn this lesson. The dominant tradition in Western philosophy for centuries favored the view that in some sense there is a single preferred description of the world. The world is given to us in preordained categories, often called *natural kinds,* and to understand the world is to be able to locate each individual in its appropriate natural kind. The theory of definition was initially tied to this enterprise of identifying natural kinds: a definition was to give the *essence* of an individual, or that set of properties or, as the Platonists first regarded them, *universals*, in virtue of which the individual is a member of that kind. There are, it was conceded, properties other than essential ones: individuals constituted a meeting place of an indefinite set of properties. This person is an animal, a thinker, an American, a body and a mind, a friend, an enemy, or a trader. This pencil is yellow or brown, hard or soft, long or short, with black or green lead, costing so-and-so much. But those properties that were not possessed by virtue of being a member of that natural kind (for example, human) were termed *accidental*, and as such, somehow not so important or so significant. For human beings, being rational was essential; being a trader was not essential.

The theory of essential definition therefore readily admitted that the "same" reality was capable of alternate descriptions: the same person is describable as a thief and as a loving father. What marks out the theory is the view that there is one description of any (natural) individual that is the "best" universally. It is when philosophers began to press the question, "Best for what?" that the theory began to erode. It has become commonplace for us to acknowledge that the choice of description rests not on truth alone, but also on relevance, and that relevance is determined by context and purpose. For the purposes of a criminal trial, the description "thief" is relevant and a better description than "loving father." For the purposes of a child-custody hearing, "loving father" is the relevant description; "thief" may not be. And for both hearings, "rational animal" is true but not relevant.

The ancient quest for complete truth continues to be so seductive that we are often tempted to say that underlying various incomplete descriptions—the descriptions, say, that are relevant to a child-custody hearing—there is a complete and true description. As a practical matter no one would imagine that such a description could be provided. But even as a theoretical matter, it is doubtful that such a description exists. The point can be made by considering maps, surely a paradigmatic case of description. Is there a single true and complete map of the earth? The answer could be yes only if we could find a way to project the features of a sphere onto a flat surface without distorting some of those features, and cartographers from

Ptolemy on have known that this is not possible. All maps necessarily contain some distortion. In elementary school we learn that the Mercator projection distorts the size of continents—Greenland, we are told, is not as large as South America, as it appears on the map. It turns out that in moving from a sphere to a flat plane we cannot preserve shape, distance, and area at the same time. We can represent one accurately, but then we must sacrifice the others; that is, we must make a decision on what our purposes are in using the map and select which features it is important for us to preserve. As a modern cartographer puts it: "There is no over-all 'best' projection for all maps. Each map represents a particular problem. The projection that is ideal for mapping Chile, which extends more than 2,600 miles north and south and an average of less than 150 miles east and west, is not the ideal projection for mapping an area like the former Soviet Union, which extended 5,000 miles east and west near the top of the globe."[8]

Mercator's map was designed to address just such a particular problem—to aid navigators in deciding which compass bearing to use in getting from one point to another. His great achievement was to make it possible for navigators to determine the required constant course by drawing a straight line on the map. In doing so, he had to sacrifice an accurate display of area, for he could not maintain the same scale throughout the map. Size is true at the equator but becomes increasingly distorted as one moves north or south. Hence, although navigators could determine what compass bearing to follow, they could not calculate distances by the Mercator map. Yet this in no way diminishes Mercator's achievement; his was a thoroughly successful solution to the problem as he defined it.

The significance of interest and purpose in the choice of a map is clear from the typologies used by cartographers: they differentiate the class of conformal maps (preserving shapes of small areas) and equal-area maps (preserving a standard scale throughout, but distorting shapes and distances), and others. Maps relevant to one purpose are not appropriate to another.[9] There are also thematic maps, designed to illustrate some special subject—distribution of oil deposits, rates of energy consumption, distribution of poverty, and so on. The United States will grow or shrink depending on what the map is to depict. A famous early example is a map of an area of London drawn by the physician John Snow in 1855 that showed the locations of every death from cholera and every water pump: it revealed that those who died had used a particular pump. More recently, Sweden has used a map displaying its "welfare landscape," showing travel times to medical, educational, and recreational services.[10]

The point is that maps, and descriptions generally, must be selective and incomplete. Certainly all maps must be accurate, but whether a given map is a good choice for a given situation is decided by what the map is to be used for. (A map might be used to project district pride—as in a Brooklynite map of the United States that has Brooklyn stretching halfway across the country.)

In our everyday world, we live relatively easily with alternative descriptions of the same things or events. The same loud noise may be perceived as a backfire or a shot according to the situation. A pain dismissed as illusory by the family practitioner may be real enough for the sufferer and the psychiatrist. Or, to take more homely examples, the library book is one thing to the stack worker, another to the cleaning person, the scholar, and the would-be censor of school texts, or member of the Society for the Liquidation of Secular Humanism. For some purposes, a whale is a fish (to the department of Game and Fisheries) and a tomato is a fruit; for others, they are a mammal and a vegetable. For some purposes, the same étude may be performed by the beginner and the professional; on other occasions, two performances by the same artist may be taken as different. An event may be perceived at the time of its occurrence differently from the later perception of it when placed in a series of events. For example, Rosa Parks, taking a seat in the front of the bus, might have been described then as being too tired to move to the back, while a later perspective marks her refusal to move as the beginning of the civil rights campaign. What was perceived in 1914 as an assassination in Sarajevo, part of an obscure Serbian dispute, is regarded now as the beginning of the First World War.

Exactly where to draw the line between perception (what we see) and conception (how we think of it) is notoriously difficult. The history of philosophy and of psychology abounds in attempts to draw this line. The great classical philosophical battle between empiricism and rationalism pivots on this point. It is no longer in dispute, however, that what we perceive is dependent, to a greater or less degree, on what we conceive. We see what we expect to see. A nice illustration is the Rosenhan study, in which eight perfectly normal "pseudopatients" were admitted to hospitals for psychiatric treatment under the faked diagnosis of schizophrenia. Although once admitted they behaved "normally," and stayed an average of nineteen days, none of them was detected as faking, and they left as "schizophrenics in remission."

> Once a person is designated abnormal, all of his other behaviors and characteristics are covered by that label. Indeed, the label is so powerful that many of the pseudopatients' normal behaviors are overlooked entirely or profoundly misinterpreted. . . . A psychiatric label has a life and an influence of its own. Once the impression has been formed that the patient is schizophrenic, the expectation is that he will continue to be schizophrenic. When a sufficient amount of time has passed, during which the patient has done nothing bizarre, he is considered to be in remission and available for discharge. But the label endures beyond discharge, with the unconfirmed expectation that he will behave as a schizophrenic again. Such labels, conferred by mental health professionals, are as influential on the patient as they are on his relatives and friends, and it should not surprise anyone that the diagnosis acts on all of them as a self-fulfilling prophecy. Eventually, the patient himself accepts the diagnosis, with all of its surplus meanings and expectations, and behaves accordingly.[11]

In one sense, then, language dictates what we will perceive as "the same." But in another, what we selectively perceive dictates what terms we employ. Where we have just "snow," allegedly the Eskimo have words to distinguish falling snow, slushy snow, snow on the ground packed like ice, wind-driven flying snow, and so on. We have words to distinguish bird, insect, aviator, airplane; Hopis have two words, one for birds, and one for anything else that flies.[12] Even so basic a perceptual matter as color may differ by the language classifications:

> The ancient Greeks and Romans classified colors not as we classify them, by the qualitative differences they show according to the places they occupy in the spectrum, but by reference to something quite different from this, something connected with dazzlingness or glintingness or gleamingness or their opposites, so that a Greek will find it natural to call the sea "winelooking" as we call it blue, and a Roman will find it natural to call a swan "scarlet"—or the word we conventionally translate as scarlet—as we call it white.[13]

In the world of mathematics and the hard sciences we find that the search for definition is continual, controlled, and conscious. The way in which chemists employ the concepts of acid and base illustrates the point. Early in the history of chemistry the acid–base distinction was made roughly by characteristics such as whether the solution had a sour taste, whether it could dissolve metals, and whether it could change the color of certain dyes (acid if, in its presence, litmus paper turns red, and base if it turns blue). Then in 1884, Svante August Arrhenius, observing that properties of acid solutions are due to the presence of hydrogen ions, redefined acid as any substance that increased the concentration of hydrogen ions in aqueous solution. Because hydrogen ions can be formed by transferring protons to water molecules, Johannes Nicolaus Brönsted and Thomas Martin Lowry in 1923 proposed the further redefinition of acids as proton donors (and bases as proton acceptors). The difference between these definitions is not just a theoretical matter; what counts as an acid also changes. Acid anhydrides are acid by the Arrhenius definition but, since they contain no hydrogen, they are not acids by the Brönsted–Lowry definition. Also in 1923, Gilbert N. Lewis suggested a third definition, which includes the acid anhydrides—an acid is any species that can accept a lone pair of electrons; a base is any species that can donate an electron pair. This definition expands the number of acids again. This might give the impression of being a shockingly chaotic situation—after all, one might say, which of these three definitions is the "real" definition of acid? But chemists live comfortably with all three definitions, moving from one to the other as convenience dictates.[14]

Even so straightforward a concept as that of "straight line" became a matter of contention at the beginning of the twentieth century in the development of relativistic physics. "The shortest distance between two points" was traditionally associated with a set of measures all of which were assumed to yield the same result: the path over which a ruler could be laid down the least number of times, line of sight, the path of maximum tension of a string, and so on. Relativity theory, though, had the path of light affected by gravitation, which meant line of sight became a questionable criterion of straightness. Now Einstein had a choice: he could say light traveled in a straight line, and therefore the geometry of space is non-Euclidean, or that space was Euclidean and light did not move in straight lines. He saw the problem as that of choosing between two different combinations of geometry and physics.[15] He chose to take non-Euclidean geometry as the true description because he thought that particular combination of geometry and physics simpler. Here the decisional aspect of conceptualization was transparent.

We can draw some lessons from the history of science on the question of how we choose among competing concepts. We see that truth alone, or accuracy, is not the only consideration. Disputes are often relativized to a theory, and the issue is often not what is true but what is more fruitful, more powerful, with easier connections to other bodies of knowledge. Aesthetic qualities too play a role; the history of astronomy is a splendid example of the role of aesthetic criteria in the guidance of theory construction.

In law, too, the struggle over definition is explicit, protracted, and controlled. Even more than in science, law attaches direct consequences to conceptual decisions. How is insanity to be defined? What constitutes a contract? What is "income" for the purposes of the Internal Revenue Service? Is alcoholism an "addiction"? Is a hearse, for tax purposes, to be classified as a passenger vehicle or as a truck?

It was once thought that judicial decision was a simple matter of deductive logic: combine the law (as major premise) with a statement of the facts of the case (minor premise), and the conclusion follows automatically. We have come to pay far more attention to the necessary preliminary step of categorizing the case at hand as a case of something, which in turn determines which laws are relevant. Then the law itself has to be interpreted—by appeal to historical argument about intent, by consistency with other laws or past decisions, or by meanings of the terms in the law. In Common Law particularly alternatives are available at each stage: law and case are mutually adjusted so that there is an appropriate "fit." Each new case puts the law to the test, and each case, by virtue of its unique features, has the potential of changing the law for the future. Sometimes the press of cases forces the evolution of a new concept, as happened with privacy in constitutional law; but where that happens, it is by finding that concept latent in earlier decisions, as the right of privacy was found to be a "penumbra" of other rights.

These considerations suggest that, in the case of legal concepts and of scientific concepts, it is inappropriate to ask what it "really" means, as an essentialist might. We see concepts change, often explicitly and sometimes implicitly, and we see constant arguments over how concepts should be defined. Reasons are given for preferring one definition over another, and in the argument some general criteria are appealed to: comprehensiveness, consistency, simplicity, theoretical power, systematicity. Yet for the most part conceptual change is urged for reasons that are relative to particular theories or particular cases. Whether chemists have made good choices in the definition of acid can be evaluated only by examining in some detail what each definition permits them to do. Whether constitutional scholars properly classified a set of cases as issues of privacy can be determined only by an examination of those cases against possible alternative classifications.

Several lessons emerge from this inquiry, partly as conclusions, partly as further questions. It is clear enough that there are always alternative formulations possible in any given problem-situation and that the grounds of selection among them are in some measure purposive. Does it follow, however, that in applied ethics we should always seek out alternatives, or should we stay with the habitual meanings that have had, so to speak, survival value? Secondly, if we envisage alternative formulations, how do we decide either correctness or superiority?

In one sense, as noted earlier, the very fact that we have a problem to resolve entails an element of doubt about proceeding in a habitual way. Some modification or alternative has at least to be considered. But the matter has deeper roots. On the whole, the habitual is so entrenched in our common approaches that creativity is dulled and opportunities are missed. Indeed, we train for the habitual. The schoolteacher asks pupils questions in such a way that they assume he or she has the correct answer, not that they are all engaged in an inquiry in which there is fresh learning. Even in testing, a "hidden figure" test will ask the subject to find the figure that is hidden, not to see how many different figures can be found or elicited. We become so used to seeing a situation in one way that it takes effort to see it in another. And if another is produced, it is assigned to the imagination, not to the "correct" account. In art we recognize now that impressionistic painting had a liberating effect in that it showed us surfaces and colors and shades rather than familiar utilitarian objects. But in social and moral thought standardized ways of seeing become tyrannical: national interest is described from the position of those in power, not in light of the needs of the people at large; ideas of success are described in terms of male attitudes of autonomy and domination rather than by female attitudes of care and responsibility. In short, our culture has not yet caught up with the demands of living in a world of change, of evaluating the habitual and the familiar against alternatives, even where we may ultimately decide to keep to it. On the first point, therefore, the answer is clearly that in facing a practical problem the consideration of alternative formulations is desirable, even where they do not immediately present themselves.

The second question, that of criteria for the most satisfactory or more satisfactory of alternative formulations of a problem, is extremely complicated. One component, of course, will be matter-of-fact correctness for some elements in the picture. If the problem is whether to enter some cooperative enterprise (partnership, marriage, joint holiday), alternative kinds of partner relations may be envisaged—strict division of tasks with each managing one's own, common work on common projects, attitudes of business relations or friendship relations. It matters in formulating the problem whether you have *correctly* assessed the capacities and virtues of the intended partner, for those qualities make one alternative possible and rule out others. Correctness here may refer to relations within the alternative (for example, whether the partners must agree in political—or for that matter, religious or moral or aesthetic—outlook is necessary if a particular business relationship is to work out) or to whether the picture envisaged in the alternative fits the situation (for example, whether the intended actual partner has the requisite qualities).

How to judge matter-of-fact correctness need not be considered at length here. In the modern world we rely where possible on scientific inquiry or on logical–empirical methods of securing evidence of this. Since we are dealing with particular situations in applied ethics, correctness will be judged more in the manner of the court of law or the detective or, most of the time, in a commonsense way rather than as a laboratory experiment. The reference to the scientific reminds us that the formulation of a problem is more like a theoretical assertion than an observational one, and that theories are not judged simply true or false but involve complex processes of establishment in which there are criteria not only of successful prediction but of fruitfulness, simplicity, and coherence within the larger assumptions of the world-outlook of science. We should not expect practical ethical judgments to be less complex—indeed, they are likely to be more complicated, for the variables entering into them are more numerous and varied than in the typical scientific situation.

It is helpful to distinguish types of situations. In one type alternatives are thought of only in a speculative way, and they are not entertained as serious possibilities. Parents thinking of the approaching schooling of their young child usually have no alternative to a public or private school where the child will spend so many years. They may have read and thought about libertarian attacks on compulsory schooling, or Ivan Illich's proposal to abolish the schools and rely on mutual arrangements of people for the interchange of teaching and learning, or have been influenced by ideas of cooperative progressive education. But unless they have extraordinary resources or are ready to fight for home education against formidable legal obstacles, the alternatives they envisage do little to resolve their problem. Most people, perhaps, will not even think of what they face as a problem in the first place, or if they do, they attempt to solve it by more active participation in the local parent–teacher association and by keeping a close eye on the child's progress.

In a second type of case, there are alternatives, and genuine ones, but no effort to think of them is made, and familiar solutions are resorted to. For example, the United States is in difficulty because of the high ratio of imports to exports. The problem is posed as changing the ratio in one or another of two ways: reduce the imports or increase the exports. The first alternative, labeled "protectionism," is for the most part rejected, on the basis of its past failure and of fear of retaliation by other countries. Governmental dictation of industrial policy is on the whole unpalatable to free enterprise. Hence, we are left with the second alternative. So far, so good. Now the problem is how to achieve increased exports. Here the stereotype is a sports-competition model. The cry goes up for "increased competitiveness," on the assumption that if we all strive to beat the competition, we win the economic game. Perhaps it is the prevalence of the sports model in society at large, with everyone urged to strain and cheer one's own side,[16] that prevents us from conceiving alternative formulations of our economic situation. Is it possible that in some respects we suffer from too much competitiveness? Some economists have pointed out that our practice of short-term (three-month) profit statements from corporations, geared to the stock market, puts a premium on immediate profit to the detriment of long-range investment. Thus our habits with respect to production and its planning, in contrast to Japan's, may be a source of many of our economic deficiencies. Even within the game model itself, the notion of competitiveness needs examination: does it promote the star system, with stress on the success of the individual winner, or loyalty, with a stress on the success of the team? Even the very ratio of imports to exports, taken to be the defining condition of the problem, raises complex questions of measurement. United States corporations producing abroad may have their sales in the United States count as imports. Perhaps there should be a greater break-up of the problem field. Some areas may be ready for international cooperation rather than competition. For example, agriculture, an economic sphere in which nations spend vast sums subsidizing their farmers, may be ready for a worldwide plan with a rationalized division of labor. Of course, such cursory ideas as these are far from solutions to the complex problem of the trade deficit, but they may serve to show the hollowness of a one-track reading of a problem-situation.

In a third type of case solutions to a largely new situation are formulated in terms of older familiar ideas. A striking example of this type is that of surrogate motherhood. The practice itself has obviously answered a definite need, and, given the traditional positive attitude in this culture to family values, the need of couples who want children but are unable to bear them evokes wide sympathy. (The need is not adequately satisfied by opportunities to adopt, although these might be considerably widened if racial attitudes and preferences were not so deeply entrenched as they still are.) Now, the situation of the surrogate mother has been read in different ways. One formulation regards it as a straight contract, within the moral discretion of the participants; as moral, there is no antecedent prohibition of the type of contract, as there is for prostitution, sale of bodily organs, and the like—participants may write their own ticket, provided they agree. A second formulation sees the case as straight motherhood—just another case of extramarital childbearing. A surrogate mother would then have all the rights that maternity endows. True, there are moral issues raised by the relation to the surrogate's own husband, if she is married, resolved probably by his consent. As for the surrogate's relationship to the people who are seeking a child and initiated the procedure, on this formulation, the eventual transfer of the child to them is seen as an act of adoption, with the consent of the (surrogate) mother. A third formulation sees the whole procedure as an abhorrent commercialization of a sacrosanct domain of social life: it is an agreement to produce a child for sale, and human beings are not to be bought or sold. (Of course, it might also be regarded as an act of love or friendship, where a sister or friend acted as surrogate from affection for the infertile person.)

A further analysis sees the situation as a largely new one, where the old rubrics fit badly and the task is to frame or design a new practice or institution—as new as, for example, joint stock companies had been in a world where businesses had been private individual or family ventures, or as organ transplants, with their associated problems of access to limited supplies. Each proposed new institution has to be evaluated for its objectives and dangers and all the different perspectives on it treated as possibly relevant relations for consideration. New problems are likely to increase with the development of new technologies, such as the case of a divorced couple struggling over legal control of frozen embryos—another problem arising from the very technique of in vitro fertilization that makes surrogate motherhood possible. (Some consideration of the problems of innovation will be found in Chapter Ten; those of institutional reconstruction in Chapter Nine.)

Grappling with cases of these kinds suggests that beyond the narrower question of matter-of-fact correctness lies the whole purposive background for the practical problem. The task of assessing different formulations is therefore itself dependent on eliciting the salient purposes of the situation. It calls not primarily for an inventory of basic values, but rather for addressing the question: what basically is at stake *here*? What are we really driving at in seeing and feeling this as a problem? It is not enough merely to say, "We have such-and-such desires." We must also ask why we have these desires, where they are likely to lead us, how they arose, and how they fit with other aims we have. And there is likely to be no sharp line between thinking of my aims and the aims of the groups or community in which I live. It is within such a matrix of reflection that I am likely to raise questions of right and wrong and the practical problem be translated into a moral problem.

The lesson of these considerations is that moral issues do not pertain only to the action with which we conclude our facing a practical problem. They enter from the very beginning into the way we see the problem itself. How this works out carries us step-by-step into the analysis of the situation itself and then into the entry of moral concepts.

CHAPTER

Six

Context

When dealing with a problem it is helpful, if not unavoidable, to consider its context. Taken narrowly, the context includes what ancient and medieval philosophers referred to as the circumstances—who the agent is, what is being done, how it is being done, who is affected, what the intention is, and so on. More broadly construed, the context encompasses the whole sociohistorical dimensions of the situation. To consider context helps clarify the situation, pinpoint where the agent can get a handle on it, revise the formulation of the problem while the view of the situation itself is being reshaped, and advance deliberation toward the resolution of the problem. This chapter explores and sorts the components that enter into context and considers the criteria for expanding and calling a halt to expansion of context.

This is not to say that appeals to context are deemed universally relevant in moral philosophy. Whether to consider context or circumstances, and if so, to what extent, remains a matter of continuing controversy. On the one hand, there are those whom we might call *absolutists*, *rigorists*, or *eternalists*. They look toward changeless norms of conduct, incontrovertible principles of moral obligation, or virtues that regardless of the kind of society or stage of development are the necessary conditions of commerce among peoples living together and that make such living possible and rich. And perhaps when found, they are taken to be discovered rather than constructed. These norms often involve a profound belief in fundamental moral attitudes that are a part of what it means to be human—fundamental intuitions shared by all who are civilized. Thus, the condemnation of gratuitous inflicting of pain, betrayal, and ingratitude, some version of the Golden Rule; absolute commitment to respect for life, promise-keeping, veracity, and a peaceful stance (at least within the in-group).

Theirs is a search for stability and the authority, autonomy, and independence of moral judgments. Sometimes they are committed to unseatable priorities such as freedom of speech, free enterprise, equality of opportunity, and rights to property.

Theirs is also a well founded and general hostility to context-bound judgments, perhaps a search for certainty, for unchanging and reliable rules and guides. It doubtless comes from our long tradition that the moral law is no respecter of persons, whether sovereign and subject, and from traditions of fairness and impartiality that are against special privilege or special excuses. Doubtless this is what powers the appeal to the United States Constitution as written and as an absolute guide, without which we would lose our way. It ties in also with a traditional moral intuitionism either that some truths are self-evident or, says William Gass,[1] that there are some acts or situations that would be repugnant to all reasonable men.

There is a pull in the other direction quite as strong, which we may call *contextualist*. Contextualism tends to see each situation so uniquely endowed with promise, resources, and dangers, as not easily to be bound by abstract principles or universal rules. Contextualists are more sensitive to change, to the incomplete control of circumstances, to the relevance of what is possible, and to the pressure of what is necessary. They are alert to mitigating circumstances and to the hardness of decision that almost always leaves some values or good unrealized, some obligations unmet, or some objectives compromised. They recognize that different moments in history offer fresh opportunities and unprecedented challenges. Perhaps there is here a regard for the spontaneity, authenticity, and autonomy of a particular decision, where one takes pride in making decisions in accordance with values that are fluid and flexible, decisions that often are the lesser of evils. Above all, they are impressed by the varieties of experiments in styles of community and self-realization. Each decision is ultimately unique. All decisions are present decisions, and past commitments have to be reaffirmed or altered, not just followed. Nor does the importance of the principle accepted diminish the value of the principle rejected. The decision is a principled rejection of a

principle that necessitates bearing the unavoidable guilt of its violation.

Both attitudes—rigorist and contextualist—come philosophically
well credentialed. Kant's work, of course, serves as the *locus clas-
sicus* of the rigorist, and Bentham's of the contextualist. But Nicolai
Hartmann calls our attention to the vast plurality of ideals that may
conflict among themselves and from which we have to choose our
principle on a given occasion, and G. E. Moore questions our ability
to discover what is right in the welter of endless consequences that
flow from the variety of contexts. Hartmann calls on us to bear the
unavoidable guilt of choice, while Moore urges us not to embark with
any trust on the sea of unavoidable ignorance.

CONTEXTUAL–HISTORICAL INQUIRY

If we are to consider context, clearly two of the initial components
will be *whose* problem it is, and what the *preliminary account* of the
problem is. For example, let it be the problem of keeping a job
during a depression or the advancing technological displacement of
workers. Take the case of a longshoreman with the job of unloading
incoming goods from ships as they dock. The time is the early 1930s
and imports are decreasing. It is not enough to say that the worker
should continue performing well so that any cutback will fall elsewhere, even though employment at that time was very competitive.
We have to grasp the mode and conditions of employment. In fact,
if we knew enough to see the question as relevant, we would ask
whether he was working on the East or the West Coast. East Coast
jobs were assigned every day through a shape-up: those who wanted
work came to the pier early in the morning hoping to be chosen for
work by the boss. On the West Coast, the longshoremens' union had
organized union hiring halls: union members were sent to fill the
openings through a rotation system, job by job without any seniority
provision, with everyone taking a turn; all shared advantages and
disadvantages thereby. The problem of keeping one's job in a growing depression was thus a different one in the two places: in the one,
it was the longshoreman's own problem; in the other, it was the
union's. In one, it meant keeping in favor with the boss, whatever the
specific means; in the other, remaining in good standing in the union,
a matter of ready recourse not amounting to a problem. In some

cases, the problem becomes the group's from the start, for example, where the whole type of job is threatened, as performing musicians in theaters were undercut as a group by the development of "canned music." After a prolonged strike, the musicians won compensation consisting of contributions to a pension fund for retired musicians, it being clear that most of the work would not be phased out. Fine shading is important in determining whose problem it is. Particularly, other people can enter in different ways: they may be part of the context as entering into the effects of the action, or more intimately as human beings affected by it, or they may be co-participants in whose problem it is. Thus a person deliberating on a problem and recognizing it as a matter of public policy already is taking the standpoint of the group: it is the group's problem being considered, not his or her own. If it remains the latter, it is like a corporation advocating some legislation because it will bring in business. Of course, there may be those who share the belief, once expressed by the president of General Motors, that what is good for General Motors is good for the country. Apart from such attitudes, a public policy issue is seen as a national or a societal problem.

The extension of relevant contexts in a given problem may carry us from a wider present into the past or the projected future. The historical origins of a problem are often relevant to its analysis. A typical example from the current scene is the problem of ethnic or religious minorities in many troubled countries. The conflict between Protestants and Catholics in Northern Ireland is unintelligible outside the history of Ireland, or that of the Turkish minority in Bulgaria outside the long history of the Turkish Empire. And the shadow cast by the oncoming future may become a strong factor in the present. Current examples are concern with the greenhouse effect and the problem of the ozone layer or the general effect of rapid technological development on industrial employment. In the longshoreman example given above, the rise of container packaging and unloading by machinery seriously affected the job market.

The most systematic advice in guiding the expansion of context comes, as might be expected, from the most systematic knowledge we possess. We begin by classifying a problem as raising psychological or social issues, or as involving cultural differences, and then turn to accumulated knowledge of such fields for help. In many personal problems as well as social issues such as criminal behavior and its punishment, psychology has been much invoked. But in ordinary personal deliberation within the larger realms of professional decision and social policy, it is the combination of the sociocultural and the historical that proves most fruitful. The remainder of this chapter is devoted to illustrating these processes and seeing insofar as possible how relevance is judged, and in particular, how dramatically a problem may be transformed in this way.

Ordinarily, we do not distinguish sharply between content and context, between the meaning of an idea, act, or behavior and its circumstances or situation. For we live *in* situations, and indeed it seems rather less that our ideas are *in* a context than that the context is an intrinsic and constituent part of understanding or of assessing what is at issue. This is the familiar point made in diagnosis. For we scarcely ever just perceive or just see. We generally identify the phenomenon as a lie, as usury, as harassment, a violation of privacy or free speech, or as an unwarranted interference by government or others in our lives. We have seen, in the previous chapter, how readily we provide a context, as for example, in asking, "How far is 30th Street Station?" whether the interest is walking or taking a cab. Or the different ways an architect, social worker, or sanitary engineer would describe a city block.

This chapter develops and extends the materials of the previous chapter. But in that chapter, the appeal was largely to methodological contexts of definition and theory, and on the whole the appeal to context was rather minimal or local, appealing most often to contemporary usage. It would have been in the purview of that chapter to have raised questions of the relevance of intention, for example, in modifying a situation—say in which X kills Y—but it needs further reference to the prevailing social institutions or arrangements that go to its justification or excuse. Even in the case of a soldier, the right to kill is not a blank check, but regulated as to time and circumstances. Again, place and time may make a difference: under Texas law, infidelity excuses killing in the immediate context of discovery—but not after forth-eight hours. Or, in another age, death resulting from dueling brought no penalty. Youth too may provide an excuse.

The cultural patterning of institutions may often be essential to understanding what is going on. For example, we may look at divorce as merely an act between two consenting adults, especially when there are no children. But in other cultures, and even in our own past, serious social consequences may give the practice a thoroughly different meaning. For example, in some East African societies where cattle are used for dowries, the dowry received for the marriage of a son may be used in turn as a dowry to marry off a daughter. If later, the son's marriage ends in divorce and the cattle have to be returned, the daughter's marriage breaks up as a consequence. Again, in a far different part of the culture—say, business— what is frowned on as immoral or illegal bribery in one part of society may be regarded as standard business practice or as standard gift giving in another. These differing attitudes may be difficult to resolve as business becomes international.

Here we want to explore this larger social–cultural–historical context and the help that expansion may give to a better understanding of the quality of the act, of the behavior, and of what is at issue. Such broadening may not only give a better understanding but point in new directions toward new avenues of assessment and decision. Often enough such expansion is unnecessary, for we can bring into play a rule or principle as relevant or apposite; here a glance at expansion is simply making sure that no objection is offered. But as often we are uncertain or uneasy as to how to identify or label the act, or the rule seems not to fit comfortably, the conflicts between rules gives pause, or the act seems to fit under two incompatible rules, or new technologies make for discomfiture in decision or create genuine disagreement and even confrontation, thereby forcing us to reconsider definitions and categories.

We may generally be unmindful of how much we import from the larger sociohistorical context. Few Westerners would see in medieval painting merely a beautiful woman with a baby rather than a Madonna and Child (as few Westerners would appreciate the musical and seasonal associations with Indian Raj paintings). Discourse generally has an audience in mind, as well as a context—for example, *cape* becomes unambiguous when the context is a discussion of clothing or a lecture on geography, as does *work* in a physics laboratory or a union meeting. More subtly, *quota* implicates exclusion to an older generation, opportunity to a contemporary one.

Particularly, we may be alerted when we have made a mistake. Or again, when we run into perplexingly different assessments, the cultural and social circumstances are often needed to make proper sense of what is going on. The Eskimo practice of abandoning the aged as the tribe moved on, and even helping them to die when they could no longer keep up, was often cited as revealing a different and more callous attitude to respect for life. But once we understand that the whole group was living on the bare margin of subsistence, that taking the aged along would risk the survival of the group, that the aged themselves expected and acquiesced in this custom, and that compensatory myths—that one would dwell in the hereafter with those bodily capacities with which one departed from this life—sweetened the planned departure, then a more appropriate comparison is to a lifeboat situation, not to disrespect for life or cruelty.

Or again, what might appear to be excessive vanity in one group of Melanesian men who spent a considerable time primping and painting themselves takes on a different quality when understood as a residue or remnant of the custom of warriors making themselves appear more fierce as they prepared for war. The British had abolished such tribal conflict, and so the primping was left hanging culturally.

We need not go so far afield, or to such exotic cultures; variations can be found close to home, giving rise to misunderstanding and often to confrontations. This is scarcely surprising, particularly in a pluralistic society. There are differently working social institutions with different degrees of effectiveness; different senses of the self, of human nature as essentially evil, innocent, or educable; different degrees of confidence in control and different models of interpersonal relations (as contractual or interactional), and different views of what constitutes the moral community (that is, where responsibility lies); changing patterned virtues and priorities of virtues and principles; and above all, differences in the extent of knowledge and technological development. And we frame different ideas of happiness and of what constitutes a rich and productive life.

There are also different views of what is regarded as a moral matter, and in what the moral enterprise itself consists. Indeed, there have been longstanding tensions in the ways that ordinary citizens and philosophers have regarded the nature of this quest. The sociocultural–historical has not only shaped what we take to be properly moral matters—affecting what we take to be right and wrong, good and bad, virtues and their priority, but also what the moral enterprise itself is about, its constraints and objectives.

In any case, moral inquiry shares with inquiry generally the need to muster knowledge to understand what is going on; that is, what are the factors involved in the situation, what are the local conditions or the specially prevailing conditions that give an unnoticed dimension to the act or possibly alter the quality of it completely. An appeal to social context may alter our perception even as to what the problems are and what remedies can be pressed into service. This calls for not only a clarification of terms and principles, testing them for consistency with applied principles and with other principles, but also a search for remedies that might otherwise be overlooked.

For example, consideration of a divorce may lead us to ask whether there are children or not, as well as what kind of immediate consequences there may be to the structure of the family and to the care of the elderly. Or again, a remedy may be sought in one direction, only to turn out, when local circumstances are understood, to lie in a far different one: thus in the problem of reducing teenage pregnancy in Washington D.C., it was thought that extending sex education would be helpful, only to find that the teenagers were becoming pregnant not as a result of ignorance but as a way of making a mark, that is, achieving something in a situation that offered few other paths to accomplishment, especially in a social atmosphere where the practice was not condemned. Again, in considering the problems of deterrence and punishment, one needs to know the variable factors the deterrent effect depends upon—how great the temptation in the particular wrongdoing, how desperate the typical plight of the wrong-doer, and how serious and how frequent society's effort to stop that action. Or, in addressing poverty, it becomes critical to know to what extent it is a phenomenon of unemployment in continued recession or dislocation of industries, to what extent unemployability is due to lack of skill and education or uneducability, and to what extent poverty has become "feminized."

Examples abound of how context diversifies meaning. Currently *quotas* mean radically different things to those who remember them as barring entry to a field and those for whom they are now enforced opportunities for entry into a field. *Famine* is quite different where it involves an unavoidable shortage of food—as in crop failure or other disaster—from where it rests on cornering the market and making food unavailable to the impoverished.[2] Principles such as freedom of speech are constantly being reclarified under the challenge by news media and docudramas, by "sextalk" telephone lines, by advertising claims, by nonverbal symbols like the flag, and by the wielding of stereotypes. Freedom of religion finds the concept of religion taxed by Satanic cults, no less than by polygamy in pockets of Mormonism, and the rejection of standard surgical assistance for children in Christian Science. Most dramatically, the current meaning of *war* and preparations for war includes the consequences for the environment as well as total destruction of human life.

It is not sufficient merely to look to the present, or even to the foreseeable consequences and the resources presently available. We also need to look to the past, with which the present is entangled. The present owes the past much of its principles, ideals, virtues, vices, what are regarded as its basic needs, and its goals in the light of what is possible. It is clear that *moderate* in Iran is not the same as moderate in our usage. *Liberal* and *conservative* need to be pegged to a historical moment and context to understand what they summarize in the way of general outlook and what issues are involved. A twentieth-century American conservative, if a devotee of free enterprise, is equivalent to a nineteenth-century British liberal, not to the nineteenth-century British conservative, a devotee of tradition and the aristocracy.[3] *Pornography* clearly changes its content. Or for that matter, even what is taken to be a moral matter changes with the times. What is judged *fornication* at one time is at another distinguished as promiscuity on the one hand and a serious trial marriage on the other.

Even discontinuities, apparent or real, raise important problems. The chivalric virtues and the seven deadly sins have almost lost their character as morality. What is praiseworthy or blameworthy changes: for example, gratitude and ingratitude lose their prominence whereas punctuality, productiveness, and thrift (the Benjamin Franklin virtues) take their place.

Of equal importance are the virtues that are diminished. Friendship, the values of community, and hospitality are stripped down or fade away entirely. Close relations become suspect in politics, especially when they confer benefits (which would normally be expected in friendship), special regard for kin becomes nepotism, and hospitality is obviated by hotels. Matters of individual and social responsibility shift back and forth: in one direction, individual liability is absorbed by insurance, while pollution, overpopulation, and health care become social responsibilities. In the other direction, tithing gives way to individual charitable (tax-deductible) contributions. The traditional legal regulation of sexual practices, fornication and adultery, gives way to individual discretion, though fresh regulation comes on the scene in the areas of on-the-job sexual harassment and child abuse. Abortion shifts its moral status from time to time and place to place. There also occurs the wholesale disappearance of what was once deemed a moral obligation—for example, the sense of honor that required defense in feuding and dueling is now rebuked as private vengeance, and retribution is left to the courts. To some extent responsibility for the aged, even parents, is taken over by social institutions.

Emotional and valuational attitudes are often out of phase with the actual state of affairs. Thus impoverishment continues to be associated with shiftlessness even when statistics indicate its major source is unemployment. Similarly, labor unions and their instruments continue to carry overtones of moral opprobrium in some quarters, approximating conspiracy, as unions in the nineteenth century were taken to be.

Now what do considerations of change have to do with dealing with problems of applied ethics? Perhaps the most important consideration is how far we need to reconsider principles under changing conditions and complex interactions. Some of them can be readily understood in terms of the complex interplay of institutions and of the articulateness of different social groups—for example, the rise of a market economy, individualism, the Protestant work ethic, and the so-called move from status to contract (at least for a given period).[4] Others are still poorly understood. Certainly some modifications are easily tolerated in morality and do not cause any fundamental change in our principles. Others, like freedom of speech, are challenged when pornography, or docudramas that mix history and fiction, lay claim to its protection. Freedom of assembly is strained by Klan marches, and freedom of religion by Satanic cults or dictation of education. And rights to privacy are strained by compulsory health tests and threatened by the extent to which our financial, tax, and medical records are available for inspection.

ABORTION AND ITS CONTEXT: AN EXAMPLE

Let us take as an extended example perhaps the most bitter policy controversy of the day, that over abortion. It is often debated as if it is resolvable by brandishing a single moral principle. One side (pro-life) says abortion is killing, and killing is wrong, therefore, abortion is wrong. Another side (pro-choice) says a woman's control over her own body is a private matter, and therefore her choice of abortion is morally permissible. It is not our object here to give a final answer to this moral conflict, but only to inquire how far attention to context, both for the principles and for the present situation of the controversy, affects the way the issue is formulated and the direction and resources in which answers are sought.

First, the principles. Both sides state theirs as if they were the sort of rules that governed decisively every case to which they are applicable. This cannot be: neither principle is without exceptions, even in the moral experience of those who invoke them.[5] Those who oppose abortion will frequently allow capital punishment or killing in war or self-defense—surely, violations of "thou shalt not kill." Defenders of choice will frequently also find prostitution (even though the choice of the prostitute) or the use of drugs morally reprehensible. The appeal to the principles underlying each side therefore marks the beginning, not the end, of the inquiry.

A contextual–historical inquiry is necessary to understand the place of the principles among the multitude of principles and rules that pervade human life. It is undeniable that both principles have great strength in contemporary consciousness. Few would deny that killing is worse than lying or stealing or a host of other "thou shalt not" principles. Similarly, sovereignty over one's own body is the first of liberties, even before speech. Yet it is salutary to recall that there were times when both principles had a lowly status. The one principle did not stop the Inquisition from arranging the killing of heretics, nor the other stop the slave trade, and both activities were claimed to have the sanction of the Lord.

Viewed historically, the principle of respect for life has had a slow growth continuous with the expansion of the moral community—it is the lives of persons within the community that were protected. In many early societies the moral community extended only to the local community, whether this be family, village, or tribe; the stranger was fair game for attack. Now all of humankind is conceived of as a single moral community, but even within it, the full participation of its members has taken long to achieve: women not fully, if even now, till this century, and children not fully yet. In the light of such a history, the various movements that agitate for an extension of the curve—antiabortionism, animal liberation, radical environmentalism —can be read as experiments on the border of the present.

The pro-choice principle, in similar fashion, might be seen as an experiment expanding the curve of individualism. In recent centuries there has been a gradual accumulation by individuals of freedom of thought and expression, of enterprise, of political decision and action, of entering any occupation, of marriage, of holding property, and, more recently, of sexual orientation. In general there has been a steady expansion of the liberty to determine one's personal goals and the shape of one's life. The acquisition by women of many of these rights has lagged behind that of men, and so can be expected to be accentuated. The pro-choice position on abortion, which in recent American legal history has been tied to the concept of privacy (in *Roe v. Wade*), may have the appearance of novelty, but privacy itself is simply a conceptual expression of the need for the individual space that growth of individual liberties requires, accentuated in a world becoming highly interrelated, crowded, and increasingly subject to interference and control by technology.

Both principles, growing out of long traditions, and now the subject of experimental skirmishing at the border for possible expansions, have their dangers as well as their long-range values. The respect-for-life principle can in practice shelter large traditional and often repressive tendencies, while the pro-choice principle can sometimes open the way to a reckless individualism that is destructive of communal ties. Therefore, in any practical situation of applied ethics, such as policy decision about permissible abortion, the values in the principles have to be examined in the broad context of their use at the time and over the whole range of social life, not simply in the specific issue under consideration.

Regarding the respect-for-life principle, how ready is our society to tolerate sacrifice of life in spite of respect for it? There are several areas that may give us startling pause. First, of course, there is war; we do not seem to be ready to give up this instrument for furthering national or group gains and interests, though they are usually cast as national security. A second is capital punishment, noted earlier, which has experienced a resurgence in the United States. There are also some less structured areas. We tolerate a large loss of life each year in automobile accidents; and there is a strong movement to use cost–benefit analysis in dealing with ecological threats to human life, as in labor processes, so that the expense of cleaning up a threat can be reckoned against the loss of life anticipated. (In a recent argument, an administrative agency wanted to reckon a human life as worth only $22,000, rather than the million dollars that had been proposed, if the asbestos damage allowed the person affected to live on for another forty years.) Again, there is the toleration of smoking, with its annual toll.

In the light of such tolerance for loss of life, the defenders of abortion might argue for parallel treatment as appropriate to their problem. The social problems to which abortion are addressed are evident enough—particularly in matters of family planning and in adolescent pregnancies, though occasionally also when medical testing reveals early on that a child may be born with a serious birth defect if the pregnancy is brought to term. The major social problems involved here have come in a context where women were bound down by childbearing; the women's liberation movement has opened the vistas of equality. That society has not faced adequately the problems of education in matters of sex and contraception is even more serious in this case than the way it has failed to face problems of alcohol, smoking, and drugs in connection with driving and other ways of death. Losses in abortion could be regarded by pro-life proponents as social sacrifices parallel to losses of life among soldiers and to automobile accidents and ecological cancers, in the cause of advancing genuine equality for women. (World War I with its tremendous losses of life was indeed labeled a war to make the world safe for democracy!) And all this is pertinent, without raising the question of whether or not the fetus is to be regarded as the sort of entity that is "killed."

The question of means for good ends also enters into the reckoning of a practical problem. The United States experimented with the legal prohibition of alcohol and reversed itself when it saw the futility as well as the harm of dealing with the matter in that way. Education in the harmful effects of alcohol abuse, some legal control of access, and fostering personal moral responsibility are the better means under these conditions. Part of the ethical decision in the case of the permissibility of abortion or its legal prohibition should surely go into the broad context of means. This is where the defenders of permissibility remind us of the scope of illegal abortion in the old days and the toll it took of life and health. Whether a question is raised in the background model of right or wrong or in that of the good and means to achieve it, the evaluation of means will be an unavoidable context area preparatory to decision.

Perhaps the most serious moral issue of the instrumental use of abortion as a means in facing damage to social well-being is likely to arise from the threat of overpopulation (exceeding resources available to support life). Some indication of this has been found in the experience of China, the world's most populous country, where once a policy of greater population stability was decided on, social promptings to abortion were apparently found in many villages. It is not difficult to envisage a world in which failures to provide contraceptive education or widespread neglect of necessary limits made abortion an unavoidable means for warding off ecological disaster. (Hume long ago pointed out that the virtue of justice held only in the middle range of available resources: given complete abundance, it was not needed; given complete scarcity, it could not maintain itself.) To ban abortion might mean setting off one population against another in wars for scarce resources. Kant, in his advocacy of the categorical imperative, said that the rule *"Fiat justitia, pereat mundus"* (Let justice be done though the world perish for it) should better be translated as "Let justice be done though all the fools and knaves perish as a consequence." But this is oversanguine; the wise and the virtuous may well suffer the same fate. The ultimate stage of population growth is not yet with us, however, and some room remains for practical wisdom.

It is surprising how much scope there has been for context-inquiry even before we reach that central issue of biological knowledge that seems relevant here—namely, whether the fetus is to be regarded as a living being amounting to personhood. The United States Supreme Court, it will be recalled, divided the period of pregnancy into three stages with respect to permissibility of abortion, with it being permissible in the last trimester only if the health of the mother was at stake. Now the recognition of biological knowledge as relevant to decision is in the terms we outlined at the outset a question of context. Ethical decision requires appeal to knowledge outside ethics itself, but it may have the task of deciding which of conflicting views in the science itself can be relied upon. It is worth noting that anthropology tells us of preliterate peoples who permit infanticide in an early period of the infant's life if it is before certain ritual ceremonies have been performed. In general, peoples have always recognized some mark for personhood, but the timing and the mark have differed. So, too, have the views about the nature of personhood itself—whether, for example, it comes in a yes–no pattern or is subject to a degree of development standard, by which earlier stages do not yield a person but a potential person. That this is a complex field of problems has become evident at the other end of life, when medical biology was led to distinguish brain death from the end of life (heart death). A case can certainly be made for the end of personhood with brain death, but it has raised a variety of legal and moral issues. The whole issue has been rendered more complex by some religious beliefs about the soul and immortality, which may play a vital part in the morality of those who hold them, but the initial question we are concerned with is the ethical issue of the legal permissibility of abortion, and in American law, with its constitutional separation of church and state, a special religious belief cannot be overwhelmingly decisive. This is seen, for example, in the case of Catholic judges who, in virtue of their judicial oath, will grant divorces even though their private religious belief forbids divorce. Such considerations show that another context relevant to decision of our issue is the fundamental legal background of the country.

If indeed the question of personhood for the fetus is a matter of serious dispute under a variety of premises and outlooks, and the lineup of opposing positions with pro-life and pro-choice as their flags threatens a split in the community, with an increase in hostilities and even violence at times, then it is precisely the constitutional background with respect to religious sects that may provide a guiding model for ethical decision. The separation of church and state in the United States Constitution reflected the realization of the social consequences of the conflict among sects and the will of an established church to extirpate other churches, as well as of course its belief in religious freedom. The resulting path is to regard profound differences—religious or moral—within a community as matters of free adherence by individuals to one or another mode of judgment, and to allow proselytizing within the limits of freedom of speech, but to forbid coercion. Such a path of decision may, in the question of abortion, help the country avoid the evils that have beset, for example, the conflict of sects in contemporary Lebanon or Ireland.

CONTEXT AND INTERPRETATION

We have not, to be sure, settled the controversy over abortion, but we have shown how inquiry into multiple contexts reshapes the moral issue for decision. This richness in restructuring the initial problem is a first, and major, contribution of context-inquiry. Others, although overlapping, may be listed.

Reference to context also helps to clarify the meaning of central terms and thus helps in interpreting principles. It does this in the first place by contextual differentiation. An excellent example is Karl Duncker's discussion of the idea of *usury*, prompted by the historical shift from regarding usury as wrong to its moral acceptance.[6] When usury was condemned, he says, it was in the context of indigent people requiring loans for survival, an area that fell morally closer to the realm of charity. When usury was later permissible, it occurred in the context of borrowing for purposes of investment and commercial enterprise; it could be seen as an indirect way of sharing in the profits by having shared in the capital formation. Hence, we have two different ideas and no moral principle governing both. A comparative analysis such as Duncker's is of great service in many areas of applied ethics. For example, in business ethics much hangs on the principle of *free enterprise*, but the meaning of this principle is very different in a setting where businesses are predominantly small (whether commercial or manufacturing), where it is a world of corporate relations, or where a major focus is on finance capital in international operations. Thus questions of government regulation, of privatization of socially necessary enterprises, even of taxation, cannot be settled by simple acceptance of the importance of free enterprise in an economic system.

A further contribution is found where context-inquiry not merely differentiates the concept but provides a historical picture of the growth of the idea in response to developing social problems. The idea of *liberty* is an excellent case in point. It entered the Western scene as a major social slogan with the development of opportunities for individual effort in commerce and production, and it was soon accompanied by the demand of intellectuals for the right to criticize. (Of course, the efforts of slaves to escape from slavery has an older tradition.) In a world of fixed *stations*, with privileges for nobility and feudal superiors, it became sharpened as the right to enter any field—the "career open to talents" of the French Revolution. In the nineteenth century, liberty became the core of a central principle protecting and advancing individuality and individual opportunity in the control of one's life. In this form it became almost the ruling ideal of Western liberalism. Twentieth-century reinterpretation of liberty stems largely from the realization that such liberty is not adequate to ensure progress in a growingly interrelated and complex society without sufficient material guarantees. Hence, the distinction is often drawn between "negative liberty," simply protecting individual rights to choose, and "positive liberty," which provides support for effective choice.[7] The least that such a historical view shows is that there is no simple appeal to a principle of liberty except in areas in which a tradition of well-demarcated protection has been established, such as freedom of speech in the United States.

Historical inquiry not only brings out the different social groups that find expression through the idea but also the value that the idea carries in a given time and place. Without such exploration of context, we are left with bare and abstract meanings. The case of *equality* is an excellent contemporary illustration, for it has been the ideal toward which most of the twentieth century struggles—of blacks, of women, of persons with handicaps, of homosexuals. Many practical decisions, such as quotas in employment or reverse discrimination or equal worth in wages, rest on the assigned meaning of *equality* and the acceptance or rejection of instrumentalities for embodying it in conduct. If the concept is not examined contextually, we find either an abstract quantitative treatment or some general distinction like that between equality of opportunity and equality of results. The insistence that equality of opportunity is what is vital and that guarantee of equality of results is not appropriate becomes the basis for rejecting many of the concrete proposals for removing discrimination—for examples, the reverse discrimination of the *Bakke* case[8] or the attempts to overrule union–employer agreements to bring up by selective promotion or appointment the group hitherto discriminated against. On the other hand, the study of equality in its historical development as an idea enables us to see it as the effort of submerged groups to participate in the full operations of society and share in its material and cultural gains. Quotas in employment become, therefore, not an issue of numerical proportions as a permanent principle of job assignment, but of whether their temporary use is the only way of making a breakthrough or whether another method can achieve that goal. (It becomes comparable to, say, giving veterans a several-point headstart in competitive examinations for civil service appointments, rather than setting permanent limits on college admission for certain categories of students.)

A comparable contribution of such inquiry is to show the teamwork of concepts in understanding a situation of moral decision. The familiar tendency to deal with one concept and resolve the issue in its terms (for example, "This is a question of liberty" or "This is a matter of equality") neglects that actual interaction of the concepts in the development of human problems. They are subject to a division of labor that undergoes modification, and sometimes, for historical reasons for a given period, one takes over the job that the other is doing. For example, Bentham made little of the idea of liberty, giving most of its work to *security*, since liberty seemed to mean primarily not being interfered with. (He was wary of what the French revolutionists were doing with liberty.) The abolition of slavery was clearly seen in terms of liberty; but the recent liberation movements have been cast in the language of equality, of overcoming discrimination. It is also possible that liberty, which in the nineteenth century was pitted by conservatives against equality, the latter being regarded as overly democratic, could not bear the twentieth-century demand for social gains, such as extension of education, social security, and various other forms of social insurance.

We may point to still another contribution to exploration of historical context, which helps us understand the relative strengths of moral ideas in different epochs. Why, for example, did Dante in his ranking of sins in the *Inferno* give the ultimate place as the most damning sin to *ingratitude*? At the lowest level of hell, frozen in the ice, Satan holds Judas, who betrayed Jesus, and Brutus and Cassius, who assassinated Julius Caesar. By contrast, for Kant, the prime principle is one of truth and honesty and keeping promises. Of course, for Dante, ingratitude meant treason to church and state; but there is enough evidence in the medieval period to show the importance of gratitude generally. When we set Kant and Dante against the background of their social systems, the mystery is dissolved. Ingratitude is the violation of the central status relation in a system of fixed social roles— allegiance to those above one in a feudal hierarchy. Bur promises in the form of contract form the basis of an open commercial society, in which everything from commercial relations, labor relations, even the very foundation of the state, is seen as issuing from the free agreement of free individuals. Once such distinctions are clear, the way is open in dealing with a particular moral decision of broad and serious consequences to go behind the principle to the important values of which it is the bearer.

It has not been argued in this chapter that all practical moral decisions are complex. Some of them may be resolvable in terms of simple subsumption under a well-established principle, as in the case of freedom of speech suggested above. We have reached the point where even Oliver Wendell Holmes's dictum, that free speech does not entitle one to shout (falsely) "Fire!" in a crowded theater, is itself regarded as too narrow. We are prone rather to ask why the theater was not fireproof to begin with or why the local ordinances about fire were too loose. Indeed, civil libertarians have gone so far as to defend the right of Nazi organizations to parade (as on an occasion in Skokie, Illinois), and they defend publishers of materials that most people would regard as pornographic and even the freedom to advocate overthrowing the government, provided it is not a conspiracy of violent action. But when so extreme a principle is automatically followed, it has behind it lessons of the dangers of censorship and how rapidly the least exercise of censorship grows into arbitrary exercise of power over anything contrary to dominant views (the memory of McCarthyism is still strong). Hence, even the apparent neglect of underlying context may have a contextual explanation! Nevertheless, there doubtless are many simple moral decisions in practice, just as there are routine cases in the courts. But perhaps questions that are settled too easily do not become problems, just as one does not go to trial on cases where the law is thoroughly clear. The understanding that context plays an essential role in moral decision remains, however, a clear and permanent guide for analyzing problems.

Seven

Formulating the Ethical Issue

We have not yet met the occasion for distinguishing *moral* problems from problems as such. Now we want to discuss the different kinds of ethical problems. The perceptual and conceptual shaping of a situation, which we examined in the preceding chapter, is sometimes guided by the move toward an ethical formulation but it rarely gets all the way there, even when we are conscious of alternatives. There is a broad borderland of vagueness, a no-man's-land in which ethical questions may be implicit or, if raised, rejected as unintended. For example, I might initially read A's behavior as aggressive, and then realize that it might rather be seen as defensive. But neither reading has indicated the *right* thing for A to have done; perhaps he *should* have just stayed cool. Or take the complex case of recognizing that what is going on in an industrial plant is creating acid rain. To view the pollution as one result of the process of production and to group unwelcome resultants with the valuable industrial products is one analytic path; to see their removal as part of the cost of production (albeit *external* costs) along with raw materials and labor is a sophisticated extension of perspective. This path points to the ethical question, "Who *ought* to bear which costs?" but does not quite ask it. We may compare this stage with the earlier history of the problem of accidents on the job. The familiar ethical judgment had been that it was better for society to let the loss lie where it fell, that the employer as a God-fearing person might, of course, contribute to philanthropy for the injured. Eventually, however, the ethical decision was for a regular system of workers' compensation supported by contributions from employers, workers, and the public treasury, since society as a whole gained from the industry. Seeing the situation in different ways leads more readily to different ethical judgments, or at least prepares the ground in different ways. For example, seeing a wife's working to put her husband through medical school not only as an act of love but as an investment brings us closer to deciding that it is right in cases of divorce to give her a share of his income. And to label certain actions of male employers toward female employees as "harassment" already suggests an ethical judgment.

Once we cross the borderland and get to ethical issues, there is usually little difficulty in recognizing them, for they are stated with a distinctive ethical vocabulary. We are all familiar with the terms *right* and *wrong, ought* and *duty* and *obligation, rights* and *responsibilities, good* and *bad, virtue* and *vice*. These are the terms that traditionally occupied the center of the stage and brought some order into the host of terms describing specific actions and ideals and attitudes, such as *honesty* and *deceit, justice* and *fairness, liberty* and *equality*. Of course there have been other general terms that were given a central position experimentally and achieved widespread use: good examples of these are *value* and *commitment*, the former involving a choice from an array of preferences, and the latter sending us to self-scrutiny to identify moral bonds.

Our familiarity with the vocabulary of ethics has both advantages and disadvantages. We recognize readily when we are in the midst of a moral issue; and we have no difficulty in shedding nonmoral uses of these terms, such as using *right* and *wrong* for correctness and incorrectness in arithmetical calculations or *value* for fetching a high price in the economic market. Yet their very familiarity can keep us from attending to the deeper differences of task that different parts of the vocabulary point to. Even sophisticated moral philosophers have approached the vocabulary from a misleading angle. They ask which of the terms are primary or which should be defined in terms of which. They divide into schools that hold either that the *right* is prior to the *good* or that *good* is prior to the *right*, with the resulting theories attempting to subjugate the greater part of the vocabulary to their preferences. Thus the utilitarians define *right* as that which produces the greatest *good* (thus making *good* primary), while Kantians define *good* in terms of the narrowed moral sense of having the kind of character that is drawn to the *right*. It is not our purpose here to pursue the controversies over ethical theories; rather we want to determine how applied ethics should deal with the vocabulary. We shall see that from the point of view of resolving moral problems that different batches of moral concepts open up different avenues. We shall study the importance of these differences for the three traditional families of ethical terms—the family of right and wrong, duty and moral law, rights and responsibilities; the family of good and bad; and the family of virtues and vices—and make occasional suggestions in regard to other terms. If indeed the different families can be distinguished for applied ethics by the *functions* they serve, then in formulating an ethical problem we have to be deliberate in the moral language we invoke lest we seek our solution in the wrong direction.

It is worth noting that those moral philosophers who have had a strong sense of the importance of the practical function of ideas have tended to differentiate ethical ideas along functional lines. For example, to take a kindred field, Aristotle distinguishes three types of rhetoric, according to whether it is addressed to the future or the past or is designed to celebrate or praise. Future-oriented rhetoric, he says, is legislative. There is a distinctive form to speech when it is attempting to determine future policy in legislation. Past-oriented rhetoric, by contrast, is judicial: it involves passing judgment on the conformity of an action with already established principles and policies. The third kind of rhetoric is the sort we find in obituaries or when we mean to praise. The distinctions Aristotle makes here seem very appropriate for ethical ideas also: good and bad for policy decision, right and wrong for conformity to established principles, and virtue and vice when we are concerned to praise and blame. The significant point in this comparison is that ethical terms need not then be reduced to a unified system by subordination; instead they can be employed with reference to the occasion of need and task. Dewey has a somewhat similar and more explicit approach to ethics: good and bad provide criteria for decision where there is a conflict of aims or goals; right and wrong and attendant concepts concern conformity to regulation that is necessary to the existence of any community; and virtue and vice reflect the human tendency to praise and blame as modes of affecting others.

From such a point of view, the formulation of an ethical question is choosing among ways in which it may be explored. And it is turning to some rather than other of the resources that the history of ethical theory offers in its treatment of ethical concepts. Instead of urging a choice among competing theories, we suggest building up an inventory of resources from the theoretical reservoir, with a clear understanding of which can be invoked from what kind of purposes. We shall deal first with the formulations that invoke moral law, right, and duty; then with those that invoke good and bad and value generally; and finally with those that are set in the moral atmosphere of the virtues.

One further preliminary point. In current usage, *ought* is frequently used simply as a moral marker and its use does not automatically put it into the right–duty family. The question "What *ought* to be done?" or "What *ought* I (or we) to do?" is often the preliminary mark of a practical moral problem. It is asked from the point of view of the agent. Which family of terms becomes the center of attention is usually set by some *interpretation* of *ought*. Thus, some writers translate the question "What *ought* to be done?" into "What is the *best* thing to be done?" thereby see it as a question of the good. Others ask "What does the *moral law* demand for this kind of situation?" and so treat it as a matter of the right. If instead the translation were "What would a perfectly moral person do when faced with this situation?" then it would be a question of virtues.

In the rest of this chapter we try to develop sensitivity to how we structure the problems before us at a given time in terms of one or another family of concepts. We shall find that some problems are better tackled by one family than another, but that the choice of family is hardly a matter of routine or something that can be learned by rote.

MORAL LAW: THE STRAIGHT AND NARROW PATH

The most formidable concepts in the right–wrong family have been those of *rights* and *law*. Think of their strength and scope. Law prescribes or commands; it does not simply invite. Law, too, is general—for all situations or occasions on which it applies. ("Thou shalt not kill" is not for Sabbath only.) Disobedience carries a penalty, whether it be punishment or ostracism or deep-felt inner guilt. Beyond all this, the ethical theory with which the idea of moral law has been associated, though varied, has always been weighty in human affairs. It has also been complex. In the greater part of Western history, moral law has been tied to a religious metaphysics in which God both implants a nature in human beings and commands the law for its expression, hence the conception of *natural law*.[1] In more recent centuries, moral law has been connected with the idea of rationality, with self-legislation and autonomy, so that a person's very being has found expression in the moral law.

Yet this very complexity has brought the idea of moral law to the verge of unraveling as questions are asked about the coupling of disparate elements. Henri Bergson pointed out that the idea of law had no necessary connection to that of command. Commands can be singular, while laws are general. Laws, as in the scientific phrase "laws of nature," do not issue commands to us. Older religious philosophy had coupled the scientific and the moral with a saving hypothesis: scientific laws are also God's commands, and since matter does not have free will, it obeys universally; humans with free will can disobey moral law. But from Kant on, the distinction between the scientific and the moral became an accepted part of ethical theory, as in the dictum that scientific laws tell us what *will* happen while moral laws tell us what *ought* to happen. Again, the use of the nature of human beings to warrant moral law was severely weakened by Darwinian evolution in which the pattern of unlearned tendencies in a species was said to be the outcome of past survival successes and hence might be out of tune with present social needs.[2] As for guilt feelings attendant upon disobedience to moral law, psychology (particularly Freudian) has shown the enormous complexity of inner formations and character structuring, tied less to the content of the law and more to emotional relations—of children and parents, of young and old, and of individuals to cultural patterns of authority.

The outcome in contemporary ethical theory has not been to reject the idea of moral law, but to separate its strands for critical analysis. Each has grown in the process. Guilt, for example, is not relegated to the psychology of feeling; it has been linked culturally and socially with *responsibility*, with *fault* when some element of violation is involved and some punishment or retribution demanded, and with *liability* when for a whole variety of reasons, not always discrediting the person involved, restitution or sharing of the cost is involved.

The element of command or prescription has also taken different shapes with varying conceptions of human relations or cultural attitudes concerning appropriate interpersonal transaction. For example, moral advice assumes a different relation to the person addressed than does moral command; it shifts the locus of decision, it involves a clear suggestion of respect. Indeed, comparative cultural study has shown that the sharp contrast of right and wrong, the view that for every question there is a decisive answer, may be to some degree a cultural specialization. A contrasting pattern is found in some Mediterranean societies, largely North African, where the central emphasis is on honor and shame, so that in resolving a dispute neither party is found wrong and so shamed. The solution, even when it goes against one side, is seen as an honorable way out of a difficulty, a kind of compromise that each side can accept.[3] The peremptory view that one side is right and the other consequently wrong is a put-down that no honorable person will accept. Nor is this kind of attitude found only in pre-industrial societies. Margaret Mead pointed out— during World War II when she was working on advice for American soldiers who would have to acclimatize themselves to British ways— that to *compromise* had different shades of meaning in British and American usage. In Britain it was what honorable people did when they found themselves at odds and stalemated over a practical problem; in America it suggested selling out your ideals. Obviously the Americans are (or were) more prone to a sharper division of right from wrong, perhaps reflecting a variant of an earlier fire-and-brimstone puritanism. In general, then, once we recognize the variety of attitudes and relations that may be found in the range from sharp command to stimulating reflection, perhaps a looser concept of *guidance* may be more appropriate for understanding the interpersonal relation in the unfolding of moral law.

The most difficult element in the conceptual heritage of moral law is that of *generality*. There is something awesome about the universal, whether it is the sweep of a law of nature telling us what will happen in *all* situations of a given sort or a legal enactment that will penalize *every* discovered deviation, or a moral demand to act *always* or *never* in a given way. Even the ordinary use of language shows that the words we use for the most part (aside from prepositions, conjunctions, proper names, and the like) betoken *kinds* of things or qualities or situations, not particular or singular ones. The *universal* so constantly enters into our very understanding of the world that we almost worship it—at least philosophers from Plato on have done so, only to be challenged by the devotees of the particular, the unique. They deny that the universal gives us the *necessity* of things but rather only the *constant conjunction* of properties to be picked out in experience—not the *essences* of things but the most convenient gathering of properties for practical use.

Perhaps the most appealing reconciliation of the universal and the particular is to be found in the epistemology of pragmatism today that finds the meaning of ideas in the practical ways they operate in experience and action. Our adulation of the universal reflects the importance of *order* in enabling us to steer our way *through* the world, to survive and plan and gain some measure of control. The basis of order is *repetition* in the flow of temporal events, with sufficient nearness of quality to give us the experience of *similarity*. The search for order is our major technique of survival; we form habits that guide our actions, and in the conflict of habits we develop ways of deliberating. Thus knowledge, from ordinary experience to the heights of science, serves to guide us. *Order* becomes *ordering* and *regularity* becomes *regulating*. (There is this wisdom in the ancient coupling of laws of nature and laws of morality.) The appreciation of the unique, the singular, and the unrepeated is only now coming into focus. For the greater part of the past, it was dismissed in intellectual reflection as the *accidental*, the *contingent*—just what happened. It was appreciated, of course, in art and in interpersonal relations such as romantic love. It began to be taken seriously with the rise of probability theory. And now it seems to be acquiring scientific respectability in studies of turbulence and chaos in mathematics and physics and in the historical and evolutionary orientations of cosmology and biology. Applied ethics, which focuses on the problematic aspect of the particular situation, is thus especially concerned with the place of the general in the particular. Any understanding of moral law for practice has therefore to go in some depth into the character and types of regularity.

The concept most commonly used today in studying regularity is that of *rule* rather than that of law. Rules, whether explicit or implicit, guide us in thought and action, in knowledge and language and morality, in institutional behavior and in common practices. Indeed, to ask for the rules in any context, from games to crafts and social relations, is to ask for guiding general procedures. Such breadth of the concept of rule transfers the most important questions to the types or order of rules involved and to their specific scope. Some philosophers (Dewey for one) took rules to refer to habits of action, and used the concept of *principles* for guides to analysis.[4] But on the whole this kind of concern would be met today with a distinction of different functions of rules. What has doubtless given this concept such wide currency is the opening up of studies in so many fields that show the deeper, often hidden order in human action—for example, the deep grammar of linguistic use, or the gamelike quality of mathematics, or the hidden mechanisms of the unconscious. Moreover, even ethical theories that have rejected the emphasis on rules have been reanalyzed in rule terms. For example, in "situation ethics" the moral judgment captures an intuitive grasp of the situation in its particularity. But it is always possible to say "If the same situation occurs, even though you believe it never will, do the same thing." Thus situation ethics is understood as asking for many low-ordered rules rather than general high-ordered ones. Another possible challenge to the usual rule schema is to offer only one highly general rule, such as the Golden Rule. The debates are thus over the order of rules, not over the use of rules as such.

The traditional use of a moral-law or moral-rule schema has been to present the rule and apply it directly or through deductions from it to the problem at hand. Historical and cultural features have supported this habit. The paradigm of our morality is a set of commandments—the Decalogue of the Judeo–Christian tradition. The comparison of the moral and the legal reinforces it: the legal is seen as a system or rules or laws, and so is morality. Each may, of course, take different linguistic form: for example, the imperative "Thou shalt not kill" or the indicative "Killing is wrong." And the directive character may be sharp and peremptory or (less often) only predictive, as in "Don't do it or you'll be sorry." Clearly the simplicity of the rule schema is belied by the many serious controversies over it.

Jesus in the Gospels is plausibly interpreted as opposing the spirit to the law and, while not denying law, giving it a secondary place. In the Hebrew tradition, Hillel has a similar attitude in the attempt to reduce the law to the Golden Rule. Sometimes rules are criticized on the basis of a distinction between external conformity, which is taken to be without value, and inner spirit, which is taken to be the true locus of morality. Thus a line of criticism can be traced from Augustine ("Love and do what thou wilt") through Abelard (for whom only the possession of a right intention counts) to Kant (who claimed that only actions motivated by a sense of duty count). Sometimes the disputes over rules are carried on in the terminology of interpretation, where the letter of the rule remains sacrosanct but its meaning changes. This form of debate requires that the rule itself not be challenged, but the sides line up as "rigorous" or "flexible." The confirmation hearings of Supreme Court nominee Robert Bork made us all aware of this kind of dispute raging in constitutional law between

"originalists" and nonoriginalists; the dispute is over the range of discretion we are permitted to exercise in the application of the rule.
This is merely a modern version of a very old quarrel.[5]

Rules vary considerably in type of function, as well as relation to
authority as a source. If the source is a lawgiver, divine or human,
rules are an expression of will. Take games as the model, and rules
have a less direct source in authority, representing something like
defining conditions. It matters not on whose authority a flush beats an
inside straight; what matters is that you must abide by it if it is poker
you wish to play. Then take grammar as the model, and rules become
something like patterns of behavior, regular and ordered, but not necessarily a matter of awareness on the part of those abiding by them. It
matters a lot which sense of rule you have in mind when speaking of
professional ethics as rule-governed activities. If you mean it in one
sense, explicit organizational codes is the appropriate place to look.
If you mean it in another, it is the regular behavior and responses of
the professionals that is the focus. Thus Charles Bosk studied the
morality of surgeons by observing what they do and say and analyzing the patterns that underlay their actions and words, even though
the subjects of the study were incapable of expressing those patterns
in the form of rules.[6]

In the light of the variety of types of generality and functions of
generalization, it is obviously desirable to examine differences of
kind in rules and their significance, and thereafter turn to considerations that guide the use of one or another type in resolving moral
problems.

Different Kinds of Rules and Their Significance

The classification of types of rules has not been intensively pursued
in moral philosophy. Sometimes they have been distinguished in
terms of moral importance or weight, as for example the traditional
separation of venial and mortal sins, or the common judgment that
"Don't injure" has precedence over "Don't lie." There are obvious
linguistic differences in how rules are expressed: negative or positive; permissive, advisory, or obligatory. Rules can sometimes be
weighted by their source, a rule from a higher authority having precedence, and clearly the question of the authority of a rule is important
to its appraisal.

Kant classified rules (imperatives, in his terminology) by whether they were hypothetical or categorical. The former were either rules of skill that tell one how to accomplish a given end, technical rules in essence, the acceptance of which depended on one's desiring that end; or they were prudential rules, largely empirical generalizations about what brought success in the pursuit of happiness, and Kant was ready to assume that everyone wanted one's own happiness as an end. Yet this universality did not make a prudential rule moral. Moral rules were categorical imperatives, without ifs or buts, issuing from legislation by the self directed to all rational beings. This classification was governed by his interest in setting off what he regarded as truly moral rules from the rest, and led to a significant narrowing of the moral domain. Moreover, it is not clear that there is a distinct border between the prudential and the moral, depending on the kind of end pursued and its consequences. For example, the rules, "Don't smoke," and "Don't take mind-altering drugs," have the same form, and yet the first is at best prudential (possibly technical), since risking health and even death in return for certain satisfactions would not fall under Kant's criteria for a moral rule. On the other hand, "Don't take mind-altering drugs" might well count as a moral rule on the grounds that the activity it condemns threatens reason itself or the self.

Abraham Edel has suggested a phenomenological set of types for moral rules or laws, that is, a classification based on how we feel about them or more strictly what qualities they have in the field of our "vision."[7] He lists four: must-rules, always-rules, break-only-with-regret-rules, and for-the-most-part-rules. Against Kant's view, he argues that there is room for morality in all these types. The most important thing is to keep them apart, not assimilate them all into one type, and to determine under what conditions each is usable. The must-rules are the most formidable. They hover over every situation and to break them is felt as utterly damning. Kant felt that way about his categorical imperative, and his provocative essay, "On the Supposed Right to Tell Lies from Benevolent Motives," set off a long train of controversy, because he argued that one must not tell a lie even to a would-be murderer who asked whether the intended victim was in your house. (We shall extract the lessons of this controversy later.) The Victorian prohibition of female unchastity was often cited as another illustration before contemporary sexual liberation made sexual behavior a private or individual matter. On the whole, there has been a tendency, with some relaxation of moral dogmatism in the

contemporary world and with psychoanalytic exploration of the irra-
tionalities of the superego, to render this type of moral rule suspect.
Edel, however, argues for it as a possible type: he cites a statement
issued by the French Resistance under the Nazi occupation, headed
"The duty to kill," in which every Frenchman was urged as a duty to
come back into the war.

Whatever the theoretical controversies about must-rules—whether
the *mustness* is a quality separable from the rule part—it seems likely
that everyone has a moral threshold that he or she will not overstep.
Sartre's "Rather death than . . ." is a good indicator;[8] so is the common, "I couldn't live with myself if I did that." An example is abhorrence of cannibalism—"rather death than eat human flesh." But perhaps a more common example is revulsion at the idea of becoming an
informer. Its precise analysis is not easy—it is felt perhaps as an
ultimate disloyalty to an essential group. Again, in many ethical theories, empirical knowledge may enter into what becomes an absolute
moral judgment because of the overriding importance of consequences. The injunction against drug use given above may be one, or
even the prohibition of smoking if issued on an airplane during take-
off or in gasoline storage facilities.

Always-rules are familiar enough to be taken for granted. They are
empirical and they were given the central moral position in Utilitarianism with its tendency to legislate and to gear all moral rules to one
ultimate end of general happiness. They clearly derive their significance from the importance of the task on which the agents are engaged—the patient caring for the infant, the staff in a nuclear plant
keeping an eye on the appropriate level indicator, the doctor keeping
up-to-date with newly discovered treatments, and so on. In general,
role-rules have this character, for they are lessons of experience about
the responsibilities inherent in the enterprises that generate the rules.

Break-only-with-regret rules reflect the fact that every complex
moral problem admits more than one rule in its structuring, so that
complete concentration on only one requires at least some justification. A reader of Kant's essay about lying, mentioned above, will
wonder initially why this great philosopher did not at least invoke the
rule of saving life along with that of not lying. (The British moral
philosopher, Hastings Rashdall, argued that under British law Kant
would have been held responsible as an accomplice before the fact
for the death of the man pursued.) John Ladd, in his exploration of
the ethics of the Navaho, set up a situation in which he paralleled the

Kantian picture, and by different questions tried to lead the informant to say whether he would tell the truth or lie to the would-be murderer. But all he got was that the Navaho would reason with the intruder, remind him of people who went to jail for violence, and the like. Finally, when Ladd asked what he would say if the pursuer threatened his life if he would not answer, the Navaho replied that he would then have no choice—he would have to take away the gun from the would-be murderer. In short, the Navaho structured the problem wholly under the rule of saving a life, not that of honesty in discourse.[9] Why then did Kant not consider both? The answer is found in the little essay itself. Kant goes on to argue that if one told a lie and made a mistake, so that it gave an indication of where the man hiding in your house had gone without your knowing it—perhaps he had heard the early part of the conversation and sneaked out—you would be responsible for his death because it followed from your lie. If, however, you told the truth, then natural events would be the cause, not you! Underlying Kant's argument, then, is a profound belief in the unreliability of nature with respect to human aims. One is reminded of Sartre's short story ("The Wall") in which a man is tortured by Nazi captors to find out where the underground leader is. He resists, enduring the torture, but finally, to get a respite, says, making it up, "He's in the cemetery." Imagine his feelings, shortly after he is released, when he learns they have indeed found and killed the underground leader in the cemetery! It is probably a lesson of experience that prompts the army to warn any captured soldier not to make up stories, but to stick to the Geneva Convention—give name, rank, and serial number, but nothing more.

It may very well be that the relation of a moral rule to the build-up of the self is a key to its phenomenological status. We may have no self-investment in a purely empirical moral rule—that is simply the way the world is. But a must-rule, if violated, indicates some damage to the self. Perhaps Kant was correct in referring categorical moral rules to the self, but wrong in tying them to universal legislation rather than personal development.

Break-only-with-regret rules can be construed in different ways, probably with the same result. They can be seen as valid moral rules that have weight, but are outweighed by other moral rules—their weight nevertheless counting up to a point. Such rules are thus rules of reckoning, not rules of immediately effective action. Or they can be seen as rules of analysis, giving one aspect of the situation and leaving others to be independently explored, with the summing up to be carried out thereafter. Some moral philosophers have appropriated the term *right* for these—they are rules of right, but they are only prima facie, and the final result of their comparative reckoning will yield one's *duty* in the situation. As for the *regret* part, there is again a difference of opinion among moral philosophers. Some (utilitarians, for example) feel that the rule that has some weight but is outweighed in the situation has made its contribution and there is nothing to regret. Others (for example, Nicolai Hartmann in his *Ethics*) feel that an outweighed rule involves a value that has been thwarted, and though it was rightfully done (as in telling a lie to save a life), there is a burden of guilt ("unavoidable guilt") for the agent, which must be borne, and that simply to drop that episode of the loss of value is inimical to self-respect.[10]

The fourth type of rule—for-the-most-part rules—raises no serious theoretical issues. These rules are probability guides where guidance is possible, in a situation whose elements have already been analyzed. There may be moral recklessness in betting against the odds in some types of important problems, but there may be moral wisdom if much is at stake and going with the odds surrenders major values. It depends also what is risked—and people do occasionally risk their lives on bets, for example, in trying to save others.

There are other bases on which rules can be compared. One is degree of abstractness of the terms used in the rule. Some rules are high-ordered rules (such as "Do no harm") leaving most of the work to be done in concretizing them toward a particular situation, while others are low-ordered rules (such as "Never represent both parties to a divorce suit") that practically call for immediate application. We may think of this as the question of the *distance* of the rule from the situation.

Rules differ in *scope*. In one sense this has to do with the population covered by the rule, which to some extent overlaps with the distinction Kant was making between different types of imperatives. Kant seems opposed to any moral rule less than universal (see his rejection of using prisoners for medical research), but he does acknowledge, without developing it, in the *Metaphysics of Morals*, that circumstances matter. But we accept that physicians, for example, are bound by rules that do not apply to everybody. It sounds odd to our ears, but the first code of medical ethics had a section that was intended to govern the obligations of the general public to the profession of medicine, listing obligations its members had to physicians. Now the code governs only physicians.

A second issue in scope has to do with how general moral rules, which apply to everyone, take a different cast in different fields. Take the rule of honesty, which is enjoined on all enterprises. It is enmeshed differently in law, medicine, business, religion, or teaching.[11]

Rules can differ in their *degree of aspiration*: whether they are intended to set minimum standards or to set forth ideals of perfection. The lawyer's Code of Professional Responsibility is divided between canons, which are ideals, and disciplinary rules, the violation of which may incur expulsion from the profession. The canons recommend behavior, the lack of which does not lead to disciplinary action.

Rules can differ in the *severity of sanction* that uphold them—mere disapproval or disappointment at one end, and severe sanctioning at the other. This is distinct from the deemed importance or function of the rule—for example Bentham argued that some matters of morality are best left unsanctioned by the state because of the dangers involved in their enforcement.

A further distinction greatly relevant to professional ethics is that between *constitutive* and *summary* rules.[12] Constitutive rules underlie institutions, and to the extent that professions can be considered institutions, their morality might be regarded as constitutive of the profession. This would constitute the strongest connection between the rules and the aims of the profession. As the argument from Plato's *Republic* has it—to be a shepherd, one must act for the benefit of the sheep.

Our inquiry into types of rules suggests that rules have been much overplayed in traditional ethics. It is the type of rule and the degree of generality the particular rule admits of that tells us whether rules are central or peripheral to a particular reckoning of moral application. Of course in one or another sense of *rule*, rules we always have with us. But that itself tells us very little—about how serviceable what kind of rules will be in what kind of problem structuring.

How Autonomous Is a Legalistic Ethics?

There is one further matter to be considered before we get to the serious business of determining how applied ethics can operate in relation to a legalistic ethics—that is, a morality that is formulated as either a system of moral laws or a set of human rights. This is the familiar claim of the autonomy of such a morality. We saw that in opposition to Utilitarianism (or Consequentialism) or a virtue ethics, a legalistic ethics employs the concepts of *right* and *obligation* or of *rights* and *duties* as underived and not dependent on notions of good and value. And this means that the system of moral rules or the list of human rights was in some sense prior or autonomous. We also indicated, at the beginning of this chapter, that to commit to one or another of these conceptual families was to structure the inquiry along a different avenue. What happens, then, when we structure a practical moral problem in terms of the rule orientation we have been examining, and what determines us to go along that rather than an alternative course?

The general conditions for invoking a rule formulation—having in mind not just the unavoidable sense of rule but a system of middle-range rules selectively attended to and applied—are a degree of complexity that requires ordering and that cannot be handled ad hoc as well as some degree of division of labor that requires more than a common ordering. Both of these are central to a large community's having a continuity of communal life. These are necessary conditions for peace and order without which a community cannot survive, and as the community grows larger it calls for general regulation in one form or another. Division of labor sets specialized tasks off for different fields, so that individuals assume special roles giving rise to special obligations required for adequate performance. Accordingly, when such conditions and such needs are foremost, we turn to a rule system of regulation. Of course, there are competing modes of trying to satisfy the needs: a common goal will sometimes secure the unity and order required, but the variety of means and the diversity of goals may make this a less dependable path.

The social and historical conditions for adopting a system-of-rules approach have not been studied sufficiently in ethical theory. One neglected dimension is the historical entrenchment of the judicial as against the legislative aspects. Quite literally, the immemorial laws of the Medes and the Persians, the laws of the gods to which Antigone appealed against the ordinances of the rulers, and the English common law, which hemmed in legislation, are all signs of how late the idea of human beings setting forth their own ends struggled to the fore. Its present prominence is the result of the increased rapidity of change that makes constant readjustment to changed conditions unavoidable. But what the idea of legislation does to the theory of a system of rules is to shift attention from obedience to rules to the establishment of rules. Hence it focuses directly on justifying reasons for their adoption and so breaks through the alleged autonomy of rules as such. For example, why not have a strict, legally enforceable rule of truth-telling as against limiting strictness to legal oaths and affirmations, or why not a general rule of truth-telling with expected areas of equivocation—for example, not only politicians talking to journalists during campaigns, but even priests asked about information they could have learned only in the confessional?[13] And certainly we expect the family that hid Anne Frank to lie when grilled by the Gestapo. Would morality here do better with a virtue of honesty that allowed moral judgment in particular contexts than with strict obedience to an absolute rule? Or else reclassify the rule as a break-only-with-regret type.

The twentieth century has had a large-scale example of the formation of a set of rights in the development of the United Nations Universal Declaration of Human Rights. Both the discussions around its production and the controversies over what rights to include and what interpretations to give them have shown amply that any legalistic morality, whether a system of rules or a list of rights, is set in a justifying background that goes far beyond the system or list itself.

It follows that applied ethics has to be sensitive in approaching a problem as to whether to focus on it as a matter of finding moral rules to obey or rights to protect or advance. And that sensitivity has to come from examining the conditions of the problem and how nearly they approximate the conditions that would support a legalistic approach. Take the three areas of applied ethics that have been distinguished. Policy formation has a legislative rather than a judicial character; it will less frequently be a matter of adhering to an established system of rules, unless the particular problem concerns an already well-structured, rule-organized area. For example, policy on AIDS testing involves already ordered rules of individual civil liberties as well as generalizations of social structures conducive to medical success. But policy formation in an area in which there is a conflict of goals or a large-scale controversy about means, as in economic life, may better be structured within the family of goods, means, and ends. Some problems—such as coping with the use of drugs—may waver between a legalistic approach through the criminal law and an educational approach that employs the virtue framework. Difficult, then, as it may often be to render explicit the underlying assumptions that guide our moving along the path of one moral language family rather than another, applied ethics cannot disdain a greater sophistication in this respect.

In personal decision, one is immediately close to the particular, for the question is not just what a person should do but what *I* should do, and the features of the I and its situation are taken to be relevant. Hence one might expect that rules invoked would be rather of the more general kind of *principles*, higher in the range of types and more complicated in the way they function. Perhaps the best source for examining a system-of-rules morality in application would thus be in the third area, that of professional ethics. Here explicit adoption of *codes* to play a governing role in the morality of the professional should help us study the relation of rule and purpose, of selection and emphasis in relation to the conditions of professional practice. This is considered in the next chapter.

THE GOOD: ENDS AND MEANS

Ethical questions tend to be presented along the avenues of *good* and *bad, better* and *worse*, the *best* thing to do, when we are either pursuing definite goals or are uncertain which goals to pursue. The means are the control points for action, the ends are the goals pursued, and goods represent the criteria for selecting one rather than another end. Now humans are constantly wanting, desiring, seeking, aspiring. We live and move among a welter of aims and goals and ends, and so to embark along the avenue of the good is the most natural thing in the world. Indeed, we have often to be reminded that some of the ends are out of bounds and we should shift to the right–wrong avenue before we start traveling their road. (It is just as in driving: we make a turn onto a one-way road, and just after the arrow we should have noticed, we see "Wrong Way.")

For a great part of the history of ethical theory, the analysis of *the good* has been central. It was taken for granted that if we knew the human good, we could figure out what kind of conduct was right and wrong and what kind of character was virtuous. The good at bottom was what our natures prompted us toward, through the mass of circumstances and distractions that life experiences provide. Some theorists sought a single ultimate end—usually labeled well-being or happiness—on the assumption that the chief task would then be to find the proper road to happiness. Others diversified the good or fastened attention on general unavoidable means for its achievement. It is not our present task to pursue these theories, but it is useful to extract from them a variety of formulations that might increase the instruments available for applied ethics.

Types of Good

Platonic and Aristotelian ethics, the first to appear on the theoretical stage, saw the good as nothing less than *a form of life of a community*. Thus happiness was not to be equated with pleasure of short duration; no novelist under this conception would write of how the draftee about to go into battle experienced the good on a three-day pass packed with romance and adventure. In short, moral judgments cast in terms of the good would refer to a life pattern, and they would refer to the ways of a community, not of a lone individual. Having determined the good, one could then ask as an individual what part of it one might attain in the light of one's capacities and conditions.

To the individualism of the later ancient world the Stoic ideal of individual self-sufficiency through extreme self-control and the Epicurean ideal of personal happiness entered the theoretical stream. Medieval religious ethics developed the communal ideal within a framework of individual transcendence. A this-worldly individualism grew from the sixteenth century until it reached the enormous proportions of the contemporary world; in the past two centuries it is clearly seen in the ideals of political liberalism and economic individualism. Individualistic ethical theories have been built on the idea of individual happiness (pleasure), individual desires, interests, and preferences, with the social interpreted as the rules and institutions most successful for maximizing individual choices. (This is where the utilitarian slogan of the greatest happiness of the greatest number found its place.) In recent decades there have been attempts to restore a social meaning to the idea of the good as a criterion for social policy. Some have experimented with the notion of "quality of life," which reflects the fact that longevity has more than doubled over a great part of the world, that urban life requires a high degree of regulation, and that the threat of exhaustion of basic resources demands more long-range planning. Others have offered a more pluralistic account of the good as a varying assembly of goals under different world conditions at different times to serve as criteria for judging more specific goals or ends. An older paradigm for such construction would be Hobbes's development of a whole ethics on the need for securing peace and order within a society.

Applied ethics, faced with this inventory of patterns of the good need make no antecedent decision; it can focus on the specific problem of any particular inquiry and select its conceptual tools from the wider array. Clearly, decision about a whole range of issues of social policy—what to do about the ozone layer and its thinning, the garbaging of the oceans, acid rain, and so on—is better carried on with concrete social goals than with indirect derivation from the summation of individual pleasures. Decisions about problems of professions and professional behavior might also be more readily cast in terms of the social aims of the profession, although the theory of individual rights of patients, clients, or customers may help with some problems. The solution of a problem is easier when the social and individual aspects pull in the same direction. For example, the individual's desire for free speech has a social bulwark in a democratic bill of rights. Careful analysis is required where there is the appearance of conflict between individual and social; for example, in disputes over prohibiting pornography, the issue turns out to be not the desire of the individual versus the interest of the public, but the conflict of two public interests, one in diminishing pornography, the other in not diminishing free speech.

Even in that segment of applied ethics that deals with the personal and moral decisions, contemporary formulation in purely individualistic terms might require correction by tracing the institutional assumptions in the background. This is examined in detail in Chapter Nine. Another element here is the fact that many problems of personal decision turn on questions of desirable character, and so on the theory of virtue rather than simply of the good.

Ends and Means

In the context of action over time, the ends in ethical judgment are ethically certified goals; the means are the steps of action taken to achieve the end. Ends and means are the preferred categories for raising ethical questions; such as whether the end justifies the means, whether willing the end entails willing the means, whether a good end can be achieved by evil means. Such questions point to serious issues, but their formulation often obscures rather than clarifies them. The initial concepts themselves require more careful analysis.

The chief danger in dealing with an *end* or *goal* is to isolate it for contemplation as if it were a gem whose sparkle is to be admired. Ethical language has tried to capture this aspect in the notion of "intrinsic value," relegating the relations the goal may have to other goals and human situations as "extrinsic value" or "instrumental value." Unfortunately, in human experience, goals are not so well behaved. Even jewels shine differently according to the light upon them, and (as we have seen) context makes a great difference in how something is beheld and understood. There is no easy road in practical situations to separating and appraising ends in isolation. Ordinary shopping experience confirms this: yes, it's beautiful, but where will it fit, how will it interfere with things around it, how much attention will it need, how often will it have to be repaired, is it fragile, can I really afford it? As the difficulties pile up, the item becomes less and less an end (something to be pursued) and more an aesthetic object.

The common tendency to see the selection of end as an ethical matter, but the selection of means as a factual matter—will it effectively bring about the end?—is very misleading. It is belied by the contrary tendency to see anyone who believes that the end justifies the means as unscrupulous. But clearly the question whether the end justifies the means gives us only a framework for specific questions: some ends justify some means and others do not. The end of being elected president does not justify arranging for the assassination of the opposing candidate. It does not even justify encouraging derogatory rumors about him or her. It may justify recalling past mistakes in the opponent's record. *Means* is a very limited category. It is important in practice because the means for achieving an end are the points at which we act to secure the end. But just because the means comes before the end and will help bring it about, it does not follow that it is more significant ethically than, say, the consequences of achieving the end, which come afterwards. So the real situation is that there are lots of complex relations in which working for an end is enmeshed, and ethical assessment of the end includes ethical assessment of many of these relations—for example, the consequences of using a given means, the place that end will have in relation to other ends held or pursued, the consequences of all these, and so on. Practical wisdom with a large measure of insight and experience is required in deciding to work for an end and in working for it. Applied ethics has at least to face these issues.

A further important feature in practice is that the border between ends and means is not always clear, that what is a means in one respect may well be very like an end in another. John Stuart Mill pointed this out in the case of liberty. Its importance in a liberal or democratic social order is such that while it is clearly a means to ensuring greater freedom of expression and so the greater likelihood of new ideas and of invention, yet it becomes so integrated in the way of life as to be part of it, not just a mere means to it. Mill accordingly thought of liberty as a *constituent* of the good, invoking the relation of part to whole, rather than antecedent cause. The lesson for practical moral judgment is that if the categories of means and ends are used in analyzing a problem, attention should be directed to how the element in question functions in the situation, not simply to an antecedent classification of types of means and ends.

A final point to be noted is that although the formulation of the inquiry in terms of good–bad or of right–wrong takes us on different roads, this does not prevent items from the one coming into the analysis of the other on various occasions. Thus, a business use of cost–benefit analysis to determine which course of action is better with a view to profit as the end, might be stopped with the objection that it would be wrong to endanger lives by one of the proposed courses of action. Similarly, an inquiry into what is right or wrong in a given matter might meet the objection that a given course pointed to by the rule of right involved would yield a great evil to certain of the parties involved in the case. Clearly, there are ready crossovers in practice between these two major avenues, without affecting the general direction of movement. (They are not like turnpikes with fixed exits involving long detours.) One reason for this flexibility is, of course, that each family uses the concepts of the others in its own way. Those starting with the good often conceive of the right as rules of what has in experience been found to yield the good; and those starting with the right have, as we suggested earlier, their own view of the moral good.

Goods and Values

In the twentieth century the idea of *value* has become very common and the term is used widely for what is of worth. Of course, it extends far beyond ethics, since there are aesthetic values, religious values, economic values, and so on. Sometimes value is almost a synonym for good, but sometimes it focuses on an essential element within a complex good. Thus "intellectual values" will refer to the variety of joys to be found in doing intellectual work, for example, the excitement of the process, the education of the self in that process, and the contributions to human knowledge and well-being. Similarly, "family values" will embrace the joys of love and parenthood, the community of a small group, the strength of mutual assistance and responsibility, and so on. It is often helpful in a practical problem of the good to assemble an array of the values involved; that enables us to see how they are affected by proposed solutions and what will be strengthened or sacrificed in going one way or another.

In dealing with goods and values, the analog of the different kinds of rules in a legalistic morality is the different levels of abstractness. A simplified hedonism would have us estimate which of two alternative courses of action would yield the greater pleasure. But is an idea as abstract as pleasure susceptible to this kind of reasoning? Erich Fromm, in *Man for Himself*, attempts to distinguish a variety of pleasures that would make it more pertinent to ask what kind of pleasure is involved rather than to sum them against one another. He distinguishes qualitative differences by examination of psychic sources. One is relief from painful tension (as in hunger, thirst, falling asleep, etc.); these he calls *satisfaction*. A second is rooted in psychic tension and the pressure to allay irrational desires and needs (e.g., sleepiness due to repressed anxiety, alcoholic dissipation, the sexuality of a Don Juan). These irrational desires have an insatiable quality and yield an *irrational* pleasure. A quite different pleasure comes from abundant or surplus energy and it is manifest in play and creative achievement; its pleasure he calls *joy*. We need not follow him into his theory of happiness as coming from inner productiveness. It is sufficient to recognize the variety of what is homogenized in the pleasure idea, a variety that appears when it is dealt with concretely in terms of source and specific quality.

The same kind of concreteness is required in dealing with all sorts of goods. For example, friendship is a good, abstractly speaking. But friendly associations, as Aristotle analyzed them, fall into general types. He lists: friendships of utility (that may include business relationships), friendships of mutual pleasure, and friendships of common devotion to the same ideal. The field of the good is too complex and too varied even to suggest a uniform mode of classifying levels of abstraction. An important part of dealing with a practical problem is to find the appropriate level of generality for the material at hand.

VIRTUES AND VICES AND THE MORAL ATMOSPHERE

Virtues and vices, described in the ethical tradition as states of character, have played a large and honorable part in ethical theory. For a time in the twentieth century they were lost in the background, partly because psychology in its behavioristic mood found the concept of character problematic and became particularistic about behavior patterns so that "character traits" seemed erroneous abstractions. (For example, honesty was found to have different meanings and to generate different attitudes depending on the kind of situation involved.) In part, too, the Kantian tradition homogenized virtue into simply the readiness of the will to do its moral duty.

The problem of getting behind behavior did not go away. It became especially clear from psychoanalytic theory that the same behavior might itself have a different meaning depending on its source within the self. Thus industrious behavior might come from a rational way of dealing with a job or from a neurotic necessity to keep busy, and loving behavior might issue from genuine affection or from a feeling of inadequacy requiring dependence. So one cannot avoid going behind behavior to examine the social underpinnings of virtue, for example, in the interpersonal phenomenon of praise and blame, so widespread in social relations. There is also the perennial task of every generation, to educate the young with concern that each child become a certain kind of person and not just a performer of certain prescribed actions.

The history of the virtues in ethical theory shows divergent yet complementary tendencies. One is toward the multiplication of virtues until they become almost a total phenomenology of the person in the variety of typical situations in which humans find themselves. The other is toward a generalization in which virtue becomes one and is equated with a *moral atmosphere* pervading the life of the individual in the community. Both of these repay study for the leads that they offer in dealing with practical moral problems.

On the side of multiplicity, one might even pluck virtues and vices from the dictionary in alphabetical order, and either in the form of noun or adjective: for example, *autonomy, bravery, charity, discretion, envy* (or, if you insist on a virtue, not a vice, then *emulous*), *fairness, gratitude, honesty, integrity, justice,* and so on. In the history of ethics, however, virtues have tended to appear in clusters, related to some psychological or social theory, and functioning to guide criticism and education in the path marked out by some implicit task. For example, the best-known Platonic virtues—wisdom, courage, temperance (or self-control), and justice—come with a psychology in which the first three primarily fit different capacities of humans (parts of the soul, Plato puts it) coupled with different social roles. Thus wisdom, the virtue of the intellectual part, fits the rulers; courage, the virtue of one's spirited will, the military and the administrative segment of the state; and temperance, the virtue of self-control of the appetites, fits the mass of the people who are to accept and obey. Justice is the virtue of the whole self and its parts when they are in good condition and doing what they are best fit to do. The whole virtue constellation is thus geared to the task of securing what Plato regards as a well-ordered society. In the subsequent Christian ethics, the task is to strive for a purity of soul in one's individual relations to God; the seven deadly sins thus include pride, avarice, anger, gluttony, lust, envy, and languid indifference.[14] When we come to the Calvinist virtues, Max Weber's familiar thesis is to show how well industriousness, thrift, sobriety, and justice fit with the needs of accumulation in the early phases of capitalism. Again, one has only to read Mill's *On Liberty* to see how initiative, autonomy, liberty, and rationality fit the pattern of a liberal society—almost defining it. Nor is the mode of analysis different for individual virtues. We have noted earlier how gratitude as a central virtue involved the feudal pattern of stations, with ingratitude to those above constituting treason; and how keeping one's word and promises became the central virtue of a commercial society that required a goodly measure of trust. Similarly, the spectacular rise of punctuality is almost made to order for industry; just as loyalty and obedience become the central virtues of the military in the organization of mass armies and war between nations.

What can applied ethics learn from these lessons of the history of ethics? It can reverse the order: identify the kinds of practical problems in the handling of which one has to involve character; pinpoint the tasks that are set in those problems; and then look among the virtues for the kind of character relevant to those tasks. For example, there are problems that cannot be handled by rule when rule is too rigid and the problems too complex; nor can they be handled by specifying the good involved, for that good is too general and the specific goods to be sought may be precisely what is at issue. The only course may be to appeal to the judgment of a person of a given character, just as one might in a problem of craft production appeal to the hunch of the experienced craftsman. A legal example may be helpful. To take care of the kinds of cases in which the rigidities of rules may lead us astray, the law has conceptions of equity, areas of judicial discretion (as well as practical discretion of prosecutors and juries), and types of problems—for example, in the obligations of trustees or in the operation of responsible management—where the appeal is to *good faith* or to *reasonable care*.

The contexts in which questions of the virtues are likely to arise for applied ethics are probably greater than we may think; we may not put them together because they are different in type. One is clearly the virtues invoked for the professional. Reliability and keeping confidences play a central role in law and investigative journalism; truth in advertising is a notorious problem; trustworthiness and honesty in accounting; care and sympathy in nursing; and so on and on. Sometimes there is an explicit problem of reconciling opposite virtues— the traditional problem of fairness and mercy in justice; the scientific aloofness of the surgeon and fellow feeling with the patient.[15] A quite different set of contexts in which concentration on one or another virtue becomes relevant is that in which no other method of decision is available than the holistic intuitive judgment of a person of experience. What kind of character do we want for such a judgment in a case of that sort, given its complexities and particularity? To look for particular virtues is thus an essential part of the practical business of handling that problem. It is worth noting that this might apply also to oneself. If I am told of a given dilemma that the problem is such that ultimate decision is up to me, what sort of a me would I want for deciding that? Surely not one who acts on whim, or through special favoritism; here my ideals of virtue—of good judgment, perhaps of impartial consideration of alternatives, of unrelenting search for the facts of the case—all become pertinent. In short, practical moral judgment in large scope lives and moves and breathes in the atmosphere of the virtues and makes implicit or explicit selections among them.

We turn now to the second tendency in the history of the theory of virtue—the tendency to treat virtue as one rather than a host of different states of character. Ancient ethical theory debated whether virtue was one or many, whether one of a list of virtues was the more fundamental; indeed, whether a person could possess one of the virtues without possessing all of them. Kantian ethics stressed the unitary task of willing what was one's duty. Kant's underlying assumption appears to be that virtue and character are always at risk, that the supreme task at every point is to do one's duty motivated by respect for duty. We need not here follow these traditional controversies, but it is important to recognize that there is a fairly definite meaning in the way in which people today speak of a *moral atmosphere* within a given society. It is perhaps clearest in the common complaint that the moral atmosphere (like the ozone layer?) is being thinned and in danger of disappearing. The sense of social obligation and responsibility is vanishing from much of professional life, yielding to the pursuit of gain. Corruption in politics, insider trading in the stock market, dangerous shortcuts in corporate activity—in manufacture and in construction—as well as overcharging (especially in government contracts) are only a few signs of moral degradation. The lack of trust is evidenced in the resort to law as the sole means of redress, particularly in the high incidence of malpractice suits. Field after field shows such deterioration. Perhaps the most depressing evidence of what has happened is found in sports, an area often set aside in the past from the workaday world and treated in an almost religious spirit. A team's goal used to be to play a good game, win or lose. Then the sole end became to win. Then the cooperative spirit, the essential team spirit, itself becomes secondary to the star system. Now individual competitiveness is all.

An arena in which a deterioration of the moral atmosphere becomes a particularly acute practical problem is the schools. This is made even more urgent by issues of delinquency and youth crime and drug use. It has become more complicated than in previous centuries because the electronic media engender models that take a powerful hold on the young. The schools are no longer the central focus of moral education along with the family. More powerful than any single institution, whether family or school, the general moral atmosphere has become decisive.

There are, of course, trends, both in theory and in practice, that counter the general deterioration. A sizable part of the feminist movement has stressed the ethics of care and responsibility in the hitherto submerged outlook of women in contrast to the aggressive individually self-oriented success morality of men. (Whether this is a natural difference or a cultural one does not concern us here.) At any rate, the dimension of care and responsibility has now powerfully entered the stream of ethical theory. Medical students in the 1960s forced into the curriculum at many places some attention to the attitudes of doctors to patients, and particularly to the dying patient. Paradoxically, today the area in which moral attitude is most prominent is not how to face life but how to face death, both on the part of the dying and the social milieu. The hospice movement for the dying was to a marked degree an outcome of such concerns. It became a more widespread issue in part because of increased longevity and the developments of techniques for prolonging life. The irony is that, whereas in the past the virtues of facing life were brought to bear on facing death, today the virtues facing death should help restore the importance of fundamental moral attitudes toward facing life.

The existence and quality of the moral atmosphere depends on the character of the moral community, which in turn reflects the practices and institutions of society. As we have seen, the moral community is an in-group, within which there is mutual respect, mutual concern, and mutual responsibility. We have noted, too, the way in which the moral community has grown over history from the time when it was just the kin-group to the global family of today. But the growth is uneven, strong in some aspects and weak in others, and this is mirrored in the moral atmosphere. Edward Banfield describes a village in southern Italy that was still turned in morally on the extended family or kin group and could not believe that projects proposed by central or national authorities were intended for their welfare.[16] Of course, one would have to know what experience they had had with such projects. Economic studies of Third World countries report that peasants sometimes will not volunteer labor for road building even though the road would greatly benefit them personally. In their experiences plans for such a road have sometimes been changed in the building to run it closer to a large landowner's property and not, as intended, along the poorer peasants' route.

The existence and power of a moral atmosphere is not something that can be conjured by rhetoric or even persistent indoctrination. It is rooted in the practice of peoples, in there being a community of common aims and purposes, of organized ways of cooperating and helping one another. It becomes thin and can even vanish where there is total emphasis on individual self-regarding activity, the pursuit of gain at the expense of others, and the evaluation of human activities in terms of acquisitive success. Fortunately this seldom happens.

The point about a moral atmosphere is that we can count on moral behavior in ordinary contexts and do not have to take special measures of inquiry or enforcement. If we were to analyze our common behavior, we might be surprised to find how much of it is held together by a kind of moral cement; there need be no deliberate invocation of moral rules. Ordinary conversation is not packed with lies. We go to work on time—whether to teach a class or because the machines will be starting up—because of the enterprise on which we are engaged, not usually for fear of sanctions. When we undertake a task, we try to carry it through and do not usually ask whether we could make a greater profit if we abandoned it in the middle. The operation of an office or a factory involves a measure of politeness among its occupants, but much more is needed for effectiveness. The history of twentieth-century psychology of management has a long chapter about the different inducements that have been tried in the workplace, from a musical background and a good cafeteria to the workers' deciding their own distribution of tasks. At present there are even suggestions of greater participation in management itself. Such efforts can be seen as attempts to improve the moral atmosphere of the enterprise, to have participants share aims in common and feel responsibility for its successful operation, not simply to see it as a source for extracting personal pay. Some suggestions may even prove counterproductive: for example, merit pay with merit judged by the managers may set the workers against one another; this competition, though it may increase production for a time, diminishes the sense of community; it is particularly destructive of morale when norms are pushed up for all on the basis of the higher production.

Such experience shows that the question of moral atmosphere as a pattern of virtues in general or in a given context is a highly practical one. It may be the first problem found in analyzing a deteriorating situation, and its remedying may be more important than any particular technique of removing specific deficiencies. The analysis of a problem in applied ethics has therefore to be sensitive to this dimension of virtue in a concrete way that will lead to a diagnosis of the practices and institutional behaviors that have generated the deterioration.

The analysis of virtues and how they function in practical moral problems reinforces and extends the conclusion suggested at the end of the discussion of good. Just as we saw there that exploring a situation through the good may cross over at specific points into judgments of right and wrong, so here too, consideration of virtues, their relevance, and how a moral atmosphere may be restored or improved may carry us into proposing specific goods as ends to be sought or suggesting rules to be standardized and even enforced. In effect, the strengthening of virtues becomes an end invoking means, and judgments of right and wrong guide the search and effort. If we generalize this for the three avenues of opening up a moral question through the different families of concepts, we see not only that the choice of opening moves sets the tasks and general strategy, but once this is under way the resources of the other approaches can be called upon for assistance. And in the outcome of a complex case, the results may extend across the whole board.

HOW APPLIED ETHICS CHOOSES ITS ETHICAL VOCABULARY

We have seen how the specialized families of ethical concepts set the formulation of questions in different directions and made some suggestions of the kinds of situations that point to one or another way of starting. It is this practical basis of formulating the ethical issue that now concerns us.

Take the simplest case of a moral injunction against killing. Minimally it is the moral rejection of a certain kind of action. But how is it to be understood? One path (A), following the right–wrong family, says killing is against the moral law, the binding regulation of the community. A second path (B) is that killing destroys life and life is a universally recognized good. "Thou shalt not kill" and even "Killing is wrong" would be immediately construed as an injunction not to destroy what is of high worth. A third (C) turns to the self of the would-be killer: "Don't be a killer," the kind of person who is reckless of lives. (A) sends us to regulations that hold a community of persons together and enable them to lead a life in common; (B) to criteria for ordering goals or ends; and (C) leads us to the character of the actor as shaped in conduct.

It is not difficult to envisage types of situations that would prompt one or another formulation. For example, (A) has the prescriptive peremptoriness that would curb temptation in a violent quarrel (recall that the temptation situation is Kant's paradigm for the moral situation). (B) would fit situations that call for care in driving or in dealing with machines or tasks that are dangerous. (C) is particularly apt for people who have had to kill (e.g., soldiers after a war) but who, we hope, will not have been brutalized by their experience. Of course, each of the formulations can bring the other in as ancillary to itself.

Whole moral philosophies can be seen in similar fashion as context-based in their conceptual preferences. Hobbes, for example, builds his entire theory on the need for order in a community that is being torn apart in the conflict of ends. It is a striking instance of how a paramount means (peace), necessary for any stable ends in a community and so universal and necessary, is made the core of an ethics. Although Hobbes's theory presents many natural moral laws for the ordering of society, each is clearly geared to a central function; for example, equality of treatment of persons is ordained simply because men will be turbulent if they are regarded as inferior. An ethic of virtue is most clearly seen in the Stoic theory, where the whole of the world is taken to be so unstable and so in flux that no reliable order outside the self is regarded as possible. On the other hand, a life lived in the closeness of common association, in the performance of far-flung tasks, or in the continual emergencies of common dangers, will call for detailed regulation of rule and role: for example, a Spartan society living as an armed camp, the life of a disciplined army, a monastic order, or even the holding together of the vast Roman empire.

From cases that focus on moral agreement, we turn to the complex situations of applied ethics where there is doubt about the correct or agreed-on outcome. Take the familiar problem in recent American enterprise when the consciousness of risk to health and life in the workplace poses the problem of what is done. Suppose the owners of the enterprise recognize the existence of the risks but find that remedying the situation is so costly that they would have to give up the enterprise. Suppose further that it is a company on which the town depends largely for work and livelihood and the general well-being of the community. How is the moral issue to be formulated?

A ready virtue formulation is sometimes provided: that it is a matter of greed on the part of management ready to profit at the expense of the health and life of the workers. But management may say rather that it is a difficult situation in which it is doing its best with limited resources; it has to show a profit to have continued investment; it can pay for an insurance policy for workers, with health and death benefit provisions. Its books are open and its accounting honest. Perhaps, as a mark of its sincerity, management will move its offices to the shop floor to share in the risks that workers take. (Compare a regulation that all managers of nuclear installations have to live within five miles of a plant.)

While the virtue aspects may lie in the background and come to the fore in many cases where the books are not open and insurance not so readily offered, the critical element in the situation is the decision of each worker to continue working. Here the problem is formulated as one of the right of the individual to decide whether or not to take risks. A person's life is his or her own; risks are taken in all sorts of contexts—in driving cars, in plane travel, in drinking, and in eating habits. It is up to the individual to make a choice. The core of the management case is thus a rights formulation. If it is argued that the choice has coercive elements because the worker's livelihood and family well-being may be at stake, the answer is that there are always different values in choice and some choices are hard.

An opposing view might see the situation as not individual, but one of social policy to be judged in terms of the good or social well-being. It need not deny that types of situations might have as their outcome that the social good lies in following the path suggested by the individual rights formulation. For example, suppose that we are faced with a desirable social task, say, building a tunnel under a river. And suppose—to continue in the mood of ideal good will in which we have been exploring this problem—that the managers call the workers together, report to them that some of the tasks are dangerous, that past experience is that half a dozen apparently unavoidable deaths occur every time a tunnel is built, that the best equipment known would be used and the best available knowledge, and that no one would be forced to do the dangerous jobs; the dangerous work would be done only by volunteers with special pay and special insurance. It would be justified by the social need for the performance of the task and the social lack of other instrumentalities. It would not be justified if there were robots that could perform the dangerous tasks. (Contrast the relatively cavalier way in which we treat requirements for driving automobiles.)

It is precisely this difference that might be offered against the individual rights formulation of the workplace example. The case before us is one in which we have the knowledge to remedy the defects that are injurious to life and health; we are not burdened by ignorance. Again, in the instance of the tunnel, we assume the social desirability of the product. We have then to ask whether the same holds for the product of the enterprise in the workplace example, apart from the generic features of providing work and pumping money into the town. It makes a difference whether the product is a luxury—say, one among many varieties of beauty cream—or a necessity. The formulation in terms of social good has to envisage some possible losses (as the rights formulation one envisaged the loss of health or life) but it depends what they are. In a free enterprise economy, businesses may be expected to rise and fall, and some suffering is anticipated. If, however, the product is valuable, then why not have increased prices? Surely it is wrong to have part of the cost paid by workers rather than consumers. If this means an inability of that enterprise to compete, then given the importance of the product, why not assist the enterprise through the general tax fund, preferably through long-range loans? In effect, something similar is done when public money is used for cleaning up past pollution while also charging the enterprise that gave rise to the pollution itself.

The moral stance of the formulation in terms of social good is that it is bad social policy to allow continuation of the worse when we know the better; it is the ideal of a caring community that takes advantage of the frontier of knowledge on behalf of its people, rather than continue in the ways of the past that at best perpetuate harm and at worst open avenues to greed and exploitation. In this parting of the ways, the mode of ethical formulation of the issue plays at least the part of a traffic officer.

The move in one direction of formulation does not of course prevent a shift as fresh problems arise in the further progress of the inquiry. After we have agreed on a consideration of the social good in this kind of case, we may have to face the further question of what components enter into that social good. And in some ways the original question of costs versus lives may reappear in this fresh inquiry. Thus, should we include cost–benefit reckoning within our account of the social good? How urgent is the removal of asbestos from schools, or the cleanup of polluting dumps? If benefits are to be reckoned in monetary terms, and saving lives constitutes a major part of the benefits, then the value of a life will have to find some monetary expression. For example—in an actual case that gave rise to much moral indignation—it was suggested that since the effects of asbestos might take many decades to arise, a life lost should be reckoned at only $26,000. With the benefits so reduced, cleanup might be stretched over a much longer period. It is not surprising that there has been considerable objection to the use of cost–benefit analysis in cases involving human life, even though courts have often had to determine damages where the loss of life was involved. The moral objection here can find formulation in different ways. A right–wrong one would be simply that it was wrong to assign a limited value to a human life. Kant expressed it in terms of good or intrinsic value by saying that a human life had infinite worth. The same idea is also involved in the refusal to rank persons with respect to worth, but to see every person as inherently worthy of respect.

It should be clear by now that the different ethical formulations are not separate from one another, that one may move from one to another at different points in the development of a moral inquiry, but that often where we start from may make a difference in opening up the scope of inquiry or closing it unduly.

Eight

Jurisdiction, Roles, and Occupations: The Regionalization of Morality

The notion of jurisdiction has its most familiar setting in the law. On it depends who is to decide a case, how (the rules by which) it is to be decided, and what is to be decided. In the United States the jurisdiction of federal courts differs from that of state courts; criminal cases are conducted differently from civil cases. The idea that different offenses should be routed to different courts is an ancient one. Classical Athens had such a division. Roman law differentiated between public and private law, each with its own rules and agencies of decision. Indeed, the growth of Western law paralleled growth in notions of jurisdiction. For several centuries Western Europe had to grapple with the strange notion, now called personal law, that individuals before a court were subject to the laws of the land from which they came. The resulting conflicts can only be imagined. It constituted a considerable conceptual breakthrough when, about the eleventh century, the jurisdiction of the territory was adopted. Subsequently, many battles were fought over differences between ecclesiastical and secular court jurisdiction (it was a substantial privilege for the clergy not to be subject to secular courts). Even as late as the eighteenth century, we find John Locke in the *Second Treatise* discussing the justice of applying local laws to aliens (who have not given consent to those laws).[1]

The attempt to construct a concept of jurisdiction for applied ethics is motivated by a variety of phenomena in ordinary life and in moral philosophy. They generate collectively the feeling that there are *regional* differences that make a difference for moral judgment, areas

or provinces that are governed by their own moral rules, and background principles that decide in which direction judgment is to be
steered. A good case can be made for such a view in the forefront of
moral decision, but a comparatively good case can be made for the
view that jurisdictional lines are themselves being steered and experimented with under the guidance of a still deeper background in which
a common morality dictates where there are to be regional differences. This chapter has, accordingly, to deal with depths below
moral judgment and depths below depths.

A perplexing and perhaps unresolvable difficulty is how to differentiate jurisdiction from context. It has been a persistent theme of this
volume that application of law or rule, and even meaning of concept,
must always be negotiated through a particular context. As a first stab
at distinguishing the notions, we might say that the context of an
action differs from its jurisdictional aspects in two respects: first,
context includes *all* the circumstances of the action, and second, as a
byproduct, contexts as a whole are unique. Jurisdiction is decided, in
contrast, by some selected salient features, and those features are
repeatable. It is that the action is kidnapping that places the act within
federal jurisdiction, and kidnapping is, regrettably, a repeatable phenomenon. That the kidnapper wore a blue coat is part of the context,
and it may even be a vital piece of evidence, but it is irrelevant from
the point of view of jurisdiction.

On the other side, we need to distinguish jurisdiction from the
topic of conceptualization, or how we decide to conceive an act or
event. Is the action a lie, or a lie-to-save-a-life? Are children in the
house of a suspected terrorist surrounded by police to be thought of
as hostages or as suspects? This appears more general a question than
that of jurisdiction. To narrow it even further, we may say that jurisdiction has to do with the regionalization of morality by virtue
of some social category into which the persons involved fall. Is it
morally relevant that the lie told is by parent to child, or by police
officer to suspect, or psychiatrist to patient, or client to lawyer, or
politician to constituent, or teacher to student, or coach to athlete, or
salesperson to customer, or chief executive officer to stockholder?
The category of jurisdiction, therefore, refers to an intermediate
range between the abstract conceptualization and the concretizing
context.

The closer analogy to our topic of jurisdiction in the domain of law
is not so much lists of defined offenses that distinguish criminal from

civil law, or federal from state, or statutory from constitutional, but laws that pick out classes of persons to impose special burdens on or grant particular privileges. The immunity from local prosecution enjoyed by diplomats is a good example of a case where the law carves out a region, defined by characteristics of persons, whose jurisdiction preempts other jurisdictions. It matters not whether the action charged against the diplomat would ordinarily be a federal or state matter. The status triggers another jurisdiction.

Jurisdictional recognition is familiar enough. We expect, for example, that family and friends will count more than strangers. But we have come to make distinctions: in private business it is perfectly all right to give preference in job appointments to relatives and friends, but in political life this is considered nepotism and favoritism and can be a punishable offence. Yet even in political life the broad maxim "Reward friends and punish enemies" is recognized to have a place, within limits.

Most relevant to today's applied ethics is the whole phenomenon of professionalism and professional ethics.[2] Various professions and occupations formulate their own codes of conduct, and their rules, though ethical in intent, do not always jibe with common notions of morality. A good example is the way in which the commonly accepted obligation to tell the truth and be honest is repeatedly challenged—and not just as a matter of behavior but as a matter of principle—in various occupations, an exception to the obligation being either a special privilege attached to the role or even a new obligation attached to the role. Think of the engineered deceptions of advertising and the practiced sleight-of-hand of the experienced negotiator. Journalism, with all the best of intentions to present "All the News That's Fit to Print," selects, often shades, according to owner or editorial policy, and distorts what is covered. Physicians have often felt justified and even obliged to withhold from patients the seriousness of their condition. The legal profession notoriously dismisses placing on each legal practitioner the obligation to seek the truth and chooses instead the obligation to present the strongest case, even when that involves ignoring or distorting evidence and laying traps for witnesses. Running for political office involves the studied manufacture of campaign promises, often with little intention or expectation of their being fulfilled (especially when they are scarcely mutually consistent). In the Iran–Contra hearings, the testimony of Oliver North and John Poindexter suggested the justification of a higher law of falsification, reminiscent of Bismarck's famous remark: "What a scoundrel a minister would be if, in his own private life, he did half the things he has a duty to do to be true to his oath of office." Even science, for which the pursuit of truth is the essential aim, often resorts to deception as a matter of experimental design.

There are three possible positions one might take on the degree of moral legitimacy of regionalizing of morality: none, some, or all. The first position denies that there can be any regionalization of morality; morality is the same for everyone; it is never the case that the obligations or rights of an individual are determined by any status or role or category that person fits into. The second position says that there are regions, but that they do not exhaust morality, that outside all regions, so to speak, there is a domain of morality that applies equally to everyone (let us call that, *ordinary morality*). The third position says that there is in morality nothing but regions—that the right or the good action is always determined by the category of persons involved. In turn, moral conflicts can be classified as of four kinds: (A) intra–common morality (for example, kindness versus honesty), (B) common morality versus region (for example, the general obligation of truthfulness versus an advertiser's obligation to make the best case for the client), (C) region versus region (for example, a lawyer's obligation to represent the wishes of a client versus a physician's obligation to act in the best interest of a patient), or (D) intra-region (for example, a physician's obligation to act in the patient's interest versus the obligation to abide by the wishes of the patient). The first position above admits only (A). The third position admits only (C) and (D), while the second position admits the possibility of all four types of conflict.

Of the two extreme positions, on the face of it, it is the first that has the strongest appeal. The idea that at least in the eyes of morality all human beings are equal and deserve equal consideration lies at the center of both formative ethical theories of the modern age—that of Utilitarianism and of Kant. Indeed, Bentham's formulation of the principle of utility in the first place was motivated by his hostility to a kind of regionalization—the quasi-feudal mélange of rights and privileges he found present in British common law of his day. Adopting as his slogan, "Everyone to count as one, and no one as more than one," he attacked differential taxation, differential legal liabilities, differential political representation, and various other privileges. His recommendations on international law could have been written as a response to Bismarck:

> But ought the sovereign of a state to sacrifice the interests of his subjects for the advantage of foreigners? Why not?—provided it be in a case, if there be such a one, in which it would have been praiseworthy in his subjects to make the sacrifice themselves. Probity itself, so praiseworthy in an individual, why should it not be so in a whole nation? Praiseworthy in each one, how can it be otherwise in all?[3]

There is no reason to suppose, however, that Bentham would have opposed any and all regionalization; he would only have asked that privileges pass the test of the principle of utility. The privileges he attacked were those whose justification was solely that they were a matter of tradition and whose functioning was to advance the causes of what he liked to call "sinister interests" (the "special interests" of our day). In his proposed constitutional code he did not hesitate to specify duties persons had by virtue of their positions or offices, but the shape and nature of these offices in a society reconstructed on the basis of the principle of utility would now have a rational and nonarbitrary foundation and would function in the general interest. Similarly Mill, although he was less exclusively concerned with institutions than Bentham, did not hesitate to attach duties to roles. In *On Liberty*, he observes that whereas individual liberty includes the right to get drunk, this did not apply to the "policeman on duty." Parents, he felt, should have the primary role in education of the young, and not the state. And he fully supported "intermediate generalizations."[4]

Thus Utilitarianism, at least the classic version of Bentham and Mill, does not support the view that regionalization is never legitimate. Insofar as they were suspicious of and attacked role-privileges, the objects of attack were those that failed the utility test. Further, for Bentham and Mill role-duties and the secondary rules of common morality have the same root.

Kant's view is a more intimidating obstacle to regionalization. For one thing, his famous rigorism in the matter of moral rules, such as the absolute condemnation of lying, would seem to be incompatible with any nuanced shading for professional reasons. If Kant opposes lifesaving as justification of a lie, he is unlikely to approve a physician's deception of a patient in order to protect the patient from mental distress. His condemnation of treating others as means includes using human subjects in medical experimentation, even when it is likely to advance knowledge and has the consent of the subject:

> What, then, is to be said of such a proposal as to keep a Criminal alive who has been condemned to death, on his being given to understand that if he agreed to certain dangerous experiments being performed upon him, he would be allowed to survive if he came happily through them? It is argued that Physicians might thus obtain new information that would be of value to the Commonweal. But a Court of Justice would repudiate with scorn any proposal of this kind if made by the Medical Faculty; for Justice would cease to be Justice, if it were bartered away for any consideration whatever.[5]

Nonetheless, it cannot be inferred from this that Kant would never find roles relevant in determining what is right. Toward the end of *The Metaphysics of Morals* he observes that when it comes to applying the fundamental rule of morality, circumstances become important.

> What conduct is suitable according to distinctions of status, age, sex, state of health, affluence or poverty, and so on? These considerations do not provide so many kinds of ethical obligation (for there is only one kind, namely, that of virtue in general), but only kinds of application (corollaries). They cannot, then, be set up as sections of ethics and as members of its systematic division (which must follow a priori from a concept of reason), but can only be appended to it. But even these applications belong to a complete presentation of the system.[6]

Kant never developed these observations systematically and so it is not quite clear how far he would be willing to take them, and whether they have the potential of softening his rigorism. But insofar as he concedes the relevance of distinctions of status to suitable conduct, he must find it compatible with the Categorical Imperative that roles are relevant. What he denies is that such distinctions are *independent* sources of morality. But then so would utilitarians.

At a deeper level, Kant's conception of the self raises questions for any ethics oriented toward roles. He is eloquent in his claim that it is the individual human being who is the sole source and sole object of the moral law. It is the human individual as person that is the source of dignity and worth, not individual as lawyer or teacher or engineer.

> But man as a person, i.e., as the subject of a morally-practical reason, is exalted above all price. For as such a one (*homo noume-non*) he is not to be valued merely as a means to the ends of other people, or even to his own ends, but is to be prized as an end in himself. This is to say, he possesses a dignity (an absolute inner worth) whereby he exacts the respect of all other rational beings in the world, can measure himself against each member of his species, and can esteem himself on a footing of equality with them.[7]

Roles are fundamentally standardized modes of participation by an individual in some segment of an enterprise. They involve habits of action, stable attitudes, assumption of specific obligations, and share with promises and contracts the predictability of type of response to standard situations. In a role, one "plays a part," carrying the metaphor of the actor as well as indicating participation with others.

Difficult philosophical problems have clustered around the relation of role and self, or person and role. Interestingly, the derivation of *person* is often ascribed to the Latin *persona*, which means a mask and refers to the actor's standardized mask that indicated his role— for example, in the comedies, the mask might indicate the irate father, or the wily slave, or the innocent young man (who will get into trouble and be rescued by the slave at the expense of the father). The philosophical difficulties in the relation of role and person parallel those in the relation of habit to self, and are perhaps easier to see in the case of habit. Sometimes habits are thought of as a drag on the self, a routinizing of the self through which its vital activity and creativity are crowded out. On this first conception, self and habit are fundamentally in opposition. On the second, sometimes habits are thought of as useful mechanisms, providing the capacity for instantaneous response without reflection. On this conception, habits do not constitute the self; they are instruments of it.[8] A third conception regards habits as fully constitutive of the self and integral to it. Here habits are the repository of past experience, the mechanism by which learning is internalized and consolidated, as if, in an intellectual metaphor, they were the library of the self, part of its mansion. The self is a cluster of habits of thought and feeling.

Similarly different attitudes are taken to roles. Parallel to the first attitude above to habits is Sartre's view. In *Being and Nothingness*, there is an often cited passage where he describes being in a café watching a waiter. There is something strange about the waiter, Sartre writes—he is too perfect a waiter; he moves just as a waiter should, responds just as a waiter should. What is he trying to be? asks Sartre. He is trying to *be* a waiter, is the answer; he has thrown his whole being into the role. Now, for Sartre this is a deadening of the self, a turning away from the free choice and creative activity that is the "essence" of self. It is one thing to engage in waiting on tables; it is quite another to be a waiter, and this no one can ever become. We can learn to *play* the part, but we cannot *become* it. Presumably, then, the professional is one who engages in certain activities based on knowledge, expertise, and skills. In some sense, people are not engineers, they are people who engineer; people are not parents, they parent. The self cannot be dissolved into a single role, or even into a cluster of roles, no matter how numerous; it permeates all their activity.

At the other extreme, the consequences of a wholly role-analysis of human life can be seen in the literature of ancient Stoicism, which made considerable use of the idea of "office" or role. Thus Epictetus writes: "Remember that you are an actor in a play, the sort the playwright wants: if he wants it short, then short; if long, then long; if he wants you to act a poor man, you're to act even this cleverly; so too for a cripple, an official, a private citizen. For this is your concern, to play well the part assigned to you; to choose the part is another's role" (*The Manual* [17]). The result is to abandon the effort to control the direction of one's life, and to accept what comes in the shape it comes.

The third attitude to roles takes the intermediate position. Those who take this position are less inclined than a Sartrean to disparage roles as a whole. The playing of a role does not necessarily imply narrowing and constriction of activities and interests (although, of course, it may). But we can differentiate between roles by the degree to which they are integral to the self or the degree to which they are constitutive of the self. Some roles—for example, parent, scientist, or artist—may well be regarded as shaping particular selves, not as wholly external to the self. The role of parent is not to be regarded as a kind of deadening of the human being who parents; to the contrary, being a parent can yield occasions for growth and development of personal capacities not otherwise easily available. Phenomenologically, roles can be felt differently by those who have them. A person who is both a parent and a corporate executive will often think of one role as somehow "closer" to her "real self" than the other, as more *expressive* of what she thinks is fundamental to her. It is not that there is a bare self somewhere behind all roles; to think so is to look on roles as merely functioning as means to something beyond it, as if choosing a role is always a means to the achievement of some personal enjoyment beyond the role itself. One can, of course, play a role successfully while seeing it as merely a means. One might choose a career for the sake of the financial rewards it will bring, which can then be employed toward one's real pursuit. But, despite the many jokes to the contrary, parenting is not for the most part a means to something else for those who do it.[9]

Whether a given role enters more or less into the constitution of a particular self depends on many factors, some personal and some social. In any society there may be some classification of roles along these lines, so that some roles are regarded generally as more integral to the self than others, as more capable of conferring meaning on a person's life. Thus in contemporary America, a role with the prestige of physician is considered such a one. That a person would organize her whole life around the role of physician is not considered exceedingly odd, so that all her activities, responses, and interests are oriented toward medicine. That is the meaning of her life; if asked who she is, she identifies herself as physician first. So the social judgment is that the role of physician is sufficiently weighty to bear this load. On the other hand, occupations of low prestige are likely not to be considered capable of this. If a person whose occupation is repairing television sets looked on this as *the* source of meaning in his life, he is likely to be the object of pity, if not ridicule, by virtue of the social judgment that such an occupation should not enter so closely into the constitution of the self. Obviously, societies will differ on the relative placement of various occupations. It is said that in Russia the medical profession has less prestige than in the United States. Obviously, too, societies differ on what roles are available—the role of *shaman* is no longer an option for us, while computer programmer is unavailable in technologically undeveloped societies. And roles may be cut differently—in one society, the role might be simply merchant, with no further delineation of kind of merchant, while in another the role of grocer might be considered significantly different from that of jeweler. Furthermore, there may be some difference among roles in the degree to which they are "moralized," that is, in the degree to which a person in that role is assumed to be engaging in morally worthy activities. Consider the difference in the way in which the media would treat the case of income tax fraud when the allegation is made against, say, a member of the clergy, as opposed to an allegation against a salesperson of used cars. Beyond the social expectations, there is also the consideration of personal choice. The fact that medicine is considered weighty socially does not mean that each person in that occupation sees it in the same way; correspondingly, a person can choose to wrap a life around being a magician, whether or not contemporary society considers that odd or pathetic.

Roles can be seen as a specification of the phenomenon of regionalization. As jurisdictional boundaries are marked out, roles get a delineation within the domain. The jurisdiction of "politics" can be marked out so as to create the roles of "politician" (or "representative") and "constituent"; or it can be marked out so as to create the roles of "monarch," "courtier," and "minister." The domain of the family can be so designated as to create, as can be seen in Aristotle, the roles of "head of household," "wife," "child," and "slave." The boundaries of the familial will vary depending on whether there is a "role" for uncles, aunts, and cousins. In contemporary America the choice of whom to marry is considered a matter of personal liberty. The family may be concerned, but it is not given the right of disapproval. In India, among traditional families, that choice is a family matter, which means the boundaries of familial jurisdiction are drawn differently here and there. But the specific difference of jurisdiction can be translated into the terminology of roles by asking what the expectations are regarding the roles of parent and child in each system. In India one of a father's responsibilities is choosing a bride of good family for a son and providing a dowry for a daughter. Similarly, there will be differences in the role requirements of children. Thus, the boundary differences are "cashed out" in role differences.

Given this relationship between role-differentiation and regionalization, the considerations given above about roles should apply equally to regionalization. The Sartrean view of role as apart from the self corresponds to the view that regionalization is separate from common morality; the view that the self is nothing but a cluster of roles corresponds to the view that morality consists of nothing but regions; and the intermediate position on roles corresponds to the view that morality contains both a common content and variously moralized regions. As the argument above pointed in the direction of the intermediate view of roles, it points equally toward the intermediate position on regionalization.

By placing the issues of professional ethics in the context of the larger category of the regionalization of morality, we wish above all to emphasize that the difficulty of resolving conflicts that arise from a seeming clash between the requirements of common morality and professional ethics is not a peculiar one with, in principle, some special characteristics of its own. Rather, we wish to argue that morality is pervasively regionalized and that differences among conflicts are at most matters of degree. That is to say, we do not need to develop one way to deal with conflicts of common morality and regional morality, a second way to deal with regional versus regional differences, and a third way to deal with intraregional or intra–common morality differences. This is so because regional moralities are structured in a way that mirrors common morality.

Sometimes the attempt to mirror common morality is quite explicit and self-conscious. When, in the 1970s, Congress, concerned over reports of scientific activity of questionable morality, established the National Commission for the Protection of Human Subjects of Biomedical and Behavior Research, the commission went about its work at first by tackling piecemeal some subdomains of the problem— defined by categories of research subjects, such as prisoners, children, and institutionalized persons—and only later, in 1978, attempted to sum up the bases of the recommendations they had previously made. This report,[10] intended to provide "common points of reference for the analysis of ethical issues in human experimentation," offers three principles and three implementing categories through which the principle is applied. The principle of respect for persons ("Individuals are to be treated as autonomous agents, and persons with diminished autonomy are entitled to protection") is implemented through the device of informed consent; the principle of beneficence ("Do not harm, and maximize possible benefits and minimize possible harm") through the device of risk–benefit assessment, and the principle of justice ("The benefits and burdens of research are to be distributed fairly") through the device of selection of subjects. What is of interest is to observe the implied relation between common morality and the region: to the commission, common morality consists in the three principles, the intermediate categories are what are needed to *apply* them to the domain. To the extent that there are conflicts resulting from the application of the principles within the domain of human subject research, the conflicts are intra–common morality conflicts being carried over into the region. It is hard to see on such a model how conflicts of the common morality versus regional morality sort could arise. The relation is simply one of application.

At other times it does not appear this way. There are three ways in which conflict can arise, or at least appear to arise. One is where the regional obligation is stricter than the common-morality obligation. A case of this is the interpretation by the medical community that the Hippocratic "Do no harm" forbids a physician from administering a lethal injection even with the authorization of the state carrying out an execution. The conflict here is not severe, since "Do no harm" is surely part of common morality as well, although perhaps there it is not so stringent. Another type of conflict arises where the regional obligation appears to be quite independent of common morality. The commercial aspects of the early medical and legal codes are good examples of this. The ban on advertising, for both professions, for example, is not obviously based upon any specific ethical obligation contained in common morality, nor the prohibition on charging a lower fee than one's colleagues. Examples like these can lead to a cynical public view of the profession, because it interprets the ethics code as a compilation of claimed privileges rather than a list of obligations. The third type is where the common morality obligation and the regional obligation contradict one another—as in the Machiavellian claim that princes have a moral obligation to lie, cheat, and steal for the good of the community.

These conflicts are most salient when the regional morality is structured by a code. Codification is but one way to regionalize, but it represents regionalization at its most explicit, most self-conscious, and most formal. When people talk nowadays about conflicts, it is usually with codes in mind. We have seen an explosion of such codes in recent years, to the point where it is commonly a point of ridicule, as if the aspiration of a group to the status of professional required a code to live by as a necessary condition. However, it should be noted that codification represents also a particular form of morality, a legalistic morality, configured around rules, rights, and obligations. We have seen in the previous chapter what the character of this type of morality is, and we observed that legalistic morality conflicts with good-based morality and virtue-based morality. It is therefore not surprising that codes should come into conflict from time to time with common morality, since its family type in common morality also does. In fact, all the arguments in common morality among the different types get replayed within the region—should the domain be regulated by rules, by good, or by virtue? Thus Charles Bosk's study of the ethics of surgeons suggests that the effective morality is one of virtue rather than one of rules.[11]

Professional codes are a relatively recent phenomenon. The two oldest full codes—one for the legal community and one for the medical—are of nineteenth-century vintage. Codes differ among themselves in length, in what they take the force of the "rules" to be (mere guidelines, statements of ideals, statements of strict obligations, and so on),[12] what the source of the authority of the code is (whether it is legally enforceable or not), whom they take as their audience (just the practitioners or the general public).[13] There are also obviously differences in content. Each major code seems to have a "sore point"— concepts designed to deal with particularly sensitive practices— which gives a particular emphasis to the code. This selectivity is true of all codes. We pointed out earlier that one can ask about the Decalogue, why the emphasis on honoring parents and not on parental responsibility for children? For the legal code, the sore point appears to be the confidentiality owed the client—why is it not the ideal of justice? Journalism's sore point is also confidentiality—and one might well inquire why it is not truthfulness. The sore point of the American Psychological Association's code is informed consent in the context of deceptive experimental design—why not fraudulent research or plagiarism?

Many find the very attempt to structure a field by a code objectionable. Some of these objections reflect the standard criticisms of rule-based moralities, for example, the idea that rules are too general to be capable of anticipating all contingencies. Other objections reflect an implicit preference for a virtue-based structuring: Consider Samuel Bard's injunction to physicians in 1769: "Let integrity, candor, and delicacy be your guides."[14] In 1883, Lewis S. Pilcher made objections to the first code (1847) of the American Medical Association that well represent the sorts of criticisms these codes have received ever since. He argues that it has fostered "a class of men who think much of the strict letter of the code, often to the forgetting of its spirit—medical Pharisees"; that it has introduced into the profession a "spirit of censoriousness," making "every man a spy upon his neighbor"; that most provisions are ignored, and that discipline under it was uneven—the powerful in the profession were immune to its provisions.[15] These criticisms to a considerable extent echo the standard criticisms of legalistic morality. A somewhat newer criticism of codes is that codes are a public relations show, a sham intended to mask or make palatable the economic monopoly professionals enjoy.[16]

The question of whether a legalistic ethics can be autonomous, discussed in Chapter Seven, also gets replayed for codes. We saw there that legalistic ethics at some point has to reach outside itself. The same is true of codes. At some point, the code has to consider what the aims of the enterprise as a whole are, why the boundary lines are drawn just as they are, what social good is being advanced by it, and so on. Take a relatively simple code, that of the Southwestern Ice Manufacturers' Association, adopted November 15, 1921.[17] It ties the ideal of success in business to service, hence "first, the requirements of their customers; and second, the remuneration to be considered." This statement of the aims of the enterprise leads to rules of quality and quantity; desired friendship with the public; to honesty in weights, courtesy, and prompt deliveries; to recognition of the pivotal role of the ice driver and so a spirit of cooperation and relations of partnership with these employees; finally, to the practice of the Golden Rule. The Oklahoma Ice Manufacturers' Association (December 8, 1923) is more systematic in its code, distinguishing relations of employer and employee, health, public relations, competition with others ("Abstaining from making false and disparaging statements, or circulating harmful rumors respecting a competitor's product, or his business, personal or financial standing"). It recognizes charity as the greatest of virtues and so pledges to see "that the worthy needy and poor shall not suffer from want of our product."

Though ice delivery has yielded to refrigeration, it is worth observing that the rules range from ordinary moral generality to specific problems of that enterprise. The commitment that the poor shall not suffer from want of ice is no different in type, though less exigent, than a commitment assumed by utilities companies in the latter decades of the twentieth century not to cut off gas supply to the poor or elderly in a severe winter when the bill is unpaid.

It is interesting to catch a code in the early stages of the enterprise. Take the new code for the broadcasting industry adopted July 11, 1939 (reported in the *New York Times*, July 12, 1939). Its rules vary from the most general and programmatic—for example, because of programs reaching the impressionable minds of children, to study and make available results of studies of the effects on children (reconciling the child's imagination and love of adventure with respect for adult authority and law and order)—to the most detailed itemization of allowable limits of advertising for a given length of program (e.g., three minutes, fifteen seconds in daytime fifteen-minute programs, two minutes thirty seconds in nighttime). In between are rules of fairness regarding controversial public issues.

In general, in such codes of applied ethics, the conditions that generate or support the need for rules are fairly clear. Reaching out beyond the rules is usually transparent; it is at bottom directed to the aims of the enterprise and the values supported by the relations of those who are participants or involved in its operations. At occasional points, appeal is found to precepts or rules of the common morality of the common sort—more sophisticated in later codes, often blatant in earlier ones where pledged adherence to the Golden Rule is a frequent item.

That there is no principled or essential difference between what goes on in a professional field and in common morality can be seen by example. Take the question of honesty raised above and compare its problems and use in an established field like journalism, a relatively new field like television, and the ordinary practices of human communication in everyday life. Shading the truth, holding back, selecting from a special point of view, or outright lying can be found in all of them. Journalism has had a longer time than television to try to work out devices for greater honesty. For example, there are rules about the writing of stories, such as to give the facts separately and furnish clear sources for expressions of opinion by participants, not mixing editorial opinion with the stories but relegating opinion to the editorial page, having an op-ed page with different points of view, an open letters column, and so on. The underlying value assumption is that the reader should be left to make up his or her own mind. On the other hand, in a journalistic system that takes the penetration of owner–editor values to be unavoidable, there may be (as in France) the party press, so that every paper will be understood to be presenting the view of a specific political party. Television has a more severe problem of selection given the time constraints under which it works, while at the same time its responsibility to take care is arguably greater because of this greater selectivity, as well as its greater relative impact and the fact that it is licensed to use a publicly owned but scarce resource.

In everyday life similar problems of selection and shading arise. Parents talking to young children exercise considerable selection and guide many of the things they say by what they think will be the effect on the child's development. In making promises, and then keeping them or establishing justifiable patterns of excuses, parents have moral effects. A social psychologist surveying the scene of parent–child relations in conversation might quite readily see it as a province of familial communication, parallel to television communication, with its own implicit set of ethical guidelines. More generally, the relations of people in ordinary life may come to be looked at in terms of the "games we play" and, as definite patterns are found, we would have the province of "interpersonal relations" with its own ethical code.

In the current growth of sensitivity about moral aspects of professional activity, many new problems have come to the fore. For example, book reviewing is an old pursuit, but not until recently have people begun to wonder about it from a moral point of view: is a reviewer under obligation to give a fair picture of the work as a whole, or is a review justified when it illustrates Spinoza's dictum, "Paul's idea of Peter tells you more about Paul than it does of Peter"? Are we to have a code of ethics for book reviewers, for movie critics, for art and architecture criticism, for the critic in general? Or again, take a professor writing a letter of recommendation for a student. Applications for positions may be so numerous that any asserted weakness (or the use of any adjective in a form less than the superlative) will condemn the applicant, for it gives the search committee a chance to lighten its load. Given these circumstances, should letters of recommendation conform to Samuel Goldwyn's style of evaluation of one of his pictures: "It's superb, it's magnificent, it's tops; next time, we'll do better"? Or does the present situation, compounded by questions of nonconfidentiality, mean the destruction of all utility in letters of recommendation?

Problems of practical moral judgment are numerous and pressing in all fields today, but they do not appear to differ much whether they occur in professional fields, semiprofessional ones, or in ordinary life.

It remains always open to debate whether the jurisdictional boundaries should be redrawn and whether the way in which the region is structured is appropriate. If we see a profession to be the most highly structured way to regionalize, then we can always ask whether a field should be professionalized. In the domain of health care, for example, Ivan Illich waged a powerful battle against professionalization, arguing that people generally should be given instruction in their own care rather than let every matter become a care of the doctor. A similar position has been taken about intermediate professionalism, such as midwives' attending normal births and calling doctors only when some specialty is required. The same controversies crop up in the legal field, where many now argue (as did Bentham in his time) against the monopoly power of lawyers to dictate what work only lawyers can do.

To deal with these questions, resort must be had to the fundamental aims of the field. What is it that medicine is aiming at? Or law? Or business? What level of regulation or professionalism or structuring is most appropriate for those aims? If we look to aims, we find that in many instances the supposed conflict between the regional morality and common morality derives from the fact that the region possesses conflicting aims. The objectives may be all well-intentioned: the struggle need not be between good and evil. For example, it is an old story in medicine that the field aims not only at curing the sick but also at advancing medical knowledge. A code rule may then be needed to cover the case where the treatment most likely to advance knowledge also jeopardizes cure. Similarly, in the history of business ethics, three objectives—profit for the investor–manager, living wages and safe conditions for workers, service for the consumer—jostle one another for primacy. During the Great Depression, the ideology of the business "family" embracing all three interests was not uncommon. Of the dominance of the financial market over production in the 1980s, it is often said that the profit motive has become the frank definitory aim of business ("Greed is good," in the infamous remark of Gordon Gecko in the film *Wall Street*). The widespread concern with business ethics today may reflect a basic uncertainty in the underlying objectives.

That conflict of aims is the source of moral quandaries can be seen equally in common morality and in regional morality. Take the simplest of problems in communication: being less than honest in order to spare the other person's feelings. This is a conflict between honesty and compassion. Different cultures take different paths in dealing with the conflict. In some, the speaker will tell the hearer almost anything the latter wants to hear; anything less would be impolite, and subsequent disconfirmation is irrelevant. At the other extreme is the almost intense brutality of absolute sincerity. And in between are efforts at reconciling honesty and kindness, with often a bit of equivocation. Obviously a fuller ethics has to distinguish types of situations, differentiate degrees of importance in what is at stake, types of desirable personal relations to be cultivated, and so on.

It is not, therefore, professionalism, nor even regionalization, that lies at the base of code differences, or conflicts between codes and common morality, but specific problems of conflict in the aims of the underlying enterprise that mark out the relevant region.

CHAPTER
Nine

Institution and Individual

The typical moral situation is conceived of as an individual deciding what is the right or wrong thing to do. Since the individual is engaging in the proposed action, the situation tends to be cast in individual terms. Of course, in the background are the social groups and customs and traditions and practices and institutions. If we think of all these as the *institutional aspects*, the present chapter is concerned with the *different types of relation* the individual may have to the institutional in deciding, or what amounts to the same thing, the different ways in which the institutional may enter into decision.

The first way the institutional relates to the individual is in providing means for carrying out a decision; this may be envisaged in advance and may help in making the decision. A parent decides that a child is ill and needs doctoring. It is institutionally provided that there is a licensed profession to resort to. In a well-ordered society it is possible—if the parent cannot afford the doctor—to invoke some social health provisions to take care of the situation.

This is the easy relation of institutional and individual, since the individual determination of what is right can be made separately first. The institutional aspect is tacitly assumed. Of course, compromises may be made after a social inquiry is provoked. Compare the instances of a man and a woman deciding to marry and then deciding to divorce. The former decision has fairly smooth social going (perhaps a health test or a minimum age requirement), so that the decision is perceived as almost wholly individual. The latter is more complex, and is normally seen as an institutional entanglement. In the 1920s,

Judge Ben Lindsay tried to break through the problems that engender divorce by suggesting "companionate marriage," in effect an institutional trial marriage, without children, in which the couple discovered their compatibility for a permanent relationship. At that time, when there were laws against "fornication" (defined as intercourse outside of marriage), his proposal raised eyebrows. After the law gave up dealing with private sexual matters and public attitudes changed, living together could be a casual thing, a kind of experiment, or a serious commitment.

The more complex cases are ones in which institutional features begin to enter more explicitly into the deciding of what is right and wrong. The act deliberated about may be envisaged within the context of an institutional procedure. Consider, for example, the decision to introduce the designated hitter into baseball. One may think of the question in explicitly institutional terms, as when we might object on the grounds that it would change the game or point to the difficulties involved when teams using the designated hitter play teams with no designated hitter. Alternatively, one may think of the question in terms of individual virtue with interpersonal import, as when we might object that it is unfair to certain individuals when we compare the statistics of persons playing under one rule with those playing under a different rule. Sports is pervaded by such questions, driven by a continuing revision of rules, new methods of training, even by technological breakthroughs (such as the use of new materials for tennis racquets or new designs for sailboats). Answers will doubtless refer to social considerations of legitimate competition and the role of surprise within it, unfair competition, illegal action, or upsetting the traditions of a game (i.e., invalidating the long-run statistical picture). Here many social factors enter individual decision.

The most overtly institutional cases are, of course, those in which the decision is thoroughly social from the outset. Waging a war is a clear example. Individual participation and innovation may enter in the process, but this does not make the war an individual matter, nor its beginning or ending an individual decision. (An individual may, by virtue of his or her social position, in fact make such a decision—for example, the Emperor of Japan in deciding on surrender in World War II.) This is quite different from Aristophanes's comedy in which an individual Athenian farmer decides to make peace with the Spartans, and his farm becomes an oasis of peace and plenty while his compatriots suffer. The introduction of the crossbow, or the cannon, or poison gas were social phenomena with social effects, though doubtless individual inventions and in their use affecting individuals.

Again, there are individual decisions with a submerged institutional content, where the center of gravity may lie more in the revision of the institution than in the individual agony of decision. Take, for example, a young man drafted for the war in Vietnam. He may decide to serve or run away, depending on how he weighs patriotic duty and personal apprehension. Or he may consider the social aspect, whether the war is justified. If he decides it is not, he may still choose between serving as a duty overriding personal disagreement— an unavoidable evil—or avoiding participating in evil by going to Canada. A third possibility is deciding on civil disobedience, that is, publicly refusing to serve and taking whatever penalty is involved, in order to make public his considered opposition to the war. We have here obviously different strengths of the entry of the social considerations into the individual decision.

These examples suggest that it is not helpful to make an absolute distinction between individual and social ethics. There are doubtless extreme decisions in both directions that we could, if we sought a more neutral terminology, think of as *macroethical* and *microethical*. Thus we might think of preserving the ozone layer as a macroethical task. Individuals can achieve little by their own moral action toward this end by avoiding sprays inimical to the ozone layer; it requires concerted social action. On the other hand, there are instances where the decision—with some qualifications about conditions of sincerity and knowledge and judgmental ability—is entirely "up to you" as an individual. Whatever you decide after conscientious deliberation is right for your action, even if I would decide differently for myself. But between these extremes of the clearly macroethical and the clearly microethical, there is the vast area of decision in which group and private considerations sometimes are separately identifiable and yet interwoven, and sometimes hardly identifiable separately. Here what is needed is a grasp of the different ways in which specific relation affects decision.

The foregoing considerations do not add up to a sharp division of so-called social ethics and individual ethics. There are public moral problems and private moral problems (declaring war and sexual orientation), public decision of public problems and private decisions about public problems (whether to abolish capital punishment and whether to vote for abolishing capital punishment), public decision about private problems and private decision about private problems (whether to help finance private housing and whether to get married). In many cases, what seems a private matter becomes ramified into a public one—for example, whether to smoke or not. The traditional attempt to distinguish between social and individual ethics usually rested on different philosophical conceptions of society and individuality. In older ethical theories, especially those that looked to a standard form of the human being to fashion morality, the human good and human duties were worked out in general, and the individual had to conform as well as possible in the light of interests, abilities, and situations. In the past few centuries, however, with the expansion of individualism in theory and practice, the dominant approach has been to start with individuals and their interests, preferences, and choices and construct social goods out of coincidence and agreements—whether in the economic theory of the market or the ethical theory of the greatest happiness of the greatest number. Revolts against this primacy of the individual began in the last century. F. H. Bradley, writing from the perspective of philosophical idealism, declared both individual and society to be "vicious abstractions." From the beginning, Dewey refused to contrast social and individual, but saw them as correlative: the form of decision was always individual, but the content always socially determined and socially relevant. Finally, he decided that the concepts were so ambiguous as to be practically useless; all questions of values or action in a society characterize concrete *groups*, and moral questions as well as political questions should be analyzed in terms of the interests and degrees of consolidation of groups or publics.

Some of the problems discussed in previous chapters seemed to involve a tension between the social and individual. That tension was clear in the debates over abortion in the contrast of individual principled decision (one way or the other) and sociohistorical unfolding aspects of the human scene. It entered sharply into the discussion of conditions of the workplace and whether an individual should be allowed to decide to take the risks and whether cost–benefit analysis should be used for social determination about enforcing protections. But such cases do not really involve adopting one or another fundamentally different perspective; they are rather looking partially at different aspects of a situation, exploring different relations and turning to different contexts—all of which can contribute to the fuller picture necessary for serious decision. Certainly the sorting of problems suggested earlier—as macroethical, microethical, and the large area of intermingled public and private factors—does not in the end provide a ground for two different kinds of ethics.

On the current scene, it is clear that some ethical issues can be analyzed without specific reference to (or by taking for granted) the interests of individuals. Preserving the ozone layer was cited earlier as an obviously macroethical problem, concerning the general quality and conditions of life and the organized or institutional action required to support it. Obviously enough, this issue requires and has received international attention and agreement in formulating a global policy. The individual may refrain, as a matter of principle, from using certain sprays that contain the harmful chemicals, but the moral import of such individual decision is either to maintain individual principled character, or if advertised to others, to agitate for broader awakening to the problem. Now, within the life of a nation, there are numerous comparable matters, such as national defense, distributive justice, nuclear controls, methods of dealing with crime, legal structure for many areas of associated living, disposal of wastes (increasingly macroethical), and questions of population checks (in some countries). There are, of course, no permanent lists, nor everlasting ones; the conditions of life in given periods are involved in the determination of what is a macroethical question and what moves into or out of that category. An example of dispute over such a field has been that of exploiting the resources of the ocean bed. Most nations wanted a system of distributive justice involving social division applied to these nationless resources, but a few—those who at present have a monopoly on the skills and techniques for the mining—maintained the right of exploitation in a free enterprise fashion; hence the international proposal failed of agreement.

Although such areas of macroethics seem to be set aside from individual reference in decision, there are at least two respects in which such reference is presupposed. One is the obvious assumption that the overwhelming interest of individuals is reflected in the development of an institutional policy in the particular area. The other concerns the mode of decision that it be viewed as an institutional policy. This is seen most clearly in areas in which there is controversy, or in which changes are taking place in the way of handling the given field. An obvious example is welfare support, which in this century has moved from individual responsibility and individual charity to what as a minimum is regarded as a social safety net below which no one should be allowed to fall; and in more complex form we find the institutions of the so-called welfare state. The point here is not the precise organization found but the way in which a decision is to be made—for the most part, the democratic political organization in which individuals eventually determine the outcome by their individual votes. Hence a definite stratum of individual decision, although in organized or institutional form, underlies the determination that an area is to be handled in the ways of macroethics.

Given this relative independence in which macroethics may operate, can microethics similarly operate independently? It seems less likely, since individual life and its decisions are carried on in a social milieu that impinges on every situation. Yet the array of situations in which the individual decides alone is formidable. These can be seen in the freedoms gained over the last few centuries, from freedom of thought and speech to freedom of sexual orientation. In this process, the network of group support, which has so often had a coercive character, has tended to recede: the paradigm of support used to be the extended family, then the nuclear family, and then, with the rise of divorce, it became the individual. The individual is thus left to decide alone, and often glories in that "autonomy." Perhaps one of the serious consequences for moral decision is that the formulation of the situation of decision is limited to alternatives within the narrow compass of immediate individual attention.

This isolation of the individual affects both theoretical and practical treatment of problems. Take, for example, Lawrence Kohlberg's well-known studies of moral education. He formulates problems addressed to young people, presumably in different stages of moral development, offers alternative choices, gets a response as to what is the moral choice, and asks for reasons. One of his central examples for testing the moral level of development was whether a man whose wife is suffering from a disease that might conceivably be helped by a new drug, but who is thwarted in getting it by its high price, should steal the drug. The question is set in wholly individual terms, with the man not having enough money and the druggist refusing to take payment over time. There is no suggestion of the individual inviting the support of others in a moral dilemma, as since then we have often seen appeals for public assistance or television presentation of unusual medical situations (with consequent sympathetic support from a wider public), or even of the husband's picketing the druggist to shame or frighten him or her into more lenient terms! And we may wonder what role is being played by the wife's doctor or the hospital to which she has gone during the earlier stages of treatment. Certainly development of such problems in later decades has shown this kind of problem to be in very great part a social–institutional rather than a wholly individual one. For example, when kidney dialysis was first developed the moral choice seemed to be the determination of who was to benefit from this scarce resource, hence the establishment of criteria and procedures for determining who was to live and who to die; but it quickly became a matter of public support and general availability, so that the hard choice did not have to be made on economic grounds. Indeed, the whole issue of ensuring adequate medical care for all sectors of society is on the public agenda today, although methods for securing it are disputed in relation to different underlying economic theories.

An objection to this line of criticism of Kohlberg's formulation may very well be that the appeal to public policy and to institutional reconstruction sidesteps the moral point. If, in an overcrowded lifeboat that is about to be swamped by the waves, a person has only a few seconds to decide whether to sacrifice her or his life to save the rest, it may be true but irrelevant that better and more secure lifeboats could have been, and in the future should be, built and all ships required to carry them. That may be the moral issue for a survivor concerned with government regulation of the shipping industry, but Kohlberg was focusing on the individual in the moment of choice. But he also was approaching that moment with a sharp distinction of the moral form and the possibilities of situational content. He thought that the moral issue lay in the individual's choice among principles, and moral maturity meant the choice of the higher general principles—in the particular principle of preserving life over protecting property. Moral decision consists, in almost Kantian fashion, in self-legislation by principle, not in securing the best results nor in reconstructing human institutions to enhance the quality of life.

In several respects, both practical and theoretical, we find tendencies to reach beyond the individual moral situation. One practical feature is the proliferation in our society of advisory services on everything from career counseling to teenage pregnancy. In their voluntary character these services reflect the same individualism that shaped the formulation of the moral problem to begin with, and thus seem to reconcile more collective deliberation with individual decision.

A second feature of much individual moral decision is the extent to which it has to deal with principles and standards that come from the public or institutional domain. We meet this frequently in ordinary life and in numerous professional decisions, in which the individual decision assumes the character of *moral compromise*. For example, I have told my neighbors that I will attend to a meeting of the neighborhood association, but this evening I feel tired. Can I excuse myself or am I being counted on? I ask: "What would happen if people excused themselves when they are tired?" Is my obligation then to go or to make sure others are not excusing themselves? Is it right for me, with an obviously weaker sense of duty, to profit from others' stronger sense of duty? Sometimes issues of this sort will lead not only to wrong actions becoming acceptable because they are unusual, but even because they are usual and there seems no ready way to change the pattern. Compare the lawyer who tips the court clerk to prevent his case from being postponed or the architect who tips the building inspector to come earlier (not to overlook faults in the construction), or the businessperson who bribes (note the shift from reassuring *tip* to the explicit *bribe*) an official in a foreign country to secure a contract. This businessperson will seek to justify the act by noting that it is the custom of that country, but that he or she would not do it at home.

Moralists have been quick to comment on the "slippery slope" character of excusing an individual moral decision on the ground of custom or of institutional practice that requires change but which one is not in a position to change in the particular situation. At the bottom of the slope lies the kind of moral insensitivity or hardening that will not risk reaching out to help others who are being victimized. (Are there no moral banisters to help check the slide down slippery slopes?) The history of the onset of Nazism in Germany is replete with such moral situations, and a subsequent generation of postwar young people was left in doubt about the moral sensitivity of their parents.

The range of moral response from the heroic to the irresponsible is a familiar theme in moral philosophy. Sometimes morality calls for sacrifice—the duty to act on principle irrespective of the consequences to oneself. Sometimes it appeals to the unpredictably stimulating effect of moral example: in pacifist theory Leo Tolstoy argued that an example of nonviolence in a violent setting will unlock in others a flood of human sympathy, and both Gandhi and Martin Luther King, Jr., applied this lesson in social action. Sometimes, especially in a setting of corruption and repression, it is a duty to join in rebellion. In all such cases, institutional and social assumptions enter intimately into individual reckoning of moral duty.

A more theoretical consideration of the way public or institutional factors enter into what appeared to be individual moral reckonings is found in the attention paid in late twentieth-century ethics to the role of *practices*. A notable example is found in the analysis of the obligation of promising.[1] The usual analysis appealed to intuition or to utilitarian reckoning of what consequences produce the greatest good to support the obligation to keep one's promise. The new understanding saw making a promise as *utilizing an established practice* in which the obligation was inherent. One could thus question the setting up of promising as a practice, but if one had done so, then making a promise already committed one to keeping it. To promise was thus to engage in a social act; keeping a promise was like a bus driver stopping at every designated stop or a bank clerk cashing a properly presented check. The crucial point is the social character of the act of promising; it is more like voting than engaging in an act of will.[2]

On the whole, then, individual moral decision is shot through with social content. It follows that in facing a problem of applied ethics, one of the constant points of inquiry should be what institutional background is presupposed in the formulation of the problem. Consider a few examples.

A typical one is that of the nurse who faces a difficult choice between following the strict rules in the code or cutting corners to help the patient with what is obviously needed. It may be a matter of treatment that strictly by the code should have been checked with the doctor, or of calling on a patient's relative (beyond the line of duty or even against it) to take a greater interest in the patient's condition, or any of a host of items that constitute a technical infraction. Is a morally sensitive nurse to be faced with deciding between duty and patient welfare? Is it like telling a lie to save a life or to spare feelings?

When this kind of problem becomes frequent, it is time to look at the underlying situation to which the code was addressed. When most doctors were general practitioners, making home visits and becoming well acquainted with their patients and their families, and nurses were only moderately trained helpers, the constant recourse to the doctor's approval may have been a wise precaution. Today, however, doctors are often specialists called on to deal with relative strangers at critical times, while nurses are now much more highly trained and constitute a profession in their own right, so that they can more readily assume responsibilities more commensurate with their closer relations to the patient. In short, we are dealing with a professional situation in transition under changed and changing conditions. The basic moral decision here, then, is one of social policy or professional policy, only incidentally of the nurse caught between duty and human sympathy. Indeed, the tension between nurses' associations and doctors' associations is evident today in conflicts around legislative proposals for the nursing profession. It is complicated by the addition to the staff of nurses' aides, who are now in the position of helpers with assigned tasks and little autonomy and whose existence sets off more sharply the growing professionalism of nurses themselves. On the other hand, current technological changes may help in part to restore the familiarity the doctor once had with the patient's condition and responses —for example, the detailed information via computer monitoring and readier communication from a distance. In short, the moral decisions are those of a profession in transition, not primarily of an individual in moral distress. Meanwhile individuals will still be making difficult decisions, but an awareness of the social setting can help guide or supplement action.

Another typical case in our society, in which the moral burden falls in full and often public light on the individual, is that of whistle-blower. Typically an employee goes public with a complaint about some enterprise (whether governmental or private) engaging in practices that are unlawful: ripping off the public purse (padding bills, rigging bids) or, in one way or another, endangering public health (e.g., military experiments with nuclear energy with little concern for the radiation effects on the neighborhood and then covering up; or industrial corporations destroying the environment and polluting the water supply by dumping toxic wastes illegally or carelessly). Or the occasion may be one of corruption in any agency, for example in a police force. Now the whistle-blower has to be an insider, a member of or employee within the enterprise; revelations by an outside inspector or investigator are not whistle-blowing. The whistle-blower, in one way or another, has decided that what is going on is seriously and urgently contrary to public welfare. The decision may have resulted from the growing burden of conscience or a kind of conversion in which the actions of the enterprise have lost any justification they previously had in the whistle-blower's eyes—as in a member of the

CIA or British intelligence now seeing what is being done not as heroic patriotism, but as illegal villainy. It is assumed, too, that the whistle-blower has tried unsuccessfully to bring about changes within the enterprise and has given up any rational hope of doing so. The moral decision is then to publicize the evil that is going on rather than to acquiesce in silent or hopeless resignation or simply to quit. The whistle-blower knows by this time that he or she will be treated by the enterprise as a traitor and an informer, with all the obloquy this involves, and that demotion, dismissal, or isolation and social ostracism will be a consequence. It is then a heroic individual choice, not lightly undertaken, with more than a touch of self-sacrifice for the public good.

From the social point of view, the public benefit of the action invites organized support beyond mere praise. Although the informer is traditionally a detested person stirring all the opprobrium of disloyalty to the basic group, the whistle-blower is classified primarily as one motivated by concern for the public good. Indeed, it is in the public interest to encourage their actions. For example, one finds a discussion on television entitled "Accountants as Whistle-Blowers—The New Frontier of Morality?" And there are measures that would hold accountants financially responsible for trespasses they miss or ignore on income tax reports. The whistle-blowers themselves have made some efforts to get together for mutual support. A national network assists them with legal advice in court cases for restoration of rights or for damages.[3]

There is a deeper sense in which whistle-blowing may be regarded as a social mechanism. If what it does is directed toward making corrections in the operation of an enterprise, then it is one of a class of devices that take on a fresh unity as they are looked at together. At one end are complaint departments, investigation departments, and ombudspersons; at the other, procedures to encourage evaluation and criticism by all participants in an enterprise, channels for ready suggestions and recommendations, quality inspection, and so forth. It would be a sad enterprise that had no channels for a dissatisfied consumer or buyer to rectify some complaint or that left no way but devious machinations by an employee who suffered some hurt. (The recent history of sexual harassment is an excellent case of the way in which complaints not given avenues for redress end up in litigation outside the enterprise.) Whistle-blowing thus can be seen as the extreme case where self-criticism is suppressed, and what should be provided as a normal channel in any well-run enterprise is omitted or blocked. The causes of such blockage in our society are another matter—whether they be an authoritarian model in business management or an excessive concentration on profits irrespective of public losses.

We turn now to the kinds of cases where social policy affects individuals or groups of individuals differentially and therefore requires some moral or quasi-moral justification. Consider then, first, some issues involving the allocation of goods (illustrated by private property), second, issues arising from allocation of responsibilities or burdens (illustrated by taxation), and finally, problems involving the character of social and group morality, or moral atmosphere.

Private property involves at bottom the protection, with the use of state power if necessary, of the owner against any outside use of or interference with his or her property without owner consent. To designate something as private property or to privatize some activity or enterprise is thus to turn it over to private control. Hence, social policy is embodied in the existence or creation of private property. Two opposing social philosophies concerning private property are clearly the free enterprise system and the socialist system. But the practical moral questions we meet in any system are usually about particular classes of things or activities. The serious question then is how in a particular case we decide whether a particular item is to be privatized. Take an extreme hypothetical example: as a libertarian is said to have argued in jest or in seriousness, public thoroughfares represent socialism, and hence the streets of a city should be privatized. Now it is conceivable that streets could be treated like private toll roads, that the municipality would be spared the expense of cleaning and repaving, that the owners (whether private citizens or the association of those living or working on that street) could beautify it and compete to encourage its use by pedestrians or by cars (having filled all the potholes). Let us assume, too, that modern technology has worked out a way to secure tolls without slowing up traffic. What arguments would be given for or against this unusual proposal?

Privatization, it should be noted, has proceeded apace in recent decades. Private enterprises include hospitals, medical services, schools (with repeated attempts to allow parents to choose public or private schools, using tax vouchers). There has long been private ownership of public utilities (electricity, gas, telephone), though with some state regulation. There are even private prisons to which a state or county farms out prisoners to serve their sentences. In all these ventures, private profit from the enterprise would be a guiding policy. In various countries, railroads have been reprivatized, mines and steel mills nationalized, and public housing reprivatized. Should public libraries, museums, and public universities follow?

Problems are multiplied as we move from enterprises dealing with physical things and services to patents and copyrights, the so-called intellectual property. For an author and publisher, or for an investor and associated investors, control of expressed ideas or the use of an invention is essential to their business undertaking, and so anything that makes inroads upon such property is firmly resisted. For copyrights, for example, a major threat stemming from technological advances is photocopying, since—in the case of a book—sales will be diminished if those who need it in whole or part can photocopy it more cheaply. Hence legal barriers have been erected against copying, and more are being sought today. Analogous restrictions have long held for performances of a play or public performances of music. How far should such business-oriented restrictions go? In some places libraries are beginning to charge borrowers for the time a book is kept, with some part of the fee going to the publishers or to the authors as royalties. Conceivably, in a *Brave New World* or a *1984*, we could reach the point where every time you burst into song on the street or whistled an aria from a copyrighted opera, you would be dunned for a few pennies—computer technology having made accounting and dunning a simple matter! Consider the example of prints of a famous painting. If you buy one to hang in a barbershop, will you have to pay a continuing fee for its use in business? You may claim you own the print and can do anything you like with it, but there are precedents and analogies: for example, you own a letter a public person has sent you, but you do not own the right to publish it—that is the sender's. Now if a continuing fee at the barbershop, in effect a use-rental fee, is plausible, why not at home? (You can save during vacation by taking the picture down.)

We have deliberately taken such a bizarre extreme to show that lines will have to be drawn, principles of justification offered, and then those principles reassessed at different points. There may be *critical points*—in the technical scientific sense in which a qualitative change takes place in an advancing quantitative change, as when water turns to steam or to ice. So far we have not touched the justification principles.

Before we do, however, it is meet to note that the bizarre often turns into the familiar and the important. The most recent privatization is the right to patent life forms, the creation of which is now made possible by the advancing science of biotechnology. The Supreme Court has allowed this in the case of plants genetically engineered so as to be immune to frost. It seems reasonable to grant a company the right to market its invention during the life of the patent. But farmers were made angry by the development of a modified cattle gene that would markedly improve the breed and thus give the gene's developer a tremendous marketing advantage. Would this threat of almost total control of the cattle industry be sustained in so primary an industry? What would happen as more complex forms became private property? Could a population of altered chimpanzees (the form nearest the human) become private property to work for a corporation?[4] This begins to look like a new kind of slavery.

A further extension of private property created by patent concerns mathematical operations. This does not cover the formulas that are deemed laws of nature, but the complex modes of applying them in ingenious fashion that can facilitate industrial processes. We should perhaps remind ourselves that patents are not forever, and their term—before the inventions become public property—can be fixed by legislation.

Now the principles of justification for private property are fairly traditional. We have private houses, private clothes (apart from "privates" in the army), private food, and significantly, private land (except public forests, parks, military reserves, and the like). Some societies do not allow private ownership of land, but only its rental or occupancy for the use of hitherto unoccupied land. But in most of these instances, we take individual ownership to be obviously the most suitable, most convenient, and most furthering of individuality. At least these instances do not become centers of controversy. In the case of private property for production—that is, business and industry—the situation is different. Standard justifications are that a system of private ownership and control (with some limiting demands from the organized society) yields greater initiative and productivity and rewards merit. These being acceptable and even laudable goals, privatization is encouraged as new areas arise. Critical points, in the sense indicated, have been noted in our history. When a field turns *monopolistic*, a variety of social devices from regulation to social ownership have been employed. A second critical point is found in *social importance* or *momentousness*. During World War II, the

United States found itself short of aluminum for war production and built a plant, since private industry's production was insufficient. At the end of the war the plant was sold to a private company. Secretary of the Interior Harold Ickes wanted it to become a corporation in which all veterans were given shares, so that it would belong to those who had fought the war, but private industry was wary of such innovation. Yet it would still have been a private company with a broad dispersal of shares, as today when employees of a company that is disbanding take over the business and run it together. Still a private company, its significant feature may be a different way of managing itself internally when the workers are also the shareholders. A different example of social importance is the postal system, which, unlike the railroads, so far has resisted privatization.

Among matters of social importance, a special place could probably be found for *overwhelming importance*. Suppose a process of immunization for AIDS were discovered. It is unlikely that the government would allow it to remain so privatized that only the wealthy could take advantage of it, or that the public would be allowed to be bled excessively under the right of property to set its own price. The government would probably act as a municipality does in condemning land for public use on presumably justifiable grounds, and have a court set a price, which the dispossessed owner rarely finds equitable.

In many kinds of cases, then, there appear to be standard ways of resolving the conflict of private interest and institutional or social well-being, ways that rest on the recognition of critical points in the governing moral principles under the special conditions. At that point, in attempting to solve the problem or reach a moral decision, one stops invoking the principle that has governed decision and looks to the recognized values at stake. What happens, however, where there is no recognition of standard critical points? Here, instead of letting the principle spin on, ignoring the conflicting interests on the assumption that it *is* a well-grounded moral principle, we have to go behind it to see what interests gave it that status and how they hold up in comparison when interests conflict. For this purpose, let us take up the copyright question indicated earlier, with respect to the use of photocopies.

Granted that the author and publisher have a legitimate business interest in the control of the work and its sale, the issue is how far that interest extends before crossing other legitimate interests. Is a student photocopying a chapter of the work for convenience—to read at home instead of in the library—to be equated with a publisher in a country where international copyright is not honored publishing a cheap edition and selling the pirated copies in the United States? Is the photocopying any different in principle from one student buying the book and lending it to half a dozen others? Should the publisher have a percentage when the book is sold secondhand? That a technical means of registering the student's photocopying (through use of a number, and a device that will allow the copying only by use of that number, with the library or photocopying center billing the student) is possible is no different from the possibility of printing a book with an ink that will vanish after a given time; they are both devices to limit circulation and compel purchase. The student's interest is not to make money, nor necessarily to save it, but to advance in learning. The author, too, may have other interests, such as the wish to be widely read, or to contribute to the stream of thought or of literature. The publisher, more oriented to profit, may drop the book if it does not sell, say, five thousand copies a year, while the author might be satisfied with three thousand. Or again, for a very popular novelist, the advance and the early sales may be so great that the venture would immediately be a huge business success. (Would a law terminating copyright when profits reach a given high level reduce initiative and inventiveness and reward of merit? Such legislation might be regarded as analogous to price control in public utilities.) In addition, there is an obvious public interest in the educational and cultural consequences of a wide-reading public, which may be chilled if monetary obstacles arise in libraries or college operations. A distinction would have to be made between the purposes of use—whether a business was being carried out or just a greater personal convenience served that helped learning.

Again, a more far-reaching analysis of authorship and publishing might be desirable. The situation of scholarly works published by university presses is different even today from that of commercial publications. Scholarly publications often receive subsidies from research foundations or publication funds or even corporations. The motivations in scholarly and commercial publishing are different, too. At university presses, authors are usually academics whose writing is tied in with professional research. For writers whose livelihood comes from their writing, commercial publication often gives it a special slant. Perhaps other institutional possibilities could be opened —for example, literary guilds paying a fixed price for works they accept directly from authors.

The lesson from this brief discussion of problems arising out of the relation between institutional practices and individual interests is not a simple one. It is at least a warning not to let a principle that has governed a field be automatically extended as new problems and new possibilities emerge. Another lesson is that there is a need to recanvass the basic interests at issue and consider experimentation with fresh institutional possibilities that may provide solutions, or at least compromises, more fitting to the complexity of the problems themselves.

We turn next to the second batch of problems, those concerning the differential imposition of burdens and responsibilities. Here again, we are not dealing with those that fall with agreed-on fairness on all alike for purposes that all share, but with those that are differentially allotted and therefore require special principles of distributive justice. Let us take one old problem to set the stage, and then move on to contemporary experimental ideas.

When public education was introduced in England, Herbert Spencer objected to bachelors' being taxed for it because they had no children.[5] Against this, it was argued that the community at large benefited, since educated people produced more of public value, served it better, were less likely to commit violent crime, and so forth. Such an answer implicitly accepted Spencer's claim that a beneficial measure should be paid for by those who benefited from it. In the United States, for the most part, a more wholesale criterion was used. If a measure was widely beneficial, and it was to be supported by the community, it could be supported by the general tax fund. Thus, in the earlier history of public colleges, major support came from general taxation, although it was largely children of the middle class who took advantage of those institutions.

On the other hand, the principle of differential taxing has also been clearly employed. The building of highways is heavily funded from a tax on gasoline, and thus by those who drive the highways. But some share of public support of transportation—for example, of railways—seems justified by the fact that even those who do not travel or send freight benefit from the circulation of goods all over the country. The degree of general support thus rests on the extent of convergence of general and sectional benefit. An interesting claim for such convergence was found in a proposal (that did not get far) in New York City some decades ago that the subways be free, supported only by public taxation. It was argued that much would be saved in the simplified operation of the subways, that the state already gave some subsidies to cover deficits, that in fact everyone in New York benefited from the subways through their making distant, cheaper housing available for a large working population, that there were already reduced rates for students and the aged, and that at the time many who did not use the subways paid nothing for the indirect gains their business enterprises in fact had from it.

Many recent proposals have centered around a redifferentiation of burdens toward those benefiting distinctively. For example, in higher education the burden of supporting colleges has fallen partly on the general public through taxation and partly on parents and students through increasingly higher fees. Some propose now that students pay nothing while in college but after graduation pay a certain percentage of their income for life in return for the education. This has a kind of prima facie fairness to it, in part because it relieves the intense burden that families have borne in preparing for their children's college. And people who have not gone to college are relieved of paying, at least to some degree. But, of course, much would depend on the actual figure set for the percentage. There are other factors to be considered. We tend to think of college as primarily a benefit for the student. Is it to any extent a sacrifice of time and energy, resulting in being able to be of greater service to the community? Again, for professionals, will it mean an increase in the cost of their services, just as doctors who have had a long and grueling period of college, medical school, internship, and residency have felt justified in charging high fees in return for their sacrifices. In the end, the new proposal, although simple in appearance and in operation, would have to embody a reconciliation of a set of complex interests whose index would probably be the figure set as the percentage of income due. Yet it might be the most convenient channel for dealing with the cost of higher education at the present period.

On the whole, the redifferentiation of burdens seemed a congenial path in the late 1980s to a federal government that was loathe to increase federal taxes. For example, it was suggested that the burden of providing daycare centers so that mothers could work be placed on business enterprises, in somewhat the same way that in the past workers' compensation was provided by the contributions of business, labor, and government. (The proposal has the government contribute to daycare through tax exemptions.) A similar proposal was suggested for health insurance in businesses employing more than a certain number of workers. Although on the face of it this seems to be differentiating the burdens, actually it is a roundabout route equivalent to public taxation. For the increased costs would doubtless be reflected in the increased prices of the commodities produced, and though each enterprise would pass the cost onto those who used its products, the overall result would be to generalize the burden.

Such a circular route does not hold for one differentiation that was imposed—in the catastrophic health insurance act of 1988 for the aged, through Medicare. It includes a burden that in a few years will amount to about two thousand dollars a year on those members of Medicare with an annual income over a given amount. This is to be collected through a surtax on what is paid in income tax. Thus the burden of health care of the aged is put on one segment—the wealthier—of the aged themselves. This raises sharply the question of the principles and the ethics of categorization. For example, does it follow that, given deposit insurance, bank failures should be paid for by the profits of the richer banks, rather than by tax funds? Should impoverished teachers be supported by the rest of the teachers, instead of public welfare, and impoverished members of a given religion by other adherents of that religion? It is the principles of distributive justice here that are not explicit and need to be examined.

In general, then, the belief that burdens and costs should be borne by those who gain from the activities is at best a starter for inquiry. Indirect benefits and gains range more widely than at first seems to be the case. The assignment of burdens on such a principle may be just an indirect route to general taxation, overt or disguised, which might as well be faced directly. Most of all, there are vital cases where no sharing in the burden by those who suffer seems possible. In familial morality, the obvious case is that of infants and young children. In society at large today, it is that of the utterly impoverished. Here the initiative to bring about a situation in which sharing the burden is possible lies with the social community that has allowed such poverty to come into being.

This brings us to the last of our moral problems spanning individuals and institutions—that of the moral atmosphere. Moral atmosphere was considered in Chapter Seven in relation to the virtues. Here we focus specifically on its location as an individual or a group phenomenon. An individual certainly can be immoral in action. Can there be an immoral corporation? Was the company immoral that sold infant formula abroad as apple juice that turned out to contain largely sweetened water? Or is this excessive zeal for profit to be pinpointed on individuals in critical positions within the corporation?

The narrative in linear sociological histories of the rise of individual responsibility is a familiar one. Earlier societies, the account tells us, held the kin group responsible for the moral trespass of one of its members; retribution was directed at anyone within the group of the offending individual, and feuds formed a common pattern. Sometimes the group disowned an individual, leaving him or her without protection, or even exacted punishment. Group responsibility has usually been seen as moral progress. With the growth of civilization, the account continues, moral blame became more and more individualized, and actions are judged immoral by whether they are willed or chosen rather than by whether they result in accidental and unintended harm. It follows that moral wrong, moral deterioration, and the thinning of the moral atmosphere are phenomena of the rise of individualism.

This point of view has been faced with serious difficulties in the twentieth century. Thus German youths in the second half of the century have been tormented with the feeling that their parents were collectively responsible for not resisting Nazi brutality and for the Holocaust. Americans have sometimes raised similar problems about having allowed the first dropping of atomic bombs on Japanese cities. Again, in disputes over affirmative action, some whites have complained that the evils of discrimination took place before they were born and though they are not guilty of discrimination they are put at a disadvantage in attempts at redress for the old wrongs. Others, however, argue that these are not individual matters, that the white population has nevertheless benefited from the gains of the older discrimination and a whole societal remediation is called for.

Of course, the crucial reflection and determination of attitude takes place within individual consciousness, and action in such situations is either individual or the concerted action of individuals. This is more likely to characterize programs of change. Where the action is the expression of standard and common attitudes, it has more the character of a group phenomenon. Is there any sense in which we can think of the moral outlook or the moral atmosphere as group rather than individual phenomenon?

Consider the atmosphere we outlined in dealing with virtues in Chapter Seven—the atmosphere of competition for individual success that so strikingly characterizes American society today, which we noted is not satisfied with playing a good game but insists on winning it, and not merely with being on the winning team but being a star. When the trade balance runs strongly and persistently against the United States we hear the call for increased competitiveness and not for cooperative planning on an international basis to further a community of interests. Does it make sense for a social scientist to describe the moral atmosphere imbued by competitiveness as a social phenomenon in the United States today, whereas the effort to increase cooperativeness would appear rather as a set of individual phenomena? Certainly, with the social influences on the growing child we can hardly see the competitive ambitions in most cases as products of independent individual volition.

The effort to work out ideas that would move moral decision away from a sole focus on the isolated individual struggling with an inner choice between good and evil and allow us to speak of group injustice, as well as group decision, has been growing in recent decades. For example, as early as 1971, delegates to the World Synod of Bishops were described as "moving toward a conviction that the Roman Catholic Church must broaden its understanding of sin to include the 'structural' injustice of major social institutions that many people assume to be morally neutral."[6] It advanced the idea that "injustice is not merely the result of individual sinfulness or the failure of governments or private agencies to assist the needy but that it is built into institutions and structures that most people simply regard as a normal part of modern technological society." Again, hardheaded logicians argued that judgments of the agency of social groups could be meaningful; that they did not have to concern themselves with the underlying mechanisms any more than in dealing with human individual agents we are concerned with the underlying "hardware."[7] There should be no more difficulty, for example, than in speaking of families as consumers in the economic theory of consumer demand. Of course, sociology in its accounts of societies and anthropology in its cultural descriptions—say, of cooperative and competitive societies —have rarely hesitated to use such group language or felt the need to reduce it to statements about individuals.

Such judgments about groups do require careful verification. For example, if we find that traditional Japanese culture looks askance on litigation, we will want to examine the mechanisms they employ to palliate conflicts—for example, "The Japanese government maintains free legal consultation centers and dispute resolution centers where citizens can go to discuss their problems with a lawyer."[8] Eventually, in the light of the extreme litigiousness to be found in American society, we are led to examine the role of the legal system and the ideals that are taken to govern lawyers in a primarily adversarial pattern, and what values are taken to be furthered by that system.

Interpretation of social customs often has to be many sided. Take, for example, the procedure in European hotels of handing in one's passport to be listed in a daily report to the police. One of us commented to the innkeeper of a German country inn that in America we did nothing of that sort. Her immediate reply, in a sorrowful tone, was, "Do you mean that in America a person can be away from home and no one *cares* where he is?" Although we are not inclined to treat this as the major motivation of the rule, the absence of care is precisely what has characterized American reaction to the newer phenomenon of homelessness. And the relegation of the issue to personal compassion rather accentuates than resolves the basic problem of the moral atmosphere. (It is well expressed in the title of one of Reinhold Niebuhr's books, *Moral Man and Immoral Society*.)

These considerations suggest that in facing a deteriorating moral atmosphere, while action in terms of individual moral decision and individual resolution is important, we cannot dispense with attention to institutional factors and needed institutional reorganization.

Ten

Discovery and Innovation

That there have been moral discoveries in our human past is clear enough. At given points it was discovered that slavery is wrong, that there are senses in which people are equal, that torture is wrong, and that there is a meaning to human dignity. Alongside moral discovery has come the moral impact of the expansion of knowledge and of technological discovery. While this growth has sometimes been gradual, at times it has been so rapid as to have a whirlwind effect on morality. For example, the discovery of the role of germs in causing illness came when there was still widespread belief that illness was a divine punishment that the sufferer must bear; it required a reorientation of our attitudes toward illness, in which illness excuses one from responsibility. In due course, the concept of illness itself was stretched, which raised fresh problems concerning the limits of moral responsibility. Again, while contraceptive efforts of one sort or another go back to biblical times, it was the discovery that sperm could not penetrate rubber that launched the widespread moral change of attitude toward contraception that eventually issued in the belief in the moral appropriateness of family planning. The expectation that there will be fresh technological discoveries that will affect moral attitudes has become common, although attempts to anticipate moral changes are very few. The moral effect of the automobile in the twentieth century (certainly backseat sex, but also vastly increased independence) is perhaps the best example of lack of moral foresight.

The character of moral discovery varies. Sometimes it is like entering a fresh and hitherto unexplored terrain. Sometimes it is rather the recognition of causality in human affairs that affects moral attitudes or calls for definite changes in morality. Yet there is an element of *innovation* in the recognition that change is unavoidable or that it is needed or that it is overdue or that specific changes are highly desirable or that their consequences are to be guarded against. To give innovation a recognized place in ethical theory and in applied ethics is itself an innovation.

The moral philosopher in whose work the idea of innovation was pivotal was John Dewey. His emphasis on it stems from his psychological analysis of human thinking. In human life much action and response is governed by habit and, usefully, does not require special thought. Thinking is stimulated by the problematic, which may reflect an inadequacy of habitual response or a conflict of habits. In this situation of indeterminateness one looks for or imaginatively rehearses alternatives and looks for evidence or grounds of decision. In some sense, therefore, an innovative element figures in any decision. Now the typical moral situation, says Dewey, arises not in Kantian fashion as an inner struggle between temptation and the moral law, for in that situation we already know what is right; the issue is the secondary one of getting ourselves to do what we know to be right. The really moral situation is one in which we do not know which path is the right one to follow; we are compelled to decide.[1] Dewey illustrates this with the perennial situation of the patriotic person who believes that his country is engaged in an unjust war and does not know whether to let patriotism lead him into supporting it or a sense of justice into opposing it. (He offered this many decades before the American experience of the Vietnam War.) In such situations, an innovative element is required in decision, one that will bring together and if possible reconcile the values involved, if not the actions called for at the moment, on opposing sides.

Dewey's emphasis on innovation may be rewardingly contrasted with Marxian theory. Marx's analysis of moral change and the appearance of innovation was largely *causal*; he looked for the *determinants* of shifting moral attitudes in changes in the economy and relations of production within the development of conflicts in a society. The question of human initiative in bringing about a needed change led, in Lenin's analysis, to the emphasis on a vanguard party that acquired sufficient consciousness about what was changing and what was needed. Dewey, of course, also recognizes causal factors that produce situations in which changes of moral attitude are desirable, but his attention is directed at the human response and the possibility of its pervasively innovative character. This leads him incidentally to an interesting linguistic shift. He finds the notion of *reason* as used in ethical theory too past oriented; it refers either to generalizations of the past now invoked for deduction or to lessons of past experience now presented as trustworthy inductions. But the moral situation is a moral situation because it is always a new situation. Hence a forward-looking concept is needed, and he becomes inclined—critics say almost to the point of tedium—to use the concept of *intelligence*. In any case, the intended difference is the emphasis on innovation. Partisans of Dewey's approach are likely to ask how it is that moral philosophy so long missed the significance of the innovative that had been there all the while.

In considering the role of innovation in applied ethics we may examine (1) institutional and cultural innovation, (2) ideational innovation, (3) problems in the acceptance of innovation, and (4) ethical theory as itself an innovation within morality.

INSTITUTIONAL AND CULTURAL INNOVATION

We do not always realize how many of our traditional institutions and procedures were profoundly innovative, though we may know they took a long time to grow. Take the procedure of legislation. One is startled to read in Aristotle's *Politics* of the city where, when a man proposed a change in the laws, he had a halter put around his neck and if his motion lost he was immediately hanged. The attitude to the laws as eternal and unchanging, common in earlier societies, contrasts wholly with our modern reliance on legislation as a motor force in social life. With the acceleration of social change, we know that new problems have to be faced even within a single generation.

In similar fashion, the United States Constitution was a consciously innovative experiment. The older alternatives between which it sought a middle way were absolute rule by one or the few, which people thought to be tyrannical over the majority, and rule by the majority, which people thought to be tyrannical over minorities. The innovative experiment was the separation of powers with checks and balances, an experiment still going on despite many stresses and strains.

Let us consider in greater detail the moral implications of a remarkable yet now familiar institutional innovation, that of *insurance*. Economic historians can doubtless find some predecessors of that institution in all sorts of maritime enterprises that involved patterns of sharing of risks. Its growth since Benjamin Franklin's time has been rapid and remarkable—at no time more than in the twentieth century. Consider, for example, as one of many areas which it has revolutionized, that of responsibility in law and morals for servants' or agents' actions. In law this was the problem of so-called vicarious liability. It seems on the face of it simple enough: you tell your agent or servant to do certain things for you, and if harm results to others in the process you are responsible, even for your agent's mistake. Suppose that your chauffeur pressed the accelerator instead of the brake and someone got hurt. Or suppose your chauffeur did exactly the opposite of what you ordered: you told him to take the car to the garage, but he went for a ride and an accident took place. Why should you now be responsible? Well, it might be said, your chauffeur does not have the money to pay up, but you have. In that case, the owners reply that they are being charged just because they have the deeper pockets; then you might as well look for the nearest millionaire and charge him, for the owner is no more at fault than that stranger. Now the argument generates (or at least crosses) an innovative distinction: of course you are not at *fault*, but that does not mean you are not *liable*; if there is any criminal responsibility, say if the chauffeur got drunk first, that is his. It is right for you to pay up, because in choosing to have a chauffeur you implicitly assumed the risks of the enterprise. You get the gains, you stand the losses. Such an argument with its fresh principle can spread rapidly. Employers are liable for the accidents to employees in their workshops. Manufacturers and merchants are liable for accidents that take place because of some hidden defect in the things they manufactured or sold. Soon, with the spread of industry, such questions are no longer ones of personal relations; they have become industrywide, as the increased use of machinery leads to an almost predictable number of accidents.

We need not prolong this historical glimpse. We all know that insurance as an innovative idea cut through many of these problems, that it changed the issues by spreading thin the losses over all those in a similar position. Thus automobile insurance, workers' compensation legislation, and the like become almost a mandated part of the enterprises involved. Insurance and the kindred forms of pensions take over other problems such as provision for old age, illness and hospital care, and all the familiar areas in which immediate interpersonal responsibilities that under given social conditions became difficult or impossible to fulfill over a wide range are replaced by innovative social policies. Insurance thus solves many an old moral problem.

New problems are, however, generated by the use of the instrument. They are of a different sort, initially more social in character. For example, as we have seen in Chapter Seven, the concept of *external costs* brought the costs of hitherto ignored harms of an industrial enterprise into the budget of the enterprise. The dangers and risks may sometimes be greater than an enterprise can tolerate: the costs of possible nuclear accidents are matters of conflict today, with owners pressing for limited and opponents for unlimited liability, sometimes as a way of ensuring greater caution in running an installation and avoiding further Chernobyls. (Would it be morally useful to require all members of nuclear commissions that determine policy and all managers of nuclear plants to live within five miles of the plant? After all, tradition has it that the captain goes down with his ship.) Again, questions of public policy have arisen over medical malpractice insurance, where the costs have sometimes led practitioners to abandon risky fields. In the end, serious moral problems of sharing responsibility are unavoidable. But there has been a social advance through the instrument of insurance and a moral advance in putting the basic issues on the social table, where analysis can deal with total costs, individual assumptions of effort and responsibility, and—what has often proved to be the most difficult of tasks—the removal of the area from the profit motive in whose working some people's losses become the source of other people's gains.

It would be enlightening to look through the history of morality from the point of view of discovery and innovation. Of course much of its history may be hidden from view. If Hume is correct in thinking that justice is meaningless in a world of intense scarcity and superfluous in one of full abundance (and serves an instrumental role in the intermediate states), then it must have been a discovery or an invention that moved humankind out of early edge-of-survival conditions. And certainly distributive justice had little meaning before the rise of agriculture and the relative scarcity of land. Of course we can operate with carefully analyzed contemporary meanings of a moral idea without reference to its history, but the historical knowledge will often show us relevant conditions underlying its utility. Even prominent virtues may have been innovations at one time. For example, it is commonplace in histories of morals to note that Christian *humility* as a virtue was something new in its time. Is it implausible to conjecture about a chemistry of the virtues in which they are split to yield different moral qualities and synthesized to yield still others, and all this under the demands of different conditions of life? Is this the story of *thrift* at one stage of capital accumulation becoming the vice of *hoarding* at another? Is it a virtue to be a Robin Hood in Sherwood Forest shooting the lord's game to give to the poor, but a vice to be a *guerrilla* (occasionally even labeled a *terrorist*) organizing the poor peasantry to take the land that has been kept under coercion by the few?

That there have been all sorts of cultural innovations having a moral character is evident from the cultural differences among peoples. Some are lost in the early history of humankind, such as division of labor between men and women. More local is a caste system, as in India, saturated with the idea of cleanliness, or the class system of Western medieval feudalism with its morality of fealty and loyalty. Innumerable ideals of correct or appropriate behavior have been tied to roles that have come and gone: the courtier, the gentleman, the warrior, the knight. Roles and professions, often with codes of ethics, have been discussed in a previous chapter; the proliferation of vocations can be read from dictionaries of occupational titles that list them in many thousands. Standardization and standardized expectations often add a moral tone to smoothing difficult periods of transition or situations of tension. Ceremonial rites of passage were an early ingenious innovation. Rules to moderate conflict or give it a settled form have a long history, from rules of warfare, the etiquette of dueling, down to the still invaluable ideal of civility in controversy. The development of moral elements in the conception of childhood is, on the human scale, a fairly recent innovation, and the responsibility for education of children replacing child labor a definite innovation.

Indeed, once we push our inquiry in these directions, much of the history of humankind becomes the story of innovation in which moral elements often play a constitutive role. A notable example is the recognition of money. While the early use of gold as a medium of exchange may be seen as simply a standardized commodity—one among many—serving a special function, the later use of paper money clearly has a fundamental element of *trust*. And long before that, business practice had relied on word being as good as bond, for otherwise it would have crumbled—and that before the use of legislative sanctions for contracts.

Perhaps such an analysis extends even to immediate personal attitudes to the life process. To plan ahead or take thought for the future presupposes a moderate stability in the ways of life, a stability that has not always existed and still does not for the impoverished and homeless who live from day to day. The wish for a future is of course older: before agriculture and the domestication of animals there were magical incantations to ensure growth and reproduction of species. The extent and scope of envisaged planning is thus novel, reflecting the growth of knowledge and technology. So, too, is the idea that we are always in the process of making ourselves, rather than are simply what we are born to be.

IDEATIONAL INNOVATION IN MORALITY

The suggestions offered about institutional innovation and its place in morality led us by degrees into morality itself and innovation in moral concepts and attitudes. Clearly underlying this approach is a historical orientation that looks for time and place of origin, conditions generating or supporting a moral idea, changes in the moral idea, or its relations under changed conditions. Much of this has been recognized in dealing with moral ideas when it impinges on the clarification or analysis of the ideas. For example, as we have seen, attempts to differentiate the idea of natural rights or human rights from natural law look for the period of actual shift (beginning about Ockham's time and becoming clear by Locke's) in order to see what considerations were at work. Few would doubt that some of the rights in the Bill of Rights are new. Again, during the inquiries at the time of the launching of the United Nations Declaration of Human Rights, various rights were proposed, for example, that of all to share in the cultural and material progress of their society, which would include such things as education and cultural opportunities, or their right to sue a government.

To suggest more explicitly what goes on in ideational innovation that concerns morality, let us take two examples. One is the idea of *contract* now long established, even entrenched. Although it is scarcely found in the Constitution, the right of contract was to become one of the basic objects of judicial protection, even against state welfare legislation. The other is that of *privacy*, now struggling for recognition and subject to attack in the controversies over the right to choose concerning abortion.

Basic to the idea of contract is that of promising. As we have seen in the preceding chapter, this can be construed as a practice, like an institution, which becomes regularized as an instrument of associated activity among humans, and so already contains obligation. No one compels a person to make a promise, just as no one compels a person to drive a car. But making a promise involves the obligation to carry it out (other things being equal), just as driving a car carries the obligation to have a license and to exercise care. Nietzsche, who had a strong historical sense, pointed out (scornful of the debate about why promises should be kept) that humans could not begin to think of making promises until there was enough regularity in their lives so that they could predict what they would be doing—until, as he put it, they had become "domesticated."

The idea of contract has been so influential in practice and in theory that we rarely think of the fact that it had an early history during which period it came into existence out of the coalescence of a number of special transactions.[2] We tend to think rather of the way in which it was used in the seventeenth century to declare the state in its foundations to be a matter of contract, the social contract; or of the subsequent history of law in which all sorts of human relations were interpreted, in an accentuated individualism, as being essentially a matter of contract. (The legal historian Frederick William Maitland describes contract as the greediest of legal categories.) Henry Sumner Maine saw the movement of progressive societies generally as from status to contract. Twentieth-century legal theory countered by showing how with the growth of an urban society the need for social regulation made inroads on individuals' settling most of their relations by mutual agreement.

The early history of contract (Roman) was one in which a general idea of a bond that would be enforceable was utilized for a variety of relations. There would be simple conveyance, in which an object was handed over and payment made; there could be lending and borrowing and repayment; there could be handing over something with payment remaining as debt (an incomplete conveyance); there came to be verbal exchanges with proper formalities; eventually there were promises with special conditions that made them enforceable. Contract was thus disengaging itself from special transactions that created obligations. But it still remained limited in scope: so-called consensual contracts were limited to sale, agency, partnership, letting, and hiring. A great step in the process of abstraction occurred when the idea of a "consideration" added to a promise became sufficient ground for enforcement. We need not pursue further historical detail here. The point is that contract as we now know it had a long process of maturation with different shadings and interpretations in different systems of law. In the end it became a highly general category that escaped even the classifications with which it was enmeshed on the way, and it remains a valuable idea in the maintenance of a large part of contemporary social life. Of course, it does not operate mechanically; distinctions have to be made and justified for different areas and different kinds of problems. For example, business contracts are more readily enforceable than promises in social life, and certain kinds of contracts are forbidden—for example, to enter into slavery or sell one's own organs.

Compare this with the idea of *privacy*, which is now in the making as a general category and is still subject to major controversy in its uses. The idea that one ought to have a room of one's own apparently had a religious origin in the notion that one ought to have a closet in which one could be alone with one's God. The idea that one's body is one's own and is not to be violated is apparently old, but there are serious violations of this idea in the practices of torture and in traditional marital rights of husbands to carnal relations with their wives. Both of these are condemned in the contemporary treatment of torture as the violation of a human right, and in the extension of the idea of rape to cover forcible intercourse by a husband with his wife. Though we now readily see both as violating the privacy of the subject, they can clearly be morally condemned under other rubrics: for example, both could be seen as *trespass*. *Privacy* specifically appeared in the law at one point as a right violated by the publication of one's letters, even though the physical possession and legal property of the letter as physical object was held by the person to whom it had been sent. The eavesdropper and the Peeping Tom can clearly be seen as violating privacy, as a moral matter and sometimes as a legal one. As privacy was a relatively uncharted concept, the law at least for a time was reticent about using it when other more special concepts were available. For example, it was clearly desirable to find against one who used a technological device to eavesdrop from outside on conversations within a person's home. For a time, this could be done on the grounds of trespassing because the device required a spike be put in a wall of the house. But the rubric lost its efficacy with more ingenious devices that operated from afar. The notion of privacy became increasingly attractive as a higher order right, systematizing different areas of special decision in favor of the individual—particularly in an age in which individualism was making increasing strides under the concepts of liberty and human rights. A critical point came in the affirmation of the right of privacy against the re-emergence of an old Connecticut law that had declared the use of contraceptives by a married couple to be illegal. The significant feature of this was not rejection of the law, for it violated what had by then become the general mores of the community and ran counter to the general acceptance of family planning, but in bringing it under the right of privacy. It was this decision that became a precedent for the more controversial case of *Roe v. Wade*, which on grounds of privacy marked out the scope of permissible abortion.

The significance of a moral idea like that of privacy lies in its general character, its theoretical role, and its possible scope. In this it is like the idea of contract rather than the specific right to bear arms of the Bill of Rights or the right not to have soldiers quartered in one's house except under specified conditions. In many respects such ideas function in morality as specific theories do in science: they guide inquiry, suggest subordinate laws or principles, allow a certain degree of experimentation in what will yield truth or open fresh fields of inquiry and experiment. As pointed out above, the general acceptance of the idea of contract does not imply that every promise made, on which others may rely and from the nonfulfillment of which they may suffer some losses, is thereby enforceable. So, too, the idea of a general right of privacy is not an "open sesame" to, say, the right of prostitution or the sale of one's organs. One can, however, see it being tried out in cases where a decision is felt to be morally or legally justified but does not fit easily under a traditional rubric. For example, there is a present tendency to use privacy as a basis for allowing life-support mechanisms to be disconnected from persons now brain-dead who have previously expressed the wish not to survive under such conditions. Safeguards may of course be provided to make sure of the facts and to prevent others from profiting through the legal death.[3]

Both the right of contract and the right of privacy may then be regarded as moral and legal rights that were once innovations. Both started with a core content, developed high generality, and opened the way to theoretical and practical development. Both require constant caution concerning scope and degree of application within the broader territory of a moral and a legal system. Current controversy about privacy represents to some degree a failure to see how such moral and legal innovation functions within these systems.

PROBLEMS IN THE ACCEPTANCE OF INNOVATION

The historical orientation underlying the idea of innovation may seem at first to be at variance with the dominant religious–metaphysical view that morality gives us eternal truths. There is no need here, however, for a metaphysical conflict over this issue, for what the historical orientation may treat as innovation, with its overtones of human construction and invention, can in the traditional approach be viewed as a process of discovery of what in a metaphysical sense was antecedent to discovery itself. Thus varying approaches may agree that, say, the idea of human rights is found first at a given place and time among humans, or that some specific right about which there may still be dispute has yet to be settled (whether "agreed on" or "discovered").

The more serious opposition to innovation comes rather from a deep regard for traditional ways and an unreadiness, whatever its social and psychological grounds, to depart from them. This is not a simple attitude but a very complex one with different components ranging, for example, from dogmatism to sober caution. We meet it over and over again in the history of thought, particularly at crossroads in political affairs. As for dogmatism, there has been a slow change from an idea of heresy to one of the free market of ideas. The underlying view of those who thought in terms of heresy is that one who sincerely departs from established dogma is worse than one whose departure is less firmly rooted. This attitude characterized not only the Spanish Inquisition with its burning of heretics, but it is found in Plato's late dialogue, the *Laws*, in which we are told that those who do not believe in the gods will be restrained and punished, and if they do not reform and cannot rid themselves of their beliefs, they will finally be put to death. As for the sheer opposition to change, it ranges from the veneration of the past to the fear (well expressed in Burke's attack on the French Revolution) that to make any place for alteration of the traditional is to open the door to wild winds of passion, so that even the most meaningless tradition should be kept as an object of veneration. Burke does allow for very gradual change as accommodation in a peaceful manner (perhaps in such a way as not to be noticed?). Interestingly enough, Marx also believes in the weight of the past, but sees it as the continuing interests of a dominant class when its vital economic contributions are over and it is clinging to power. Nevertheless, the growth of consciousness about the new is slow, and humankind is presented with a consciousness of problems only when their underlying conditions have matured to provide a possible solution. Liberal philosophies (such as Utilitarianism) have been most likely to cut the link with the past, to view it as a history of prejudice, and to trust the free play of the human intellect to shape the new.

If we move from the conflict of philosophical and political attitudes to the lessons of practical experience with the increasing changes wrought by an accelerating technology, we find the need to fuse the hope of innovation with the caution of tradition. The question becomes one of practical ethics when it is seen as an attitude to be fostered and encouraged in educational and cultural processes. The range of such total attitudes is revealed in cultural anthropology's study of how different cultures have been past-, present-, and future-oriented, and of how they have regarded nature in the process.[4] Our own national culture has been strongly future-oriented and has treated nature as an expendable means. It has gleefully welcomed every invention and hastened to apply it, though in the medical field it has learned to be wary of harmful side effects. The idea that some new machine actually works but should not be put to work because of possible unknown consequences and that we should move slowly has definitely been a minor note in the technological symphony, though it has been growing in our present age of nuclear energy and genetic engineering.[5]

Technological changes have not been the only area of innovation. An obviously fertile one has been political principles. Take, for example, the story of religious belief within a given state or nation. First we find a universal church that the state has to accept and can ignore only at its peril. Then we find national churches that those with other beliefs can ignore only at their peril. Then we find established churches with tolerance for other religious practices. Tolerance is here the innovative idea. Then we find the idea that there will be no establishment of religion, but religious freedom for any religious belief and practice. This is toleration fused with the idea of liberty. Finally there is the rejection of the idea of tolerance itself as a hang-over of repression. This is well recognized in Thomas Paine's view that there is a natural right to one's religious belief (which comes eventually to include nonreligious belief), so that for a state to grant religious freedom as a matter of tolerance is like, in Paine's transla-tion, "permitting" God to listen to prayers of Moslems and Jews as well as Christians. Obviously the history of religious belief has been full of innovations, though the process has been slow and painful.

The present time, with its rapid technological and social change, its fuller experience of dangers as well as opportunities, presents an appropriate setting for the development of a fresh and reasoned atti-tude to innovation, one that will appreciate it, assess its role, and be aware of required cautions. What we find sometimes, however, are periodic swings and reactions—such as from the traditional view of nature as there to be exploited by humans to a worshipful view of nature as untouchable and unalterable. Here, too, what seems at first a remote matter of sentiment or general attitude becomes a very prac-tical element in solving practical problems of pollution, of wildlife, species maintenance, use of land, procedures in agriculture, and so forth.

ETHICAL THEORY AS INNOVATION

When we study the history of philosophy, it is obvious that the philo-sophical exploration of moral beliefs that became ethical theory was itself an innovation. History of philosophy texts regularly point out that Socrates turned from the pre-Socratic investigation of cosmology and physical nature to the investigation of the human problem of how best to spend one's life. The history of ethics shows how successive aspects of morality were made the subject of inquiry, and how differ-ent ideas of the world, of man, and of method fused with moral beliefs in the shape of different ethical theories.

From the point of view of practical or applied ethics such recogni-tion—recalling that ethical theories provide applied ethics with the intellectual instruments for its work—invites us to look to the practical import of ethical theories themselves. And here the idea of the changing practical role of ethical theories under changing conditions becomes itself an important source of understanding.

Consider, for example, the central slogan of Bentham's Utilitarianism: the greatest happiness of the greatest number. Obviously, to appeal only to the greatest happiness would neglect the important matter of distribution; and to appeal to the greatest happiness of all, as Bentham was sometimes tempted, seemed too impractical. One could get along with the greatest happiness of the greatest number in such a class-dominated society as Bentham hints his society is. The slogan will do for the reform of institutions that Bentham had most at heart as central to morality. But what happens after the reform is over, as the movement toward democracy and majority rule becomes firmly entrenched? In the mid-nineteenth century we see J. S. Mill shift his theoretical attention from the majority to safeguarding minorities, most markedly in the almost absolute emphasis on freedom of thought and speech, as well as liberties of individual action. Herbert Spencer points out directly that a majority could vote democratically that a designated minority do all the dirty work of society. That minority even if given the vote would obviously find itself perennially outvoted. Hence the theoretical emphasis in ethics often shifts from general happiness and welfare to the rights of each and every individual. It is thus not surprising that, for example, in the United States of the second half of the twentieth century, the various liberation movements (of blacks, women, persons with handicaps, etc.) invoked a rights-based ethical theory; at the time, the majority was being told in election pronouncements, "You never had it so good," which was for the majority economically true, even while the minorities lacked basic liberties.

Such an understanding of the practical import of an ethical theory at a given time is clearly as necessary in dealing with a practical problem as knowing what complicated construction machinery can be set up on the terrain where construction will take place. Take, for example, the simple principle that every young person who has shown the capability and desire for higher education ought to be given an opportunity to achieve it. If accepted in New York State or in California, this means a system of colleges (universities, state colleges, and community colleges) that come within the reach of the population generally. If the principle is accepted in a Third World country just beginning to establish a public system of elementary schools, it may mean diverting money to the higher education of children of the upper classes of that society. Both are socially useful—both greater elementary general education and (over the short run) a more rapidly developed elite to introduce technological and social changes that modernization may require. But in this Third World country, the decision means a choice of the direction of social development, which is not what the decision entails in the wealthier states of the United States.

We may note, finally, that even a highly general ethical theory is subject to such analysis. Take, for example, the theory of *ethical relativism*. At the beginning of the 1930s, when it seemed to be a lesson of anthropological ideas of cultural relativism,[6] its practical import was a plea for tolerance of different life patterns—that the expanding Western world not ride roughshod over different value patterns in what later was to be called the Third World, or for that matter, of minorities in the first world, such as Native Americans in the United States. However, with the emergence of Nazism as a value pattern in Germany, the practical question became the limits of tolerance. The meaning of ethical relativism edged over into the arbitrary establishment by a group of people of a morality with no basis for transcultural or transgroup criticism. At present, with relations of economy and communication having long transcended national lines, emphasis has begun to fall on developing a global ethical outlook and embracing within it the mutual respect of peoples. At the same time, the theory of ethical relativism has shifted largely from groups to individuals, under the impact of the enhanced individualism of contemporary culture. Hence, the aspect of autonomous power to determine the basics of one's moral outlook is what seems most to threaten the sense of community. Ethical relativism seems almost to verge into an absolutism of the individual! With such varied practical import, it is not surprising that the theory of ethical relativism has either fallen into neglect, been used as a term of abuse, or been given ever-fresh ingenious constructions.

Eleven

The Decision Factor
and Its Dimensions

At long last, we reach the moment of decision. We have investigated the problem facing us, canvassed alternative solutions and possibilities, consulted advisors, in imagination considered consequences of various courses of action, calculated impact on ourselves and on others—taking care to count long- as well as short-range consequences and to assess the impact on character, sense of self-esteem, and integrity, as well as the more mundane consequences for career, health, security—and a decision beckons. It can no longer be put off. It is time to decide one way or the other, to make a commitment, to act. The stakes, we think, are momentous, and we remain conflicted, undecided, still weighing the choices. But we gather ourselves, summon up the will to decide, struggle, slide back, re-exert our will, and . . . . there, it's done. The decision has been made. It's over. It's done. What a relief. Now, to implement it.

It would be absurd to suggest the above as a picture of how decision relates to action. Even so, there are moral situations in which something like the above takes place. Some of the greatest works of Western literature offer a stage for such decisions, *Antigone*, for example, *Iphigenia in Aulis*, or *Billy Budd*. Notably, it is the stuff of great tragedies—we might call it the "Antigone-picture" of decision. But while we do not deny the psychological truth of such stories, the picture of decision underlying them has exerted an influence in ethics quite out of proportion to the representativeness of such occasions. Perhaps here ethics bears the mark of its origin in ancient Athens where the tragedy of the human condition was an endlessly fascinating topic of exploration and appreciation of the tragic was taken as a supremely human trait. Later philosophers found speculation about such situations no less seductive.

The temptation to think of decision along the lines of the Antigone-picture is especially acute in ethics. Indeed, for many, ethics is thought of as *the* subject that deals with such situations. The influence of the picture is due probably not so much to a sense that decision making in general is like this, as to a sense that it represents decision in its most complete form. Mundane decision making differs from the Antigone-picture in having elements missing. Choosing apples in the supermarket lacks momentous stakes; choosing a car in the showroom lacks the element of conflict; selecting a treatment (for a physician) lacks a threat to integrity or character. Indeed, it might be thought that it is by moving ordinary decision-situations toward the Antigone-picture that we transform the case into one of moral dimensions. Thus, add momentous stakes to the buying of apples—one is poisoned—and the morality of choosing comes into play. Add to the choice of car the fact that its cost requires forgoing paying for your child's education, and it becomes a moral matter. Add to the physician's choice of treatment the element of cost, with different treatments for the poor and the wealthy, and the choice takes on moral dimensions.

It is worth distinguishing the features that accompany the Antigone-picture in order to consider the degree to which it presents a distorted view of decision. First, decision occurs at a particular moment; we ought to be able to identify when a decision was made. Second, decisions are thought of primarily as acts of individual persons. Third, deciding is a solitary activity (at least of psychological solitude). Fourth, deciding is self-conscious—the person deciding knows that a decision is being made, and then that it is made. Fifth, decisions are accompanied by feelings of conflict—sometimes conflict over what to do and sometimes conflict of whether to do it.[1] Sixth, decision is a completion or termination of a process of deliberation. All the other components of deliberation set the stage for decision, furnishing it, so to speak, with materials—principles and rules, facts and methods, contexts, and so on. Seventh, decision transforms the situation. As a result of decision, the problem to be solved becomes redefined. (An extreme version of this is the thought that an addict who decides to abstain is no longer an addict—the decision by itself is transformative.) Eighth, the agent, so to speak, of decision is something other than that which manages the other components of the process. Perhaps it is the intellect that deliberates and it is the will that is invoked by decision. Or it may be one aspect of the intellect that deliberates and another aspect that decides. In any case, the locus of acting is different from deciding.

Historically the feature that has generated most philosophical controversy has been the last. The idea is that decision involves a kind of withdrawal on the part of the agent, like a judge withdrawing to chambers where the verdict is fashioned. The mystery of what transpires during this withdrawal, when deliberation merges into or passes over into action, has captivated philosophers and led to many endeavors to fill in the gap. Who or what is withdrawing? For many philosophers, the will, as a faculty distinct from intellect, served as the agent of decision. Decision is then thought of in terms of a relationship between intellect and will, and good decision making becomes a matter of conforming will to intellect. The exemplar of moral failure becomes a defect of will and moral education becomes training of the will, that is, "strengthening" the will.[2] For an Augustine, decision involves a struggle between intellect and appetite or passion: when decision goes awry, it is because of a countersurge of passion that sweeps away reason. All participants in the voluntarist–intellectualist controversy, which ran through the Middle Ages up to the seventeenth century, accepted the structuring of decision as a relationship between intellect and will, the disagreement being over which had the dominant role. Metaphysical voluntarism, in the vein of Nietzsche or Schopenhauer, sees decision as blind or unqualified Will. Even when the notion of a will has been given up, the basic structuring of the problem continues to echo in later philosophers. For Hume, for example, only the passions incline to action, and so he worries about how to bring reason to bear on action. For Sartre, decision is pure, unadulterated commitment unguided by reason.

Here we mean to suggest that it matters what we think of as our exemplar of decision. If we see it as in the Antigone-picture, we expect that it should be characterized by struggle and conflict. In the Antigone case, the conflict is over what is the right thing to do, a conflict between one right and another, with each side weighing heavily in the case. But it is easy to discover struggle even where the right is clear-cut and to build the experience of conflict into a formidable metaphysical theory. If you see conflict as an element in the fullest kind of moral decision, and then construe that conflict as obtaining between intellect and will, then it is in those terms that you think when considering how to improve decision making. Weakness of will may seem plausible in the case of a person "giving in to" sexual temptation against her or his better judgment (or is it weakness of intellect?). It is less plausible for a parent's hesitation to discipline a child, and less again for procrastination, and not at all for a person's unwillingness to travel by airplane, and yet all of these might be described as behavior against one's better judgment.

Decision making is, however, the most ordinary of human activities. We make decisions daily and hourly about the most mundane of matters as well as the most sublime, we make them collectively as well as individually, we make decisions sober and drunk, in merriment as well as in anguish. Not a single element of the Antigone-picture can be said to characterize every decision. Not every decision terminates deliberation, nor is every decision preceded by deliberation. The judicial decision has many aspects of the Antigone-picture, but in this case there is an element of authority or of authorization, the decision "of the court" being defined as that announced by the court in a particular form and forum. In these cases it makes sense to ask when the decision was made, as in asking when the Supreme Court decided women had the right to choose abortion. Against this, when tracing the course of a decision in policymaking bodies, such as when a political scientist inquires how, say, decisions were made in the Cuban missile crisis, there may not appear to be any one obvious point at which a decision was made, although in the whole story one can find turning points (e.g., the decision of President Kennedy when faced with two messages from the Soviet Union, one conciliatory and one belligerent, to ignore the belligerent communication and respond as if it had not been received). Sometimes the decision is identified only in retrospect when people come to realize that one particular action decided the issue, although the participants were unaware of its implications at the time.

For some philosophers decision is the cauldron of selfhood, and indeed there are decisions that may turn an agent's character in one direction or another forever. There can be moments that are turning points in people's lives. But these are distinctive and uncommon and that it is so is not a feature of decision itself. Out of decisions selfhood may be forged, but not necessarily one decision (as Aristotle said, one swallow does not a summer make).

For a less dramatic, but more inclusive, view of decision we may take a lead from Hobbes. Unlike some of his contemporaries, he disregarded talk of a will, and compared decision to the overweighing of a balance after oscillation. When deliberating, we are pulled this way by appetites and that way by aversions, and when a decision is made we can only say one of them has tipped the balance. The issue for him is how we can plan, how we can design projects on the basis of anticipated long-term consequences, how act in the present in the light of the anticipated future.

The tendency we are arguing against is that of isolating decision, either in the more traditional metaphysical form that assigns it to a separate will and so removes it from the domain of the intellect or in a form that sees decision in ethics as unique and special, so that it has nothing to learn from what we have learned about decision elsewhere.

DECISION THEORY

Most formal analyses of decision today begin with the agent faced with alternative courses of action. Each alternative has consequences or *outcomes* and each outcome has both a *probability* of occurrence and a *value* (or preference). The decision aims at the most probable achievement of maximum value. But how the problem further presents itself depends on the context of inquiry. If the perspective is that of the agent attempting to decide—perhaps the most common focus in moral theory—the theory of decision has the task of working out ways of combining belief in the probability of outcomes with the ordering of value. If, however, the perspective is that of scientific inquiry into and prediction of decisions, then it may prove useful to start with the decisions as data, work out an ordering, and move from this stage to an unscrambling of the value scale and the probability order.

Decision theory, in turn, divides decision types into three, defined by the nature of the information the decision maker has available: certainty, risk, and uncertainty. A decision is said to be "under risk" when the agent can assign probabilities to alternative outcomes (for example, the likelihood of drawing an ace in a card game or the probability of cure from a medical procedure); "under certainty," when the outcomes are known for certain (or close enough for practical purposes); and "under uncertainty" when the outcomes are so shrouded that we cannot assign them even a probability.[3] Common to all types of decision is the idea that decisions are to be made as a result of asking two questions: (1) "What will the outcome be if I decide this in such and such a way?" and (2) "How do I value (or prefer, or rank, or like) that outcome?" It is on the method of reaching an answer to the first question that the types differ. The judgment of how you regard the possible outcomes is made independently of the method of answering the first question. On the face of it, then, it appears that ethics, or how possible outcomes are valued, enters in as an independent component of decision making, when decisions involve ethical questions, and hence that decision-making theory relies on ethics and not the reverse. But as one might expect, the case is more complex than this.

Popular understandings of decision making probably see it almost exclusively as a matter of what the theory defines as decision under certainty. Arguably there are no cases of decisions under certainty: no matter how sure you are of the consequences, you could always be wrong, and so it might seem that the decision type, under certainty, is an empty category. Even so, it is a category worth exploring. There are surely cases where the possibility you are mistaken about the consequences is not an important consideration for you: it is *practically* certain. More important, absent worries about how right you are in predicting consequences, a useful emphasis is laid by methods of decision making under certainty on making sure you have surveyed all the possible consequences. Further, these methods also stress how to deal with answers to the second question above—how you value the consequences you foresee.

The best known of all decision methods is simply to list pros and cons, the advantages and disadvantages of doing something or not. Richard Nixon famously had a yellow legal pad on which he listed pros and cons of policies.[4] Although easy to do, this method makes it difficult to compare the options. Obviously, you cannot choose one over the other by simply counting the number of entries. Several reasons on one side may weigh less than one on the other side. Benjamin Franklin devised an ingenious method, now called the "elimination of trade-offs," by which to display differences of weight on either side.[5] What is interesting about Franklin's method is that he succeeds in making what is essentially a quantitative judgment by qualitative methods. But his method works best when the decision is formulated as something either to do or not to do (e.g., to marry or not to marry, to buy this car or not to buy this car).

A further more complicated set of methods, called "sum-of-the-ratings" methods, requires that the criteria used to judge the alternatives be made explicit, and each alternative be rated under each criterion. These methods differ among themselves in how the alternatives are to be rated. For example, in deciding whether to accept a job offer from three cities, you might list as criteria such things as quality of schools, quality of environment, cost of living, potential for career advancement, and so on, and rate each city on that criterion. Methods differ in how the rating is done. You might just give each city a plus, zero, or minus, or a number on a scale from 1 to 100. What these methods will not reveal is that you might value one criterion more highly than another. For example, you might regard quality of schools as more important than quality of environment, but sum-of-the-ratings methods disguise this. A city that rates 7 on the less important criterion counts more than a city that rates 4 on a more important criterion. Obviously the next step is to rank the criteria themselves, which leads to a set of methods called "additive weighting" methods. Thus, if taxes are less important to you than housing, you would assign a greater weight to the latter, and then multiply the ranking of each city by the weight of the criterion. This type of method is the most complex of the decision under certainty methods.

To the extent that these methods are helpful to decision making, it is by forcing the decision maker to make explicit the grounds of the decision. As the methods progress in complexity, the grounds themselves become more explicit. But the methods are neutral with respect to the rankings made by actual individuals; that is, it is whatever the preferences of the individual happen to be that are entered in the calculation. There is no provision for correction or feedback, at least for individual decision.

In surveying the methods, however, an interesting dimension of decision making is suggested. The differing complexities of the methods lead to the observation that choosing a method for making a decision is itself a matter of choice and can carry a cost. A certain economy of method seems a rational requirement—the complexity of the method chosen should be appropriate to the importance of the decision to be made. It would be absurd to use an additive weighting method to decide when to go to sleep and equally bizarre to use a pro-and-con method to decide a nuclear first strike.

Based upon this insight, some decision theorists have devised methods explicitly intended not to be optimizing, that is, not intended to give the "best possible outcome" to a problem. On some issues, the argument goes, we do not need the best outcome and to use a technique likely to give us that is itself unwarranted. On many occasions it is sufficient to get a satisfactory outcome. The "lexicographic" method is an example of a nonoptimizing method.[6] Here you take the *most important* criterion and apply it to the alternatives. If one of the alternatives is clearly superior to the others on that criterion, then choose that alternative. If not, apply the next most important criterion to the alternatives that were tied for first on the first criterion. If there is one that is clearly superior on that criterion, choose it. If not, then take the alternatives that now have survived the first and second round and apply the third criterion to them, and so on until you find a criterion on which one of the alternatives is clearly superior to the others. (This works only when there is a clear ranking among the criteria, and when the most important is so important to you that you are willing to take an alternative that satisfies it alone.) Another example is Herbert Simon's method of "satisficing." Here you choose the *first satisfactory* alternative. You identify the *minimal value* you are willing to accept for the criteria and then choose the first option that meets the minimal value. For example, to buy apples in a supermarket, rather than taking the time to pick out the very best ones, you choose some minimal standard an acceptable apple must meet; then when you find one that meets this standard, you select it.

One way to think of the difference between "satisficing" and the lexicographic method is that in the lexicographic method you proceed by taking each criterion, starting with the most important, and examining all the alternatives by that criterion. So, even if you can get a decision in one "round," you must look at all the alternatives, but not all the criteria. By contrast, in satisficing, you try to avoid considering all the alternatives, but you must consider all the criteria.

The most important implication of this discussion of decisions under certainty is that it draws attention to the ethical dimension of deciding how to decide a question. For some domains of social enterprise, this is hardly a novel point. Societies are often evaluated on how they come to decisions of criminal guilt and the degree to which the procedures of deciding are protective of rights of the accused. But the point has a much more general application. How is it decided that an applicant to a homeless program is entitled to state assistance? How is it decided whether to build a nuclear energy plant? How is it decided to introduce a new drug to the marketplace?

In the discussion of decisions under certainty we have moved away somewhat from the basic model of the decision situation as pictured by modern decision theory, structured around alternatives and outcomes, values and probabilities. The model is that of a tree, with each branch representing one alternative action with its predicted outcome. And, in fact, the model fits actual decision-situations more or less well. For example, consider whether the traditional picture of judicial decision fits the model: We could say that the judge is facing alternative acts—to condemn or acquit, to decide for plaintiff or defendant; that these have different outcomes—to uphold the law or to subvert it; and that the judge's value system is set by his position so as to uphold the law. Not much work needs to be done on outcomes here, because the only consequences we are interested in are whether the law is upheld; at least formally the other consequences are not the judge's business unless the law lets him go into them. Similarly, the values question (how the various outcomes are valued) has little work to do, because it is set within apparently narrow limits. The chief job lies in the logical relation of the analyzed case and the interpretation of the law. Accordingly, the legal theorist might argue that the judicial decision should not be analyzed in the way contemporary decision theory goes about it. Not that the latter framework cannot be imposed upon it, but the theorist might question the point of doing so. Better to use a judicial framework of locating relevant issues, accurate description of particulars, and explication of relations of subsumption, or some other relation of fitting or cohering.

Again, if instead of the law, we looked at a situation in which there was a single goal sought, and no other value is at issue, the sole question would be one of means. If the selection among available means raised no other question of value, the predictive side of decision theory—what are the outcomes likely to be—would have all the work to do.

Again, in great moral decisions, what is at stake is either the violation of basic commitments or an ultimate choice between two whole kinds of life. If the choice is properly formulated, then prediction issues seem to be either settled or irrelevant.

These considerations make it clear that the decision-situation can be set up in different ways and in fact has been in traditional theoretical frameworks. The way of contemporary decision theory is more general than the others, since it can show them to be special cases under different material assumptions. Decisions can be complex along the factual lines that require prediction of consequences and

THE DECISION FACTOR AND ITS DIMENSIONS 233

along value lines that require varied specification of criteria. The conditions of field complexity and field instability hold to a high degree.

It is when we turn to decisions "under risk" that the full power of formal decision theory comes to light. Discussions of decision making under certainty as they appear in current literature would be quite understandable to an Aristotle or a Plato, although they might find the terms of the discussion puzzling. This is not true of discussion of decisions under risk, which involves the quite modern application of the notion of probability. In the ancient philosophies of Plato and Aristotle, what did not happen necessarily or with universality would be scarcely knowable. Aristotle remarks in the *Metaphysics* that there is no science of the accidental.

Now the domain of human decision is, as Aristotle also recognized, not the universally necessary, about which we can do nothing, but the changeable about which we can deliberate. So it is precisely in the area of action that the accidental flourishes. This means that the ancients did not expect knowledge in the area of human affairs, only practical beliefs, maxims, knacks, and skills without conscious articulation, or habits operating without cognitive formulation.

Statistics and applied probability theory came to be seen as the study of the properties of things in groups. Concepts were developed for representing groups, and techniques for sampling and rules for credible inference from properties of the sample to the whole. Most of this is commonplace in contemporary thought. So is the revolution in our attitude toward knowledge—the realization that in application to the world our concepts have an area of imprecision, that our assertions about the world have at best incomplete evidence, and that an unavoidable "fallibilism" (in Peirce's sense) is the best we can hope for. Yet this outlook, although it appears a retreat from the older claims of necessary and universal knowledge, was nonetheless an advance in spirit. The statistically minded are an adventurous breed; there is no property of things or of humans, however qualitative on first appearance, that they will not venture to tackle. Give them an index or two for application, and they will stake out a class, and then are off to find the incidence of the property in numerical terms, accompanied by complex tests for level of confidence.

Decision theory has explored in detail how under risk decision may take place by combining information as to probabilities with the scale of values of the agent. The great achievement of decision theory has been to drive home the importance of asking both these questions. To invest in one enterprise over another simply because its possible pay-off is greater, without regard to the level of probability of gain, commits the error of ignoring the first question. (Thus, a lottery that costs ten dollars to enter and has a payoff of one million dollars with a minuscule probability is not a "better bet" than one with a payoff of one hundred dollars with a probability of .3.) This is a common error, as people often choose the outcome they most prefer without regard to the likelihood of its occurring. (In the arguments over abortion, one position argues that even if abortion were legally banned, the probability of its elimination is slight, and hence the payoff sought by the opponents of abortion is unlikely to occur.) The corresponding error of deciding on the basis of probability alone is less frequent, but remains an error.

The aim is to present an evaluative ordering of possible outcomes on a single scale. The ideal of a single scale on which quantitative distinctions of value can be made is, of course, an ambitious one. Bentham's felicific calculus is the notable historical illustration. He hoped for cardinal measurability of pleasure. That is, one would take each pleasure or pain and measure it, assigning a number to its intensity, duration, certainty or uncertainty, propinquity or remoteness, fecundity, and purity, then multiply the readings and add up for the total of pleasure or pains involved. His criteria clearly include the value and the probability aspects. The value magnitude is measured in intensity and duration, the probability in certainty or uncertainty. It is not an easy matter to decide whether the others can be wholly parceled out between the two aspects. Remoteness may be combining elements of risk with opportunities of anticipatory savoring or impatient waiting. In any case, the end result would be a number representing the value of the act, where value meant surplus of pleasure over pain.

The "trick" to "solving" decisions under risk is to find a way to combine probability and desirability—yielding the "expected desirability" or "expected utility." The solution follows from the mode of computing mathematical expectation, or the actuarial value of a gamble, yielding a formula of expected value.[7] The formula is used to pick out that decision whose expected value is highest.

The strategy of maximizing expected desirability is equivalent to acting in each decision on the policy that if continued will in the *long run* maximize gains over losses. It is a logico-mathematical parallel of the old injunction to choose under the guide of eternity—or Miguel de Unamuno's injunction to act so that if there is no immortality, people will say, thinking of you, it is a shame that there is not. A problem arises from the fact that the predictive system operates best to guide decision where the decision is about groups and long-range consequences, based upon statistical constancies that characterize many phases of human activity. More difficult questions arise when the prediction is to be made about an individual.[8]

A more serious problem reflecting matters of ethical theory is raised by the theory's separation of elements into the independent elements of outcome and value. This sounds like our old friend, the separation of fact and value rearing its head once again. There are predictive elements on the value side, especially where the utility of an alternative outcome lies in its means-value, where the probability of its bringing about the intended end would be involved. In the utilitarian theory we have to distinguish the probability of the contemplated act having the predicted outcome from the probability of the outcome bringing happiness. Similarly, beliefs (that is, the predictions we make of likely outcomes) are in part determined by our values; these enter into what sources we trust, the limits of the confidence we bestow, and the demands we make in our research. Values are in part determined by our beliefs about the objects we value. This does not invalidate the theory, but it does draw attention to the relative character of the categories by which decision theory operates.[9]

The third type of decision-situation is that "under uncertainty." Here you know what the outcomes might be, but you are unable to assign any definite probabilities to them. You do not know how likely the outcomes are. The lesson of the risk discussion still applies—it is an error to ignore the possibility that what you most prefer will not occur—and so the problem is how to incorporate in your decision the possible outcomes you envisage. Here decision theory proposes a number of strategies, turning on attitude to risk. The "maxi–min" strategy is a conservative or pessimistic one: you assume that for any decision you make, the worst outcome will occur (the "minimum"), and so you choose that option whose worst outcome is the best (the "maximum" of the "minima"). The "maxi–max" strategy is an optimistic one: you assume that for any decision the best outcome will follow (the "maximum"), and so you choose that decision whose best outcome is the best of all outcomes (the "maximum" of the "maxima"). For those who refuse to identify themselves as either optimists or pessimists, there is the "Hurwicz strategy," that involves placing yourself somewhere on a continuum of pessimism to optimism (say, you might be .7 optimistic, on a scale of 0 to 1).[10] There is also the "regrettist" strategy, in which you ask yourself how much regret you would feel were you to choose an option and have the outcome not be the best possible for that option; you then choose that option whose worst outcome yields the least regret.[11]

The above deals with risk in the technical usage of the term as it appears in decision theory. In the more ordinary sense of the term, there is risk in almost every phase of decision. The information taken for granted as fact may be mistaken, the rules invoked may be too narrow or more pertinent ones overlooked, the context may be too restricted or too diffuse, the jurisdiction may be erroneous. There are of course risks in all decisions, as there are in all knowledge. Unlike our legal system, there is no highest court to which we may submit our decisions for final review. They enter the stream of our subsequent experience, which they help fashion. Perhaps we may think of regret or satisfaction as comparable to their acceptance for review by a higher court; but any actual review is our own in subsequent learning and experience—and decision.

FURTHER DIMENSIONS

Beyond the treatment of decision in decision theory, there are some further dimensions of decision that are worth considering as they affect how we understand the process. We consider range, agency, and moral attitudes to decision.

Range of Decision

In facing a particular problem of applied ethics, an inevitable issue is whether decision is to be *long-range* or *short-range*. This is well illustrated in comparative business policies. It is said that Japanese corporations take the long-range view in their business decisions, making provision for research and investment in order to develop the field in which they are operating. American corporate executives are said to take the short-range view, doing what will yield the greatest quarterly profit, on which in turn the value of their shares may depend. Doubtless these are not isolated features of decision, but depend on numerous factors, such as degree of reliance on state help if necessary, degree of monopoly or competition in the field, attitudes of corporate community or individual profit seeking in executives, and so on. Another area in which the choice is between short-range and long-range decision is personal choice in education, where often the choice is between different kinds of lives.

In some domains we are learning that the difference between short- and long-range considerations has vital and serious effects. This is obvious in ecological problems. For example, it seems an easy matter to dispose of a relatively small load of garbage or the ash of treated garbage or the remains of polluting chemicals in so large a body of water as the ocean. But we have learned that the outcome may be the destruction of a fishing industry or the ruin of ocean beaches.

We cannot of course always choose the long-range approach. The pleasures of youth cannot all be indefinitely postponed for the greater gains of age. It is a mark of prudence to apportion the selection of range. But there are occasions in which the selection of the one leaves us in moral debt to the other that has been declined. For example, war veterans, precisely because they have been compelled to kill for what they regarded as a good and necessary cause, and were not able to pursue the long-range path of peace,[12] may feel a special sort of moral obligation afterward to engage in long-range action for peace.

Anthropologists, as we have noted earlier, have studied the difference in large-scale cultural attitudes to time: some traditional societies are oriented to the past, others to the present, and some to the future. These become practical issues of ethics in struggles over limited resources. American short-range attitudes with respect to oil consumption in driving automobiles, for example, claims partial justification in the optimistic expectation that technological ingenuity will find some replacement for oil when it runs out. The general form of the question of long-range versus short-range—for it has become a general moral question—is what we owe to future generations. So, far from being a purely theoretical question, it enters into the moral critique of many of our habits of life.

Agency, or Where the Buck Stops

Agency is the matter of who is to decide what kind of question. Any morality has some assumptions about agency. For example, the common remark in giving advice, "It's your decision," clearly marks the purely advisory character of what we suggest, and the responsibility of decision on your part. Sometimes it is amplified into, "It's your life." In public matters this often feeds into questions of responsibility, as in, "The buck stops here."

Moral tangles are avoided by clarity about agency. But there are many different patterns of agency, and the more complex problems of agency merge with the whole domain of systems of governance. In the first place, groups may be the deciding agents, as well as individuals, and within a group making a decision, there may be also different patterns of decision—for example, partition by role or skill, or a ranking of authority, and so forth. Systems of government may be viewed as patterns of agency. How complex these may be can be seen in the recent history of questions of the relation of the executive and the legislative branches of American government, particularly who is to be the agent of decision for foreign policy. The situation becomes even more complicated when the underlying theory is the constitutional one of checks and balances.

Where the subject matter of decision affects the life of members of a group, the obverse of agency is, of course, obedience. In the individual who decides for himself or herself, the obedience points to traditional issues of self-control (or lack of it, as in *akrasia*, or "weakness of will"). In cases where one decides and another obeys, the obedience has itself the character of a separate decision.

Patterns of agency are themselves to be evaluated. For example, democracy can be face-to-face, representative, or participatory. Decision about the type desirable in a given society is in effect a decision about type of agency.

Moral Attitudes to Decision

Since a decision is made among alternatives, and each proposed course embodies some values, there would appear to be some values rejected in every decision. What is to be the moral attitude to those rejections as well as to the acceptance of the successful values?

The moral attitude will depend in the first place on what happened in the decision itself. If it was a *compromise*, for example, then some part of the opposing values have been given satisfaction. The agent may feel a certain equanimity of success, unless the notion of compromise is taken to carry a sense of failure.[13] On the other hand, one set of values may have been given full scope, while another is rejected though admittedly still valuable. What here is the desirable attitude? Should the loser drop out of consideration or be subject to a special attitude on the part of the agent? The ancient Stoics undoubtedly would remind us that there is an element of sacrifice in all we do, and the appropriate moral attitude to that is resignation. Nicolai Hartmann in his *Ethics* argues for a stronger attitude. We have violated a value even though we could not help doing it and would do the same thing again. But violation of value demands a recognition of guilt, and so he develops the concept of *unavoidable guilt*. Even more, he argues that it is a necessary ingredient in the development of a self and rejects the view that we can in a religious approach be relieved of it. The self grows by bearing guilt in a realistic realization of life's situations.

Other moral attitudes are relevant to situations in which one person's decision affects another's situation adversely. This is the kind of context in which, in appropriate cases, *forgiveness* has its place. There are also situations in which even a virtuous action of ours may mean hurt for others. For example, a pacifist may be ready to accept aggression against himself or herself, but the decision may also mean allowing aggression against others that one was in a position to prevent.

Many of the issues of moral attitude become particularly pertinent to large-scale problems and may even share in the determination of decision itself. The contemporary problem of nuclear war and that of overpopulation have raised such issues. Writers on nuclear deterrence have raised not only such issues as the cost in radiation and the risk in testing to develop deterrent missiles, but also the moral point of whether it is wrong to threaten to retaliate for an attack when one knows that the devastation of the first strike and the dangers of the retaliation to life at large will make it unlikely that one would in fact retaliate. In some cases one may be led to wonder whether there is not also a moral issue about asking moral questions. For example, during the 1950s when the threat of nuclear war was strongly felt in the first surges of nuclear discovery, the question was raised whether a person taking refuge in a shelter had the moral right to shoot another who was affected by radiation and was attempting to take refuge there. One could not help feeling that morality would be better served by devoting moral energies to advancing peace rather than to marginal issues in extremis.

It is worth repeating that the importance of moral decision in the contemporary world stems from key features of modernity. The advances of knowledge and of technology have opened up vastly greater opportunities for human life, but they bring numerous unknowns that have to be mastered in the process of use. Small certainties have given way to large indeterminacies, but the ability to advance among them has been some compensation. If an element of risk and even of adventure has been added to moral decision, it is not only because we are often dealing with what is new. There is equal risk and equal adventure in staying with old patterns under new conditions. (In some cases, the revolutionary proposal may be to keep on doing what we have been doing.) If many matters that were formerly taken for granted are now subject to moral inquiry, moral decision need not always be an isolated individual task. It can also be a cooperative fashioning or refashioning of practices and institutions. The development of applied ethics in all its aspects may be indicative of deeper moral powers than we have given ourselves credit for in the past. It is well to remember that the religious outlook of the Western world regarded despair as the greatest of the sins.

Twelve

Some Theoretical Conclusions, or How Practice Educates Theory

No matter what province of applied ethics we turn to—policy decision, professional ethics, or personal moral decision—the characteristic difference from ethical theory is the necessary attention to the special conditions of the circumstances of time and place where the application takes place. Ethical theory is inclined to put this aside, concerning itself with a general and universal picture, not a complex, changing one. Even when theory appeals to features of existence, as when it takes in assumptions about human nature or the character of the moral emotions, these tend to be cast as permanent, not variable. Hence we may conclude that the way in which applied ethics or practice educates theory is by teaching the relevance of theory to complexly different and changing conditions of existence. We have therefore first to explore and illustrate such lessons, then draw out what conclusions we may, tentative though they be, about the nature and function of ethical theory itself.

THE EFFECT OF COMPLEX AND CHANGING CONDITIONS

Perhaps the best way to approach this in brief compass is to take a traditional ethical theory and show how the theory is transformed at specific points, under different and changing conditions, especially as challenged by specific problems as they develop in varying socio-historical contexts. This is not a causal account nor a presentation of historical determinism of one sort or another, but the suggestion that theories sharpen themselves by response to conditions in order to perform the moral functions for which theory is pursued—that is, to clarify, render consistent, resolve puzzles for, guide, and the like. Let us take Utilitarianism as our theoretical example, for it has a sizable history from Bentham's time in the late eighteenth century to the latter part of our own century—but it also has its ups and downs.

Bentham's use of pleasure theory in ethics came in the last quarter of the eighteenth century when in England the Industrial Revolution had gathered strength. With a rapid population increase, and technical innovation for production, a this-worldly attitude toward humans controlling their lives rather than simply holding on to the ways of the past came more firmly on the scene. Pleasure theory had been used in the Enlightenment in France in the battles with the ruling religious morality that had humans steeped in sin and condemned to obedience to the ruling landed powers. In the more advanced and rising industrial atmosphere of England, we are not surprised to find pleasure theory having more substantial content, taking for granted its secular orientation, generating ethical instruments for criticism of the existing and traditional ways, and laying plans for reform of morality and law and social institutions. In Bentham's ethics, religion is simply religious belief operating as one of the sanctions.[1] Bentham is copiously critical of traditional ethical theories that prevent re-evaluation of institutions in terms of human happiness, of moral rules that do not submit themselves to utilitarian justification. He is critical of the landed-class orientation of the laws, of the encrusted ways that profit only the establishment. If he is not yet an outright advocate of democracy in politics and still rests his hopes on wise rulers, it is a shortcoming that Utilitarianism will soon overcome.

Two serious problems are evident in his attempts to construct an effective theory. One is the meaning of *pleasure* itself (or *happiness*, which he equates with pleasure); the other is the social goal that is expressed in terms of happiness. It is each of these fundamentals that requires solution, for they are directly related to changing conditions of the life of society.

The meaning of pleasure or happiness is critical because Bentham requires some system of measurement to determine the greatest happiness that is to act as a criterion for deciding moral and social questions. For a while he tries to assume that each individual knows when he or she is more pleased and can tell you so. Of course, if one had invented a "hedonometer," as one of the later economists speculated, one could take objective readings. In his *Theory of Legislation* Bentham is at times ready to assume that for practical purposes we can use money as a standard, on the assumption that he who has more wealth has more happiness. But effectively, the criterion for a person being pleased becomes increasingly how he or she votes or chooses. The course of economics in the nineteenth century eventually replaces the idea of what yields happiness with what satisfies preferences. It is assumed that the individual exercises preferences in different domains: by voting in politics, by buying in the market, by choosing in ordinary life. In this progression of the meaning of pleasure or happiness we see the growing strength of individualism as a value in decisions of social policy. Whatever may be the sociohistorical explanation of the growth of an intense individualism from the late eighteenth to the late twentieth century—which can be documented in all fields—this sociohistorical progression is integral to the meaning of happiness in Utilitarianism.

The meaning of the greatest happiness as a social good and the supreme criterion of Utilitarianism for judging social policy has comparable difficulties. Bentham appears to have toyed with several alternatives: the greatest happiness *simpliciter*, the greatest happiness of all, the greatest happiness of the greatest number. The simple greatest happiness as a total quantity ran obvious risks in its distribution. Some people might have or claim greater capacities for happiness (particularly the refined or upper classes or the educated classes) and so ask for a greater share in the instruments of happiness.[2] But Bentham held to the view that every person counts as one. The alternative slogan of the greatest happiness of all was of course most attractive, but highly impractical. Hence the one that emerged in Utilitarianism was the greatest happiness of the greatest number. It is to the career of this idea and the way it worked that we must attend in relation to changing conditions of life.

The combination of happiness as maximal individual preference and the greatest happiness of the greatest number (at least a majority vote) obviously had a strong democratic potential. Utilitarianism was thus on the side of the expansion of democracy and its benefits by its very theoretical formulations. But note what happens as democracy makes substantial gains. By the time that John Stuart Mill is writing, in the mid-nineteenth century and later, England has seen the Reform

Bill of 1832 extend the vote, Chartism has further extended the democratic process, and socialism has appeared on the intellectual scene. It was almost as if the setting for the greatest happiness of the greatest number would be achieved. In politics this meant the democratic rule of the majority. What we now find incorporated at the very heart of Utilitarianism is the protection of the minority. Mill's theory of *liberty* is an essential part of his utilitarian outlook, and it is overtly presented as a necessary principle for the protection of the minority. But it is not simply this, for it protects the individual as the source of, and gives him or her opportunity and encouragement for, initiative, which is itself the source of material and cultural progress, thereby adding to the greatest happiness. Herbert Spencer, who is a utilitarian with biological underpinnings, is even blunter: he notes that a majority could vote democratically to have a given minority do all the hard work of the society, with that minority itself having a vote on the question.

It is worth noting that Bentham laid little stress on liberty as a basic ideal of Utilitarianism. Somewhat appalled by the use of liberty slogans in the French Revolution, he himself analyzed liberties as part of the maintenance of security, which was the primary necessity for encouraging productivity in people. Although he favors encouraging equality, that is put as secondary to maintaining security of property.

For a large part of the twentieth century in America, a utilitarian type of philosophy was the dominant approach toward advancing social welfare. It may not be cast as happiness—perhaps more often as welfare or well-being—but the differences are minimal. Many states passed legislation regulating conditions of labor for women or working hours for labor generally. Although up to the 1930s much welfare legislation was found unconstitutional by the Supreme Court, it was not on utilitarian grounds but as contrary to rights of contract. In effect, it was a rights theory that played the conservative role, Utilitarianism a progressive role, particularly in all the New Deal welfare measures to counter the Great Depression. (In such a depression, the majority suffers, not just the minority.)

We noted earlier how after World War II a human rights ethic suddenly swept the field of moral and social theory, quite eclipsing Utilitarianism. This was surprising in America, for it seemed during the Great Society programs of the Johnson administration that the well-being of the majority was receiving careful attention. Was not Utilitarianism being made a reality when the party in power could truly say to the majority, using the economic tests for well-being or greatest happiness (though in less than elegant English), "You've never had it so good"? The answer to this paradox seems fairly evident: Utilitarianism in being geared to majorities had shown strength while the battle for majorities were being fought; it failed to sharpen its theoretical apparatus to help minorities once majorities won their battles. In short, the theory, in spite of Mill's efforts, had failed adequately to integrate the changed sociohistorical situation.

Attempts had been made to broaden Utilitarianism, but without remarkable success. One way had been to give a positive content as well as a negative content to the Millian liberties. Thus freedom of thought and expression was to mean social provision of educational opportunities to give thought scope and speech relevance. Economic freedom was to mean not only free enterprise, but social organization to provide a guarantee of a job. On the whole this kind of theoretical broadening was not welcomed in Utilitarianism, and so such views shifted over into the demand of rights. (In due course, the same kind of conflict emerged in rights theory, between the old property rights and the new welfare rights.) It is worth noting that older ethical theories felt the pressure of minorities also and had to deviate from simply majoritarian formulations. For example, John Rawls starts out with the assumption that all persons are entitled to an equal share, and a proposed inequality that will benefit people has to show that it will benefit the most disadvantaged.

The greatest happiness of the greatest number during this period became identified for the most part with *cost–benefit analysis*. And this often meant that the minority had to stand the cost while the majority had the benefit. Thus we have seen the claim that in the workplace risks should be tolerated if it would cost too much (i.e., raise the cost of the product or diminish the owner's profit to the point that the existence of the enterprise is endangered) to remove the risks. This need not always be so, of course. Sometimes a whole generation may get the benefits and subsequent generations pay the costs. On the assumption of population increase, this means that the minority gets the benefits while the majority later stands the cost. But for the most part, cost–benefit analysis has acquired a bad ethical name.

It should not be surprising then that in the liberation movements of minorities (blacks, women, persons with handicaps, etc.) Utilitarianism played no notable part.

We suggest that this brief historical survey shows that ethical theories contain variables that have to be filled in by reference to conditions of existence that are complex and changing, if the theories are to have effective meaning. It is possible to state a theory with a variable, but it should be indicated clearly as such, as something that needs to be filled in. Another possibility would be to attach a date to a theory, which we do indirectly when we speak of eighteenth-century Utilitarianism and twentieth-century Utilitarianism. But we have to take the dating seriously, with more than a historical reference to its propounders.

The altered meaning of a theory under such changes as we have been considering can be viewed as a sharpening—correction, refinement, or expansion—*under the lessons of moral experience*, an experience that comes in the varieties of application under fresh circumstances. Let us take a brief illustration, not from the same ethical theory under changing conditions, but from different ethical theories dealing with the same functional element in theory. Every ethical theory has some implicit model or interpretation for such expressions as, "This is good" or "This is wrong." (In Utilitarianism, it would be, "This is pleasant" and "This is not productive of the greatest happiness in the situation.") In the 1930s, the emotivist Charles L. Stevenson suggested as the interpretation of these expressions, respectively, "I approve of this; do so as well" and "I disapprove of this; do so as well." In short, an ethical utterance reported one's own approval or disapproval and attempted to persuade others to share the sentiment.[3] From this he drew the conclusion that morality was a matter of influence rather than of rational proof. To many people this seemed to be the situation of the struggle of ideologies at that time, that is, shortly before and at the very beginning of World War II.

A different interpretation was taken by Jean-Paul Sartre from his concern with the French Resistance to the Nazis during the war. He came to see ordinary life, with all its approvals and disapprovals, disguising the critical character of moral judgment. Life had to be stripped of its ordinary amenities to make clear the moral—not the search for happiness, nor the effort to get agreement on our approvals and disapprovals, but ultimate choice in a situation that compels it, a situation faced by Sartre's colleagues in the Resistance, often under torture. "Rather death than . . ." was the basic interpretation of something being wrong.[4]

Sartre's formulation strikes a deep moral chord. But how does it compare to subsequent moral experience? In guerrilla struggles in various countries, but more particularly in cases of terrorism, there have been instances of a readiness to sacrifice life almost promiscuously for causes that are sometimes good, sometimes mistaken, and sometimes bad. Such experience leaves us with the conclusion that the element of rationality in the person's decision cannot be wholly neglected. "Rather death than . . . " is therefore not an entirely adequate interpretation. The search for a better formulation still goes on.

Both by finding part of the meaning of a segment of an ethical theory in the changing conditions of the time and by learning from our continuing moral experience to correct some part of the theory, we see how the accumulation of experience in applied ethics can broaden our conception of ethical theory. Does it also change our view of its nature and function?

THE NATURE AND FUNCTION OF ETHICAL THEORIES

Earlier we posed two views of the relation of theory and practice or application. One had a choice of theory settled first, and saw the theory consequently as established on its own prior to application. The application had no effect on the theory. The second view saw the application as in some sense testing the theory, providing opportunity for lessons that would refine or amend it or else strengthen it. Theory and application were engaged in a process of mutual aid, each learning from the other and helping to refine and improve the other.

Between these two views of the relation of theory and practice, our study has shown ample cause for accepting the second and rejecting the first. No more need be said about this in our conclusion. But this has consequences for the comparison of ethical theories with one another and for the question of choice among them, which should be spelled out.

The usual comparison of ethical theories has been to theories of science. To accept one is to reject the others since they are so often posed as competitors with mutual argument and counterargument, often recriminatory. Yet there is another aspect of the scientific enterprise that may be equally relevant: the attempt to get an all-embracing theory that will learn the lesson of all the other competing theories that often rest on a selective use of a special range of evidence. In ethics, the subject is so complex that the hope for a unified theory may be much too premature. But there is something to be said for the attitude that looks upon them as geared to possibly different aspects of complex situations, that sees them as stressing and often exaggerating in their construction what is only a particular aspect. Indeed, at times, one is led to a comparison of different theories with different instruments, which would be usable for different purposes. For example, Utilitarianism in its Benthamite form was excellent for judging institutions, laws, and social practices, but as Mill recognized in his criticism of Bentham, it had little capacity to deal with individual moral decisions. As Hume observed that justice applied only in a time when resources were moderately available, Stoicism may not be helpful in cooperative large-scale projects in an era of abundance, but it may be just the ethical theory for an era of scarcity, trouble, and potential despair. Perhaps to ask for an overall commitment to one ethical theory at this point is less useful than to ask what light different theories throw on a moral problem as part of its analysis and to see the theories as offering us different handles or different tools for approaching it. Such an approach is not inconsistent with building up bit by bit basic agreement on different aspects of theory or looking for an eventual broader theoretical agreement. But it does involve engaging the arena of practice within this widening interactive process. And it involves constantly reminding ourselves that the function of ethical theory is to enlighten and guide moral practice, that is, to help us in facing our continuing problems.

Notes

INTRODUCTION

1. Plato's *Republic* covers the materials, but not systematically.

2. For more on this story, see Chapter Three below

CHAPTER ONE

1. Thalidomide was a sedative drug sold without prescription in Europe from 1957 to 1961, when it was discovered that its use by pregnant women produced skeletal defects in fetuses and it was found to be associated with a high incidence of babies born with shortened, malformed limbs (about ten thousand worldwide). Thalidomide was then withdrawn. By contrast, in the United States the Food and Drug Administration had delayed approval of the drug and prevented the tragedy here. As a result, the FDA enjoyed widespread public approval of efforts to institute stringent standards for the introduction of new drugs—at least until the onset of the AIDS crisis, when the length of time required to gain approval of new drugs came to be seen as excessive and bureaucratic, and controversial new "fast track" procedures were introduced.

2. "Unwelcome sexual advances, requests for sexual favors, and other verbal and physical conduct of a sexual nature constitute sexual harassment when (1) submission to such conduct is made either explicitly or implicitly a term or condition of an individual's employment, (2) submission to or rejection of such conduct by an individual is used as the basis for employment decisions affecting such individual, or (3) such conduct has the purpose or effect of unreasonably interfering with an individual's work performance or creating an intimidating, hostile, or offensive working environment" ("Guidelines on Discrimination on the Basis of Sex," Washington, D.C.: Equal Employment Opportunity Commission, November 10, 1980).

3. *Meritor Savings Bank v. Vinson*, 106 S. Ct. 2399 (1986).

4. In October 1991, the nation was transfixed by the spectacle of the Senate Judiciary Committee's attempts to grapple with the issue of sexual harassment. In the midst of its confirmation hearing on the nomination of Clarence Thomas to the Supreme Court, Anita Hill, who was at that point a law professor but who had previously worked under the supervision of Thomas in the federal government, alleged that in these previous positions Thomas had made inappropriate sexually explicit remarks to her. The difficulties in deciding who was telling the truth were aggravated by racial politics (Thomas being the second African American ever to be nominated to the Supreme Court), liberal versus conservative tensions, and allegations that a Senate committee populated entirely by white males could hardly deal fairly with sexual harassment. In the end, Thomas won the nomination, but the whole affair placed the issue of sexual harassment squarely on the nation's agenda.

5. A famous case had Colgate-Palmolive advertising a shaving cream as capable of shaving the sand from sandpaper, which the advertisement demonstrated. It turned out that the sandpaper shaved was in fact Plexiglas and that it would have had to soak in the cream for eighty minutes before it would work. The Supreme Court puzzled over whether the missing eighty minutes constituted "material deception," whether it mattered that it would be unusual for a consumer to go to the supermarket to buy Rapidshave, the offending cream, for the purpose of shaving sandpaper, and whether it is legitimate to use Plexiglas rather than sandpaper in the advertising on the grounds that the medium of television made Plexiglas look more like sandpaper to the viewer than sandpaper would. If, for an advertisement for whipped potatoes, the advertiser uses whipped cream instead, because whipped cream looks on TV more like potatoes would look to a person in the studio, is it then deceptive to use whipped cream? (See William Shaw and Vincent Barry, *Moral Issues in Business*, 4th ed. [Belmont, Calif.: Wadsworth, 1989], 417–419.)

6. Willowbrook State School was an institution for mentally retarded children in Staten Island, New York. In the 1950s, scientists at the institution engaged in a study of viral hepatitis, the object of which was to confirm the efficacy of gamma globulin as an immunizing agent. What drew the attention of critics to the study was that it involved, in one stage, actively exposing uninfected children to the virus, but the fact that the subjects were retarded children tended to concentrate the ensuing ethical debate on the question of how requirements of informed consent apply. For details, see Samuel Gorovitz et al., *Moral Problems in Medicine* (Englewood Cliffs, N.J.: Prentice-Hall, 1976), 123–142, and David J. Rothman and Sheila M. Rothman, *The Willowbrook Wars* (New York: Harper & Row, 1984), 260–267. Similar questions of consent, and from the same time period, were raised by the revelation that, as part of a study in cancer immunology, patients at the Jewish Chronic Disease Hospital in Brooklyn had been exposed to live cancer cells. This case led to protracted legal proceedings against the physicians responsible. For a convenient compilation of the legal documents, see Jay Katz, ed., *Experimentation with Human Beings* (New York: Russell Sage Foundation, 1972), 9–65.

7. The Tuskegee syphilis study was a forty-year study (from 1932 to 1973) of 431 poor black men from rural Alabama who were denied treatment for syphilis in an effort to learn more about the natural history of the disease, in spite of the fact that the efficacy of penicillin became known in the 1950s and, indeed, in the face of the widespread conviction in the medical community in the 1930s that arsenotherapy was an effective treatment. Particularly shocking was the racism evident in the justifications offered for the study. It was said that Alabama blacks would not themselves seek treatment for the disease, and therefore withholding of treatment made it a "natural history" study. In fact, participants in the study were under the impression they were being treated; further, the researchers intervened systematically to ensure that treatment would not be provided, even accidentally (to the extent of requesting draft exemptions for "subjects" lest they receive treatment from military doctors). Adding to the outrage, when the details of the study became public in the press in 1972, was the revelation that from 1932 the study had been reviewed and approved by various panels of "experts." (See U.S. Department of Health, Education and Welfare: Public Health Service, *Final Report of the Tuskegee Syphilis Study, Ad Hoc Advisory Panel* [Atlanta: Center for Disease Control, 1973], and Allan M. Brandt, "Racism and Research: The Case of the Tuskegee Syphilis Study," *Hastings Center Report* 8, 6 [December 1978]: 21–29.) Although the study was halted at that point, its social effects are still with us, in the form of abiding suspicions in the African American community of the "true purpose" of public health campaigns. Attempts to develop large-scale programs to deal with AIDS have encountered severe obstacles as a result of this suspicion.

8. In 1963, Stanley Milgram, a psychologist at Yale University, conducted a series of experiments on obedience. Inspired in part by Hannah Arendt's analysis of the trial of Adolf Eichmann in Israel—a person, she thought, who was not inherently evil but a bureaucrat "doing his job," and thereby illustrating, in her famous phrase, the "banality of evil" (*Eichmann in Jerusalem* [New York: Viking Press, 1963])— Milgram set out to investigate whether in an experimental situation subjects could be forced to harm another human being. He informed subjects, who had volunteered in response to an ad in the local newspaper, that they were participating in a "learning experiment": to test whether learning a list of words would be improved if the subjects were motivated by the fear of suffering an electric shock upon failure. The subject was to read out a list of words to the "learner" (who in fact was a confederate of Milgram's), and if the learner failed to identify them correctly, the subject was to pull a lever that resulted in an electric shock to the learner. The shocking was to be progressive, that is, each shock would be of a higher voltage than the previous one. In fact, of course, the lever was not connected to electricity and no shock was given, but the subjects did not know that. The question was how far the subject would go. The results were utterly unexpected:

> Before the experiments, I sought predictions about the outcome from various kinds of people—psychiatrists, college sophomores, middle-class adults, graduate students and faculty in the behavioral sciences. With remarkable similarity, they predicted that virtually all subjects would refuse to obey the experimenter. The psychiatrists, specifically, predicted that most subjects would not go beyond 150 volts when the victim makes his first explicit demand to be freed. They expected that only 4 percent would reach 300 volts, and that only a pathological fringe of about one in a thousand would administer the highest shock on the board.
>
> These predictions were unequivocally wrong. Of the forty subjects in the first experiment, twenty-five obeyed the orders of the experimenter to the end, punishing the victim until they reached the most potent shock available on the generator. After 450 volts were administered three times, the experimenter called a halt to the session. Many obedient subjects then heaved sighs of relief, mopped their brows, rubbed their fingers over their eyes, or nervously fumbled cigarettes. Others displayed only minimal signs of tension from beginning to

end." (Stanley Milgram, *Obedience to Authority* [New York: Harper & Row, 1974])

Reactions to publication of the study included charges that the study itself had been unethical, on the grounds that it involved deception of the subjects and possible psychological damage upon their realization that they had been so willing to harm another person. The result was to intensify the debate over ethical principles governing research.

9. See Irving Louis Horowitz, "The Life and Death of Project Camelot," *Transaction* 3 (November–December 1965): 3–7, 44–47. Project Camelot was a projected study of insurgency in Latin America, conceived by U.S. Army officers connected with the Army Research Office of the Department of Defense. Through 1964, social scientists in the United States and in Latin America were recruited to engage in research to "make it possible to predict and influence politically significant aspects of social change in the developing nations of the world." In June 1965, in the midst of the Dominican Republic crisis, details of the project became known in Chile. The project was interpreted there as an attempt by the United States to recruit social science for a program of political repression, an interpretation made plausible by the sponsorship of the Defense Department—and it was immediately stopped. The resulting furor occasioned extended debate among sociologists and anthropologists over issues such as the ethical propriety of military sponsorship, the effect of secrecy and national security concerns on research, and the responsibility of the scientist for the uses to which research is put.

10. The presidential campaign of 1987, which pitted George Bush against Michael Dukakis, was memorable particularly for a television ad alleging that Dukakis, while governor of Massachusetts, had allowed dangerous criminals to go free on parole. The prominent role given the case of Willie Horton, a black man, in the ad provoked charges that the underlying message of the ad was racist, and its use came to symbolize not only a widespread dissatisfaction with that campaign but dirty political advertising in general. Indeed, out of it came the notion of "Hortonizing": to Hortonize a political opponent means to attack by negative and sleazy ads. Interestingly, a word such as this reflects the continuation of ideological struggles by other means. Thus, only liberals (the object of attack in the original Willie Horton ad) are likely to use the word. Conservatives will avoid it, even if they believe they are the object of unfair attacks, for fear of admitting that the use of Willie Horton was racist. A later example is the verb arising from the passionate disagreements surrounding the nomination of Robert Bork to the Supreme Court in 1987. Bork, a conservative jurist, was denied confirmation by the Senate, on the grounds that his legal views were "out of the mainstream." Defenders of Robert Bork, believing he was treated unfairly in the hearings, continue the ideological battle by using the term "borking": to "bork" someone is to treat that person in the allegedly unfair way Bork was treated. In this case, conservatives are free to use the term, but liberals fear its use will admit unfairness to Bork and so avoid it. In the 1990s, the term "political correctness" has a similar ideological double-edge. It is a term invented by conservatives to impugn liberals' sensitivity to language reflective of racism or sexism or any other "ism" that "puts down" minority and traditionally disadvantaged groups. A liberal forced to use the term is compelled to place it in scare quotes. One wonders whether the future career of "politically correct" will parallel those famous instances where political terms first introduced as terms of abuse are adopted by the groups targeted (for example, "Whigs," "Tories," "Quakers," "Canucks").

11. The Club of Rome was a group of people worried, in the manner of Thomas Malthus, about the relation of growth in world population to the increasing scarcity of food. Two reports were issued in its name, the first being somewhat more pessimistic than the second: Donella H. Meadows, Dennis L. Meadows, et al., *The Limits of Growth: A Report to the Club of Rome's Projection on the Predicament of Mankind* (New York: Universe Books, 1972), and Mihajlo Mesarovic and Eduard Pestel, *Mankind at the Turning Point: The Second Report to the Club of Rome* (New York: Dutton, 1974). For further discussion on the issue, see Joseph Grunfeld, ed., *Growth in a Finite World* (Philadelphia: Franklin Institute Press, 1979), and George L. Lucas, Jr., and Thomas W. Ogletree, eds., *Lifeboat Ethics: The Moral Dilemmas of World Hunger* (New York: Harper & Row, 1976).

CHAPTER TWO

1. This is not how the distinction is consistently made in popular speech. Thus, we sometimes express disapproval of a person's conduct by speaking of her "ethics" —e.g., "Barbara's ethics leaves something to be desired." As a result of the recent explosion of codes of professional ethics, another way of making the distinction is becoming quite common, one in which *ethical* and *moral* both refer to conduct but in contrasting ways, whereby *ethical* means conformity to the relevant code and *moral* means conformity with general social norms.

2. See G. Wallace and A.D.M. Walker, *The Definition of Morality* (London: Methuen, 1970).

3. A particularly egregious example is an address by Dan Drew, founder of Drew Theological Seminary. He told an audience of businesspeople: "Sentiment is all right up in that part of the city where your home is. But downtown, no. Down there the dog that snaps the quickest gets the bone. Friendship is very nice for a Sunday afternoon when you're sitting around the dinner table with your relations, talking about the sermon that morning. But nine o'clock Monday morning, notions should be brushed aside like cobwebs from a machine. I never took any stock in a man who mixed up business with anything else. He can go into other things outside of business hours, but when he's in the office he ought not to have a relation to the world—and least of all a poor relation"; quoted in William H. Shaw and Vincent Barry, *Moral Issues in Business*, 4th ed. (Belmont, Calif.: Wadsworth, 1989), 20.

4. One illustration is how the Inuit use ridicule to drive a miscreant from the community—at night members of the community shout from home to home in the village, laughing at what the person did and exposing it to public shaming.

5. Darwin, however, believed that remorse differed from regret only as agony from pain; there was nothing earth-shaking about it.

6. Consider the case of *Franglass*, the French term for words in French use that are obviously of English origin (for example, *le soccer*). Curiously, some of these *Franglass* words have themselves a French root—that is, the English word was originally borrowed from the French—but now the French itself is archaic and the French use the *Franglass* form. (See *Times Literary Supplement*, February 5, 1993.)

7. Actually, the real meaning-magicians proved to be the mathematicians who spun out whole systems of meanings, leaving it to the philosophers to tell them what they were actually doing. (This provoked moral philosophers to all sorts of appeals to "rational self-evident truths" or moral intuitions.) Some mathematicians felt more like musical composers, creating a symphony, others like explorers in a world of mathematical truth, traversing possible worlds.

CHAPTER THREE

1. An alternative way to present ethical theories (see figure on following page) might be to profile the position each takes on four issues addressed by moral philosophers. Among these issues, perhaps most determinative are the views of *human nature*: whether it is fundamentally evil or good, or merely neutral or educable, and whether it assumes a world of isolated individuals or natural sociability. Clearly the task of morals will be different depending on which view one takes. In the one case, it may be how to limit aggression so as to make living together possible; whereas in the other, with humans taken to be affiliative, the task of morals would be to ensure a richer common life, with some scope for individual development.

A second issue or dimension concerns what *elite concepts* the moral theory employs. Generally, a choice is made for priority among the good, the right, and virtue. The choice of elite concept has consequences throughout the theory. Theories that take right as the elite concept tend to the legalistic, emphasizing rules, laws, and principles, while by contrast theories of the good and theories of virtue tend to de-emphasize rules and laws. Theories that choose virtue tend to emphasize responsibility and character formation, tend to be understanding of individual violations of the law, and see the character of the actor as central. Theories that take good as the elite concept tend to be more sympathetic to changing moralities in the press of altered conditions and tend to take an enlarged view of what is relevant to a moral decision. Of course, to take a concept as primary does not mean the others are entirely discounted: whatever is taken as primary must make room for the others in a supportive role. The concepts themselves are wide-ranging and admit of many internal differences among their adherents. The good may refer to individual pleasure (as with the Epicureans), or the organization of social life (as with Aristotle), or the maximization of pleasures over pains (as with the utilitarians), or the organizing ideals or values of life. A right-based theory may place its emphasis on duty and obligations to others on rights as claims by individuals, supported by natural law or by convention. A virtue theory takes virtue, as opposed to vice, as the central organizing concept. Thus Plato uses the virtue of justice both to develop the full ideal of a state, and as a specific trait of character.

A third issue concerns the *faculty* by which each theory determines that morals are apprehended—whether by reason or experience (in both cases a cognitive faculty), or by feelings and emotions (a noncognitive faculty), or by conscience or intuition (somewhat ambiguously cognitive). A final issue or dimension has to do with the *permanence* of morals: whether the ends and goals, or the principles of right and obligation, or the dominant virtues are to be regarded as unchanging, holding for societies at all times, or whether these are changing and dependent upon context and circumstances, subject to social and historical development.

2. The term comes from the Greek. *Deon* is usually taken to be what is necessary or binding or obligatory, although etymologically it is more likely that it conveyed the idea of what was fitting rather than what was binding.

PROFILE OF A THEORY

Dimension	Options
Human nature	Fundamentally good, or Evil, or Neutral Naturally sociable, or not
Elite concept	Good (goals, ends), or Right (duty, obligation, rights), or Virtue (responsibility, character, worthwhile)
Faculty by which morality is apprehended	Reason and/or experience, or Feelings and emotions, or Conscience and/or intuition
Character of morality	Permanent, or Changeable

3. The word derives, as does *deontology*, from the Greek, in this case *telos*, meaning goal, end, or purpose. Prior to the utilitarians, Aristotle would have been the primary example of a teleologist. For Aristotle, though, *telos* is couched in a theory of development according to which each species, including the human, has built into its nature some ideal of maturity toward which it "naturally" tends.

4. Although, ironically, Bentham's term for "private ethics" is *deontology*.

5. He was particularly unfortunate in that the outbreak of the French Revolution overshadowed the publication of his major theoretical work in 1789, *An Introduction to the Principles of Morals and Legislation*.

6. In practical life Mill was often seen by his contemporaries as taking the harder line. For example, the hard-line response of the British government to the Irish Famine is often attributed to the strong convictions in "political economy" of Assistant Secretary of the Treasury Charles Edward Trevelyan, who believed that any intervention to provide food could relieve the situation in the short term, but because the situation really reflected the overpopulation of the island, in the long term disaster was inevitable. Mill himself took this as an inappropriate application of laissez-faire. Historians find particularly blameworthy Trevelyan's decision to ban the export from Ireland of foodstuffs, for example, wheat, which were untouched by the famine. "According to Free Trade doctrines the sale, by export outside Ireland, of grain and other produce which commanded a high price should provide Irish merchants with money to purchase and import low-priced foods, to replace the loss of the potato. However, the underdeveloped commercial system of Ireland made any such operations highly improbable" (Cecil Woodham-Smith, *The Great Hunger* [New York: Old Town Books, 1962], 123–124). Trevelyan was not alone in this attitude. "Officially, it was declared that no deaths from starvation must be allowed to occur in Ireland, but in private the attitude was different. 'I have always felt a certain horror of political economists,' said Benjamin Jowett, the celebrated Master of Balliol, 'since I heard one of them say that he feared the famine of 1848 in Ireland would not kill more than a million people, and that would scarcely be enough to do much good.' The political economist in question was Nassau Senior, one of the Government's advisers on economic affairs" (ibid., 375–376).

As another example, consider this: "Professor J. Laurence Laughlin of Harvard University, in preparing a college text edition of John Stuart Mill's *Political Economy*, deleted chapters and passages in which the great English thinker attacked laissez-faire on the score of its incompatibility with high productivity and good social morale, deploring existing economic inequalities for women, and spoke of 'the total absence of regard for justice or fairness in the relations between capital and labor.' In thus misrepresenting Mill by throwing out portions the author regarded as necessary to his system of thought, Laughlin may have been acting deliberately or he may merely have been rationalizing his own predilections. In his preface he stated that he was omitting that which might properly be classed as sociology or social philosophy" (Merle Curti, *The Growth of American Thought*, 3d ed. [New Brunswick, N.J.: Transaction Books, 1982], 621–622).

7. But it was not until the twentieth century that anthropology came to study morality as a distinctive field; previously it had studied the moralities and ethical ideas of different peoples, but in a way that parceled out morality among the institutions in which it operated. Thus, anthropological writings on kinship included the morality of the family; on economics, the varied moral rules in agricultural and commercial societies; on politics, the moral aspects of law and government. But, at least up to the mid-twentieth century, there were few investigations of moral patterns as such. In the twentieth century, the two writers who were interested in comparative studies followed different lines of inquiry. Ruth Benedict examined patterns of whole societies, not of morality itself; Edward Westermarck did compare moralities in different societies early in the century, but limited his attention to selected psychological aspects. The one had too broad a field of inquiry, the other too limited a concept of morality.

8. During a year's teaching in America, Ayer was invited to the Kennedy White House, where he argued with Robert Kennedy on the literal meaningfulness of religious utterances. On another occasion *Time* magazine published a photograph of Ayer holding a cocktail glass with his little finger extended as if in an obscene gesture.

9. Oliver Wendell Holmes, Jr., *The Common Law* (Cambridge: Harvard University Press, 1963), 7. (Original publication 1881.)

10. It should be observed that even in this seemingly simple case, there is some question as to how genuinely commensurable they are. See Thomas Kuhn, *The Structure of Scientific Revolutions* (Chicago: University of Chicago Press, 1962).

CHAPTER FOUR

1. A further dichotomy, that of *individual* and *institutional*, is discussed in Chapter Nine.

2. Vercors [nom de plume for Jean Bruller], French Resistance leader in World War II, "Despair Is Dead," in *The Republic of Silence*, ed. A. J. Liebling (New York: Harcourt, Brace, 1947), 82–89.

3. It is not utterly bizarre to regard this difference over the need for an ultimate authority as a central issue in the conflict between Congress and President in the Iran–Contra affair. Those who defended the President's right as chief executive to

make ultimate decisions on foreign policy, seemed to take the view that if the President did not have such power, the very notion of the United States acting becomes incoherent. What is this if not a form of protomonarchism?

4. Or, as Kant sees it, a tyranny: "That man who will admit nothing to be morally indifferent and strews his steps with duties, as with traps, and will not allow it to be a matter of indifference whether one eats meat or fish, drinks beer or wine, when both agree with him—a micrology which, if adopted into the doctrine of virtue, would make its dominion a tyranny—that man can be called fantastically virtuous." *The Metaphysical Principles of Virtue*, trans. James Ellington (Indianapolis: Bobbs-Merrill, 1964), 68–69. How such humility ties in with ideas of forgiveness and repentance is a distinct, complex question that would carry us far from the present focus on authority.

5. See Chapter Three for teleology in ethical theory.

6. Note that we say "the world around us," not "the world outside us," in order not to beg questions at the outset.

7. Tamara Dembo, "Adjustment to Misfortune—A Problem of Social-Psychological Rehabilitation," in Tamara Dembo, Gloria Ladieu Leviton, and Beatrice A. Wright, eds., *Artificial Limbs* (Washington, D.C.: Prosthetics Research Board, National Academy of Sciences, 1956).

8. Interestingly, just as the anthropologist Ruth Benedict, in her *Patterns of Culture* (1934), asserted the equal validity of the different patterns of peoples, the Western world found itself driven to deny the validity of Nazism, which came to power shortly after the book was published.

9. There is also *conscience*, which lies somewhere between emotion and reason. For a notable analysis of conscience, see Joseph Butler's *Fifteen Sermons Preached at the Rolls Chapel* (1726).

10. Even this may depend on other factors in the situation. The case of protesters lying down in front of a train was often used to make a point about comparative national character—a Nazi engineer would run over them, a British engineer would stop, and a Japanese engineer would slow the train to two miles an hour and then jump off, leaving the protesters themselves to decide whether to be run over. The story was meant to suggest Gandhi's methods were tailored to the national character of the officials with whom he was dealing. One might speculate about American national character in such a story; presumably it would have followed the pattern of the British. But the situation needs also to make allowance for individual differences. In the 1980s, we witnessed a tragedy in the Pacific Northwest: when an antinuclear activist lay down on a track, the train accelerated and ran over his legs. Perhaps American national character is indicated not so much by the action of the engineer (at least so one hopes) as by what followed—the victim sought redress by a civil suit for damages, and won.

11. Martha Wolfenstein and Nathan Leites, *Movies: A Psychological Study* (Glencoe, Ill.: Free Press, 1950).

CHAPTER FIVE

1. Compare with *contempt of court*, which is a technical judgment, not implying a state of mind on the part of the person in court. Whether you *feel* contempt or not is not the issue.

2. In the debates that followed the Supreme Court's ruling, nothing so reminded us of the traditional legal wisdom, *De minimis lex non curat* (the law does not concern itself with trivia), than the arguments over the relevance of the placement of the U.S. flag on a garment. In the weekend following the decision, the President's wife was photographed with the flag on her shoulder (or was it her chest?). Was this acceptable, and indicative of respect, while sewing the flag into the seat of a trousers indicates disrespect—or would it matter that the garment was a pair of jeans, or torn jeans?

3. Jeremy Bentham, *Deontology, Together with A Table of the Springs of Action, and The Article on Utilitarianism*, ed. Amnon Goldworth (New York: Oxford University Press, 1983).

4. *Commentaries on the Laws of England*, vol. 4 (1769), 216.

5. C. K. Ogden, "Bentham on Sex," in Jeremy Bentham, *Theory of Legislation*, ed. C. K. Ogden (London: Kegan Paul, Trench, Trubner, 1931), 482.

6. Ibid., 479.

7. Ibid., 482.

8. Wellman Chamberlin, quoted in John Noble Wolford, *The Mapmakers* (New York: Vintage Books, 1982), 77.

9. See Wolford, *Mapmakers*, 82–83, for a chart outlining different types of maps and how they are used.

10. Ibid., 317.

11. D. L. Rosenhan, "On Being Sane in Insane Places," *Science* 179 (January 19, 1973): 250–258.

12. Benjamin Whorf, *Language, Thought and Reality*, ed. John B. Carroll (Cambridge: MIT Press, 1956).

13. R. G. Collingwood, *An Essay on Metaphysics* (Oxford: Clarendon Press, 1940), 195.

14. "The Brönsted-Lowry theory accounts for almost all aqueous acid-base chemistry. Therefore the Brönsted-Lowry concept is most often intended when the words acid or base are used. The Lewis definition is useful when discussing transition-metal ions, however." John W. Moore, William G. Davies, Ronald W. Collins, *Chemistry* (New York: McGraw-Hill, 1978), 384.

15. "Geometry (G) predicates nothing about the behavior of real things, but only geometry together with the totality (P) of physical laws can do so. Using symbols, we may say that only the sum of (G) + (P) is subject to experimental verification. Thus (G) may be chosen arbitrarily, also parts of (P); all these laws are conventions. All that is necessary to avoid contradictions is to choose the remainder of (P) so that (G) and the whole of (P) are together in accord with experience." "Geometry and Experience," from Albert Einstein, *Ideas and Opinions* (New York: Dell, 1964), 231.

16. Consider the degree to which the "war on drugs" is pervaded by sports metaphors: what is "Just Say No" but "stepping up to the plate," or to "Win one for the Gipper." Is the appeal in the bumper sticker "Support Your Local Police" a request for increased salaries for them, or an appeal that the public should *approve* what they do, cheer them on?

CHAPTER SIX

1. William H. Gass, "The Case of the Obliging Stranger," *Philosophical Review* 66 (1957): 193–204.

2. One wonders whether the mid-nineteenth-century Irish Famine—due to a failure in the potato crop—would have so seared the Irish memory had there been no food available in the country. Instead, in Irish memory, the starvation of multitudes is linked to ships laden with wheat and cattle leaving Irish ports, sometimes bound for New York or Boston, there to be purchased by charitable organizations and returned to feed the Irish people.

3. In very recent times, whether one is conservative or liberal seems to be fixed as precisely as the decade—pre-1980, conservatives were in favor of balancing the federal budget; post-1980, liberals were in favor.

4. "Status" refers to a condition of society in which the position of a person is determined entirely by family or social class. By contrast, a "contract society" is one in which positions are determined by voluntary agreement of individuals. The distinction is made by Henry Maine in his *Ancient Law* (1861).

5. See Chapter Seven for a typology of principles: in the terms offered there, these principles are often used as if they were *must-rules*, when in fact they are at best *break-only-with-regret-rules*.

6. Karl Duncker, "Ethical Relativity? An Enquiry into the Psychology of Ethics," *Mind* 48 (January 1939): 39–57.

7. Thus arises the battle over the welfare state, with one side saying that it advances liberty and the other that it diminishes liberty in the name of security.

8. The *Bakke* case (1977) was one of the first to present the issue of affirmative action, or "reverse discrimination" (to its opponents), to the United States Supreme Court. Allan Bakke had applied for admission to the University of California medical school at Davis and had been rejected. It turned out that of the one hundred places available sixteen had been "set aside" for minority-group applicants. Bakke, who was white, sued on the grounds that if it were not for the "set aside" he would have been admitted, so that he had suffered for his race. The California Supreme Court ruled that Bakke should be admitted and also forbade the University from taking race into account in any way in their admissions decisions. Fearing that the latter part of the ruling threatened its efforts to increase the representation of minority groups in medical schools, the university appealed to the United States Supreme Court, which affirmed Bakke's own admission, but reversed the California Supreme Court's ruling against any use of racial classification. The United States Supreme Court did agree that a flat quota system would be unacceptable, but it seemed to allow the principle of affirmative action, provided it was implemented in a more complex and subtle way. The Court distinguished invidious racial classification from benign, according to whether the classification is intended to help the racial group or to injure it. It proposed that the standard for benign classification should be less stringent than the customary "strict scrutiny" to which invidious classification is subjected. This proposal is the famous "intermediate standard," and much litigation on the question remained in the offing. (For a convenient summary of the case and the law involved, see Ronald Dworkin, *A Matter of Principle* [Cambridge: Harvard University Press, 1985], 293–315.)

CHAPTER SEVEN

1. The listing of *natural rights* under legalistic morality is an individualization or privatization of this conception.

2. T. H. Huxley made just this point about aggressive impulses.

3. Cf. *Honour and Shame: The Values of Mediterranean Society*, ed. J. G. Peristiany (Chicago: University of Chicago Press, 1966).

4. John Dewey and James H. Tufts, *Ethics*, rev. ed. (New York: Henry Holt, 1932), 305–306. Also in John Dewey, *The Later Works*, vol. 7, 1932: *Ethics*, intro. Abraham Edel and Elizabeth Flower, ed. Jo Ann Boydston (Carbondale, Ill.: Southern Illinois University Press, 1985), 275–283.

5. For example, one can point to the struggle over how to interpret Roman law in the twelfth century between Bulgarus, who defended *ius strictum*, or law strictly interpreted, and Martinus, who saw room for *bona fides* (good faith). Consider Justinian's maxim: *Semper in dubiis benigniora praeferenda sunt* (In dubious things the more benign interpretation is always to be preferred) (from *Digest*, 50, 17, Num. 56).

6. Charles L. Bosk, *Forgive and Remember: Managing Medical Failure* (Chicago: University of Chicago Press, 1979).

7. Abraham Edel, *Ethical Judgment: The Use of Science in Ethics* (New York: Free Press, 1955), chap. 2.

8. Jean-Paul Sartre, "The Republic of Silence," reprinted in *The Republic of Silence*, ed. A. J. Liebling (New York: Harcourt, Brace, 1947), 498–500.

9. It was also to the benefit of the would-be murderer: "The fellow comes with a gun and says where's that fellow I'm going to kill him. And then I tell this man he had a gun. [a lie] Yes he came in and came just a little while and he went on. I don't know which way he just run on. [a lie] Then I want to tell this man: You don't want to kill this man. What's the trouble? If you kill this man, they're going to kill you, too. So just stop and put your gun down. [Ladd: What if he says, if you don't tell me where he is, I'll kill you.] If he said that way . . . I say you no good and you's going to get into trouble. So I is taking away the gun. Until we find out what you done it to us, and until we—and see what the officers will say—That's the only thing that good for him." John Ladd, *The Structure of a Moral Code* (Cambridge: Harvard University Press, 1957), 378.

10. The issues here are similar to those discussed in political morality as the problem of "Dirty Hands." See Michael Walzer, "Political Action: The Problem of Dirty Hands," *Philosophy and Public Affairs* 2 (1973): 160–180, and Alan H. Goldman, *The Moral Foundations of Professional Ethics* (Totowa, N.J.: Rowman and Littlefield, 1980), chap. 2.

11. See Richard Cabot, *The Meaning of Right and Wrong* (New York: Macmillan, 1892), and Sissela Bok, *Lying: Moral Choice in Public and Private Life* (New York: Random House, 1978).

12. See John Rawls, "Two Concepts of Rules," *Philosophical Review* 64 (1955): 3–32; John R. Searle, "How to Derive 'Ought' from 'Is,'" *Philosophical Review* 73 (1964): 43–58, and Searle, *Speech Acts* (Cambridge: Cambridge University Press, 1970), 33–42.

13. Cf. Richard Cabot, *The Meaning of Right and Wrong* (New York: Macmillan, 1936).

14. Henry Sidgwick, surveying this list, suggests it is geared to the problems of the monastic life (*Outlines of the History of Ethics*, 3d ed. [London: Macmillan, 1892], 129).

15. Plato in the *Republic* likened the virtues appropriate to a guardian to those of a good watchdog: friendliness to friends of the owner and savage hostility toward strangers.

16. E. C. Banfield, *The Moral Basis of a Backward Society* (New York: Free Press, 1958).

CHAPTER EIGHT

1. And in the nineteenth century similar difficulties arose for legal jurisdiction in British India: "There was a dual system of the Crown's and [British East India] Company's courts in Calcutta, Bombay, and Madras, which lasted until 1862. . . . In addition different codes of law were used: British law for British subjects, and Hindu and Muslim law for civil cases, and Muslim law for criminal law, except in Bombay, where Hindu criminal law was used for Hindus" (Javed Majeed, *Ungoverned Imaginings: James Mill's "The History of British India" and Orientalism* [Oxford: Clarendon Press, 1992], 25).

2. Subsequently we will speak in terms of occupation rather than profession, since we wish to avoid the complicated issues involved in how a profession is to be defined. There is a long-running debate in sociology over what characterizes a profession—for example, autonomy, control of access to the group, control by the members of the occupation of standards of performance, and some commitment to service. These conditions prove hard to apply—what degree of autonomy? How is the commitment to service to be put into practice, and in what amount? Is control of entry compromised by state involvement through procedures of certification? The problem is exacerbated because having a profession has become to some extent a matter of prestige—professions being occupations of high prestige—and by the activity of state bodies in setting standards of performance. For our purposes, it is sufficient to speak of occupational roles.

3. From *The Works of Jeremy Bentham*, ed. John Bowring (Edinburgh: Tait, 1838–1843), vol. 2, 537.

4. "It is a strange notion that the acknowledgment of a first principle is inconsistent with the admission of secondary ones. Whatever we adopt as the fundamental principle of morality, we require subordinate principles to apply it by: the impossibility of doing without them being common to all system" (*Utilitarianism* [1863], chap. 2).

5. *The Philosophy of Law: An Explosion of the Fundamental Principles of Jurisprudence as the Science of Right*, trans. W. Hastie (Edinburgh: T. & T. Clark, 1887), 196. This is a translation of *Metaphysische Anfangsgründe der Rechchtslehre*, Part I of *The Metaphysics of Morals* (*Die Metaphysic der Sitten*).

6. *The Metaphysical Principles of Virtue*, trans. James Ellington (Indianapolis: Bobbs-Merrill, 1964), 134. This is a translation of *Metaphysische Anfangsgründe der Tugenlehre*, Part II of *The Metaphysics of Morals*.

7. "Concerning Servility," ibid., 97.

8. "In the first place, a habit is a form of executive skill, of efficiency in doing. A habit means an ability to use natural conditions as means to ends. It is an active control of the environment through control of the organs of action. . . . Any habit marks an *inclination*—an active preference and choice, for the conditions involved in its use. A habit does not want, Micawber-like, for a stimulus to turn up so that it may get busy; it actively seeks for occasions to pass into full operation" (John Dewey, *Democracy and Education* [1916], chap. 4).

9. Why is it taken as a joke (ordinarily) when parents say they live for the day when the children will move out of the house? Isn't it that it places the whole role of parenting in the category of the joke about pounding one's head against a wall so that, one says when asked, it will feel so good when it stops? Pounding one's head is an absurd means toward the end of feeling good. Similarly, having children would be an absurd means for securing the feeling of relief that comes when the children move out.

10. National Commission for the Protection of Human Subjects of Biomedical and Behavioral Research, *The Belmont Report: Ethical Principles and Guidelines for the Protection of Human Subjects of Research* (Washington, D.C.: Government Printing Office, No. OS 78-0009, 1979).

11. Charles L. Bosk, *Forgive and Remember: Managing Medical Failure* (Chicago: University of Chicago Press, 1979). Interestingly enough, Bosk found that the most important event in the physician–patient relationship—if we are to judge by the code and by issues raised in litigation, and the aspect most emphasized by modern medical ethics, namely, the obtaining of informed consent—is the responsibility of a resident, not of the attending surgeon, who manages everything. Informed consent is apparently not deemed an important task.

12. As one might expect, the legal code has the most explicit consideration of these differences. It operates on three levels: canons, ethical interpretations, and disciplinary rules. The American Medical Association (AMA) backtracked from a long list of rules to a short list of ideals. The American Psychological Association gives guidelines and then presents cases to help interpret the guidelines.

13. In the First Code of Medical Ethics of the AMA (1847), the section on "Duties of Patients to their Physicians" was as lengthy as "Duties of Physicians to their Patients."

14. *A Discourse upon the Duties of a Physician* (1769), partially reprinted in Stanley Joel Reiser, Arthur J. Dyck, and William J. Curran, eds., *Ethics in Medicine: Historical Perspectives and Contemporary Concerns* (Cambridge: MIT Press, 1977), 17. These virtues are recommended for relations with fellow physicians.

15. "Codes of Medical Ethics," in ibid., 36.

16. See Jeffery L. Berlant, "Medical Ethics and Monopolization," in ibid., 52–65. He points out how attentive the AMA was to public opinion, dropping the idea of obligations of patients in 1903, and introducing the rhetoric of public service only as late as 1912.

17. Edgar L. Heermance, *Codes of Ethics: A Handbook* (Burlington, Vt.: Free Press Printing Co., 1924), 239.

CHAPTER NINE

1. John Rawls, "Two Concepts of Rules," *Philosophical Review* 64 (1955): 3–32.

2. See Philippa R. Foot, "Approval and Disapproval," in *Law, Morality, and Society: Essays in Honour of H.L.A. Hart*, ed. P.M.S. Hacker and Joseph Raz (Oxford: Clarendon Press, 1977), 229–246.

3. See *New York Times*, December 12, 1982, 97.

4. Vercors [Jean Bruller], *You Shall Know Them* (Boston: Little, Brown, 1933).

5. "I should deny the equity of taking, through the rates, the earnings of A to pay for teaching the children of B" (*Facts and Comments* [New York: D. Appleton, 1902], 83–84).

6. *New York Times*, October 28, 1971, 20.

7. Isaac Levi, *Hard Choices: Decision Making under Unresolved Conflict* (Cambridge: Cambridge University Press, 1986), 152.

8. *Americans for Legal Reform* 8, no. 4 (July–Sept. 1988): 4.

CHAPTER TEN

1. This is the central theme of John Dewey, *Theory of Valuation* (Chicago: University of Chicago Press, 1939).

2. A useful account of the early history of contract in Roman law is to be found in Sir Henry Maine's *Ancient Law* (New York: E.P. Dutton, 1917), chap. 9.

3. In at least one legal case, the Supreme Court has taken no action, leaving it to states, and states are experimenting. See the *New York Times*, December 6, 1987, sec. 1, 41. It could, of course, have been a legislative matter allowing will of a certain sort, but it appears as a constitutional right to privacy.

4. For a study of different cultural orientations to nature, see Florence Kluckhohn and Fred L. Strodbeck, *Variations in Value Orientations* (Evanston, Ill.: Row Peterson, 1961).

5. The fear of deleterious consequences emerged with the development of supersonic airplanes and the suggestion that the atmosphere might be affected. It was accentuated in the Club of Rome reports predicting exhaustion of natural resources and overwhelming pollution. The development of genetic engineering and the possibility of creating new forms of life have raised fresh fears of devastating consequences of a misstep or an unanticipated mutation. While there is a strong general impression that the modern world cannot resist applying new inventions immediately, some studies show there have been long delays in many cases, often because of the entrenched interests of existent technologies that would be seriously affected economically by the new inventions. (See, for example, a story on "The Barriers to Innovation" in the Business Section of the *New York Times*, Sunday, April 16, 1989, which recounts how even radio and television could, on the basis of existent knowledge, have been developed earlier but for economic resistance.)

6. Ruth Benedict, *Patterns of Culture* (London: Routledge and Kegan Paul, 1935).

CHAPTER ELEVEN

1. The famous dilemma-situations—Antigone, Captain Vere in *Billy Budd*, Agamemnon—have conflict in the form of right versus right. In other cases the issue is whether one has the strength to carry through into action what one believes to be right, even though it conflicts with one's desires or one's interests. Plato's *Apology* presents Socrates in such conflict. The case of Abraham and the sacrifice of Isaac (Genesis 22) might be interpreted either way.

2. It is hard to see how the vice of "willfulness" can be explained as due to the *weakness* of will.

3. Technically there is a fourth type, namely, decisions under conflict: when a decision is made in a context where an opponent is likely to seek advantage. But this can be considered a subcategory of the others. Chess play involves decisions under conflict. It can be analyzed differently depending upon the information you have of the ability of your opponent. If you are playing a grandmaster, you are virtually certain that whatever move you make, your opponent will respond in the way most disadvantageous to you. If you judge your opponent to be moderately competent, then it is a case of risk, where you need to estimate the likelihood of the other player's knowing your weak points.

4. A poignant case is a list generated by Darwin when he was considering marrying, reprinted in *The Autobiography of Charles Darwin, 1809–1882*, ed. Nora Barlow (New York: Harcourt, Brace, 1958), 234. There he lays out in one column the reasons why he should marry (the pros) and in a second column the reasons why he should not (the cons).

5. Franklin called it his "prudential algebra." He explained it in a letter (September 19, 1772) to Joseph Priestley responding to a request for advice:

Dear Sir: In the affair of so much importance to you wherein you ask my advice, I cannot, for want of sufficient premises, advise you *what* to determine, but if you please I will tell you *how*. When these difficult cases occur, they are difficult chiefly because while we have them under consideration, all the reasons *pro* and *con* are not present to the mind at the same time; but sometimes one set present themselves, and at other times another, the first being out of sight. Hence the various purposes or inclinations that alternately prevail and the uncertainty, that perplexes us.

To get over this, my way is to divide half a sheet of paper by a line into two columns; writing over the one *Pro*, and over the other *Con*. Then during three or four days' consideration I put down under the different heads short hints of the different motives that at different times occur to me, *for* or *against* the measure. When I have thus got them all together in one view, I endeavour to estimate their respective weights; and where I find two (one on each side) that seem equal, I strike them both out. If I find a reason *pro* equal to some two reasons *con*, I strike out the three. If I judge some two reasons *con* equal to some three reasons *pro*, I strike out the five; and thus proceeding I find at length where the balance lies; and if after a day or two of farther consideration, nothing new that is of importance occurs on either side, I come to a determination accordingly. And though the weight of reasons cannot be taken with the precision of algebraic quantities, yet when each is thus considered separately and comparatively, and the whole lies before me, I think I can judge better, and am less likely to make a rash step; and in fact I have found great advantage from this kind of equation, in what may be called *moral* or *prudential algebra*.
(Benjamin Franklin, *Autobiographical Writings*, selected and edited by Carl Van Doren [New York: Viking Press, 1945], 280–281)

6. This gets its name from its similarity to finding a word in a dictionary— look under the first letter, then the second letter, then the third letter, and so on, until you find the word you need.

7. The formula is $EV = p^1v^1 + p^2v^2 + p^3v^3 + \ldots p^nv^n$, where EV is the expected value, p^1 is the probability of a given outcome and v^1 the value of that outcome, p^2 the probability of a second outcome and v^2 the value of that second outcome.

8. This is in part the source of the outrage that follows upon the use of these methods to place a value on a single human life. Thus engineers may calculate what the public is willing to spend to improve the safety features of a roadway and then estimate for each level of spending how many lives would be saved. They then conclude that the maximum level of spending (for example, in tolls) that would be tolerated by the public (at what level of toll would they stop using the roadway?) indicates how the public values human lives. It is when the calculation is applied to a single case that the whole enterprise appears bizarre.

9. A further problem lies in the use of the term *preferences* to refer to the evaluation of the outcomes. There are epistemological grounds for minimizing the differences between the values scale and the actual set of preferences revealed in the decisions. The term *preferences* is often used indifferently for one or the other. Sometimes it refers to the ordering in the value scale—as in John's preference for beauty over intellect; but often it refers to the actual decision—to prefer A to B is to decide for A against B.

10. See L. Hurwicz, "What Has Happened to the Theory of Games?" *American Economic Review Supplement* 43 (1953), 398–405.

11. For an elementary introduction to these various strategies, see John R. Hayes, *The Complete Problem Solver* (Philadelphia: Franklin Institute Press, 1981), and for a more challenging treatment, see Michael D. Resnik, *Choices: An Introduction to Decision Theory* (Minneapolis: University of Minnesota Press, 1987).

12. World War I was billed as the war to end wars.

13. As pointed out in Chapter Seven, Margaret Mead observed that Americans and the British differ in their attitude to compromise—what the British see as honorable compromise Americans may see as selling out one's ideals.

CHAPTER TWELVE

1. Interestingly enough, among Bentham's contemporaries, William Paley defends an apparently religious ethic that calls on humans to carry out the will of God but then attempts a proof that God intends men for happiness, and hence we can judge God's will by what will most advance human happiness. See, for example, Paley's "Reasons for Contentment, addressed to the Labouring Part of the British Population," in *The Works of William Paley*, vol. 4 (London: George Cowie & Co., 1837), 391–403.

2. There need be nothing esoteric about this, as if a measuring instrument were required for greater capacity. Take an obvious phenomenon still present: all people, including laborers whose children do not go to college, pay taxes. Out of these taxes colleges are supported, to which children of the upper middle class secure readier admission. These are being allotted "greater happiness."

3. Charles L. Stevenson, "The Emotive Meaning of Ethical Terms," *Mind* 46 (January 1937): 14–31, and *Ethics and Language* (New Haven: Yale University Press, 1944).

4. Jean-Paul Sartre, "The Republic of Silence," reprinted in *The Republic of Silence*, ed. A. J. Liebling (New York: Harcourt, Brace, 1947), 498–500.

Index

Abortion, 14, 43, 82, 83, 99, 125, 190, 216, 218, 227, 234; and context, 126–131

Absolutists, 117

Affirmative action, 14, 15, 206, 259 n

Agency, 237–238; and consensual contracts, 217

Antigone, 150, 225, 226, 227, 263 n; the play, 224

Applied ethics: and alternative problem-formulations, 112; analogy of applied science, 4–5; choosing a vocabulary, 138, 164; and comparative analysis, 132; concerned with problematic, 7, 142; criteria of correctness in, 113; emergence as movement, 2; and jurisdiction, 169; labels for, 7; learning from history, 159; relation to science, 82; relation to stabilities, 32; relation to theory, 61, 241–248; three areas of 7, 151, 241; why movement seen as new, 2–6

Aquinas, Thomas, 35, 36, 39, 101; and *Summa Theologica*, 2

Arendt, Hannah, 251 n

Aristophanes, 188

Aristotle, 35, 71, 101, 227, 233; and the accidental, 80, 233; Athenian democracy, 37; and the changeable, 233; community, 35, 153; equality for women, 35; family roles, 178; friendship, 2, 157; and the good, 254 n; merit, 65; metaphysics, 36, 233; and the natural, 69; and *Nicomachean*

Ethics, 2; and *Politics*, 2, 211; and probability, 233; teleologist, 255 n; types of rhetoric, 138

Arrhenius, Svante August, 110

Augustine, 35, 36, 37, 101, 143, 226

Austin, John L., 52

Authority, ultimate, 63–68

Ayer, A. J., 51, 52, 256 n; and *Language, Truth, and Logic*, 51

Bakke, 133, 259 n

Banfield, Edward, 162

Bard, Samuel, 181

Belmont Report, 262 n

Benedict, Ruth, 256 n; and *Patterns of Culture*, 257 n

Bentham, Jeremy, 11, 35, 36, 37, 38, 40, 41, 44, 45, 61, 64, 88, 104, 133, 149, 172, 173, 185, 222, 234, 242, 244, 248, 265 n (*see also* Felicific calculus, Pleasure theory, Utilitarianism); contextualist, 119; and deontology, 255 n; institutional change, 3; and *An Introduction to the Principles of Morals and Legislation*, 255 n; and stabilities, 31; and *Table of the Springs of Action*, 104; and *Theory of Legislation*, 3, 243, 258 n

Bergson, Henri, 140

Berlant, J. L., 262 n

Bill of Rights, 215, 218

Billy Budd, 224, 263 n

Bismarck, 172, 173

Blackstone, William, 104